Sabine Dreher

Neoliberalism and Migration:
An Inquiry into the
Politics of Globalization

Sabine Dreher

Neoliberalism and Migration: An Inquiry into the Politics of Globalization

LIT

Für meine Eltern

Bibliographic information published by the Deutsche Nationalbibliothek
The Deutsche Nationalbibliothek lists this publication in the Deutsche
Nationalbibliografie; detailed bibliographic data are available in the Internet at
http://dnb.d-nb.de.

ISBN 978-3-8258-8187-0

Zugl.: Bremen, Univ., Diss., 2001

A catalogue record for this book is available from the British Library

© LIT VERLAG Hamburg 2007
Auslieferung/Verlagskontakt:
Fresnostr. 2   48159 Münster
Tel. +49 (0)251–62 03 20   Fax +49 (0)251–23 19 72
e-Mail: lit@lit-verlag.de   http://www.lit-verlag.de

Distributed in the UK by: Global Book Marketing, 99B Wallis Rd, London, E9 5LN
Phone: +44 (0) 20 8533 5800 – Fax: +44 (0) 1600 775 663
http://www.centralbooks.co.uk/acatalog/search.html

Distributed in North America by:

Transaction Publishers
New Brunswick (U.S.A.) and London (U.K.)

Transaction Publishers
Rutgers University
35 Berrue Circle
Piscataway, NJ 08854

Phone: +1 (732) 445 - 2280
Fax: + 1 (732) 445 - 3138
for orders (U. S. only):
toll free (888) 999 - 6778
e-mail:
orders@transactionspub.com

CONTENTS

List of Abbreviations   *iii*

Preface   *vi*

1. Globalisation as a Political Project   **1**

The Globalisation Debate   *1*
Migration and Globalisation Research   *7*
Globalisation as Project? The Neo-Gramscian Perspective   *12*
Conclusion   *20*

2. Institutional Asymmetry in the Global Economy: Freedom for Capital – Restricted Migration   **25**

Embedded Liberalism   *26*
Institutionalising Liberalism Worldwide   *29*
Migration in the Global Political Economy   *42*
Liberalism and Migration Policies – Towards a Postnational Constellation?   *49*
Conclusion   *67*

3. The Neo-Gramscian Theory of Globalisation   **71**

Conceptualising Hegemonic Transformations   *72*
Crisis and Transformation: From the Pax Americana to Neoliberalism   *77*
The US and Globalisation   *86*
Migration in the Neoliberal Project   *90*
Conclusion   *101*

4. 'Equality Stops at the Water's Edge': Neoliberal Ideas on Migration Policy 105

Neoliberal Theory and International Migration *107*
Private International Fora: The Trilateral Commission *113*
The Organisation for Economic Co-operation and Development *116*
Conclusion *139*

5. Immigration and Labour Market Restructuring 143

The Neoliberal Approach to Labour Market Restructuring *145*
Contesting the Global: Free Trade, Migration and Sweatshops in the United States *148*
Restructuring German Capitalism: Temporary Workers in the New European Division of Labour *168*
Conclusion *188*

6. Global Citizenship and Territoriality in a Global Political Economy 191

Globalising Citizenship? *194*
Migration and Territoriality *205*
Neo-Gramscianism as a Theory of Globalisation *213*
Closed Borders – Open Societies? Normative Implications *224*

Bibliography 227

LIST OF ABBREVIATIONS

AAMA	American Apparel Manufacturer Association
ACLU	American Civil Liberties Union
AFL-CIO	American Federation of Labor – Congress of Industrial Organization
AIP	Apparel Industry Partnership
Awo	Arbeiterwohlfahrt
BDA	Bundesvereinigung der deutschen Arbeitgeberverbände
BUGA	Bundesverband des deutschen Groß- und Außenhandels
CBI	Caribbean Basin Initiative
CDU	Christlich Demokratische Union
DGB	Deutscher Gewerkschaftsbund
DOL	Department of Labour
EU	European Union
FAIR	Federation for American Immigration Reform
FDI	Foreign Direct Investment
FDP	Freie Demokratische Partei
FLA	Fair Labor Association
FLSA	Fair Labor Standards Act
GAO	United States General Accounting Office
GATS	General Agreement on Trade in Services
GATT	General Agreement on Tariffs and Trade
HDB	Hauptverband der deutschen Bauindustrie
IG BAU	Industriegewerkschaft Bauen-Agrar-Umwelt
IIAIRA	Illegal Immigration Reform and Immigrant Responsibility Act

ILO	International Labour Organisation
IMF	International Monetary Fund
INS	Immigration and Naturalization Service
IRCA	Immigration Reform and Control Act
MAI	Multilateral Agreement on Investment
MALDEF	Mexican American Legal Defence Fund
MFA	Multilateral Fibre Agreement
NAFTA	North American Free Trade Agreement
NAM	National Manufacturers Association
NIEO	New International Economic Order
NIF	National Immigration Forum
NRF	National Retail Federation
OECD	Organisation for Economic Co-operation and Development
OSHA	Occupational Safety and Health Act
SPD	Sozialdemokratische Partei Deutschlands
TNC	Transnational Corporation
UN	United Nations
UNHCR	United Nations High Commissioner for Refugees
UNITE	Union of Needletrades and Industrial and Textile Employees
WHD	Wage and Hour Division (Department of Labour)
WRAPP	World Wide Responsible Apparel Production Program
WRC	Worker Rights Consortium
WTO	World Trade Organisation
ZDB	Zentralverband des deutschen Baugewerbes
ZDH	Zentralverband des Deutschen Handwerks

PREFACE

When I started this research project about the politics underlying the global economy at the end of the nineties I encountered much scepticism. Many took globalisation simply for granted, most chose to ignore the lopsidedness of the globalisation process that I seek to explain where conditions for capital to move freely have improved dramatically over the years whereas it has become increasingly difficult for migrants to cross borders. The fact that within the European Union the freedom to move is now greater than before has been used as one counterargument. This overlooks the fact that many immigrants in Europe are not entitled to it (see chapter one), and it contrasts with the decreased freedom to move into the EU.

The terrorist attacks in the United States have changed the parameters of globalisation research to an extent that some have even announced the need for a post mortem on globalisation theory (Rosenberg 2005), ignoring those who, from the very beginning, pointed to the precarious nature of globalisation (Gill and Law 1988; Cox 1987). One consequence of the attacks is that they have brought the political conditions that are required for the smooth functioning of a global market into the open. As my research shows, the global market place (or 'globalisation') is constructed by specific interests and global power configurations. The case that I am looking at is the contrast between the institutionalised freedom to move for capital but not for labour. Now, after the terrorist attacks in 2001, it has become obvious that "globalisation" is dependent on and can be changed through politics. In the absence of an effective global authority, a global market needs to be guaranteed by the territorial state system (in which the interests of the more powerful take preference over other interests).

This book arises out of a dissertation at the University of Bremen in 2001 in the Institute for Intercultural and International Relations (InIIS) that would not have been possible without the support many individuals and institutions: Above all, thanks are due to Hannes Lacher who read and critically discussed various drafts. Special thanks also to the other members of my immediate support group: my parents, Ulrike Ahrenberg, Wolfram Rogers, Thomas Faist, Birgit Locher, Sonja Borski, Andrea Liese, Ruth Augustine, Alex Kamber and Sevda Alankus. My two dissertation supervisors, Thomas Faist and Michael Zürn as well as Dieter Senghaas, Eva Senghaas and the InIIS colloquium have made sure that the dissertation stayed on track. Thanks are also due to Kees van der Pijl, Henk Overbeek and Magnus Ryner who invited me to present my research in a workshop at RECIPE in Amsterdam.

Financing for my research was provided mainly by a grant for a research project on Denationalisation of the Deutsche Forschungsgemeinschaft to Michael Zürn (see Zürn 2005; Beisheim et al. 1999); Thomas Faist's offer to cooperate in the TSER Research Network (financed by the Commission of the European Union) on 'Comparative Social Inclusion Policies and Citizenship in Europe: Towards a New European Social Model' helped me to develop the German case study; Lastly, Prof. Dr. Jouni Suistola and Prof. Dr. Zeliha Kashman made sure that I found a new institutional home base at Near East University in Nicosia in the Northern part of Cyprus. I am very greatful for the help and encouragement that I received from so many people over the years.

Herrenzimmern, September 2006   Sabine Dreher

1. GLOBALISATION AS A POLITICAL PROJECT

The Globalisation Debate

Some three decades ago, the notion of interdependence came to express "a poorly understood but widespread feeling that the very nature of world politics [was] changing" (Keohane and Nye 2000: 104). By the end of the nineties, the idea that we live in a very different world from the one that existed until 1945 (or 1989) had become widely shared in the western world and beyond. But few would have accepted the notion that interdependence, as a situation in which developments in one state have effects in others, remained adequate as the key concept through which we can grasp these changes.[1] Instead, the concept of globalisation has come to express a feeling that the central international tendency is not simply one of increasing sensitivities and vulnerabilities between states, but a process of global integration that calls into question the state-centric foundation of much of International Relations theory, including interdependence theory itself (Jones 1995).

The initial theories of globalisation that emerged in the 1980s and early 1990s particularly emphasised the importance of transformations

---

1   For Keohane and Nye (2000: 105), globalisation is to be understood as increasing interdependence; globalism is then understood as a situation of interdependence not simply between two countries, but between a number of countries involving multi-continental connections.

in the structure of the world economy. They held that interdependence belonged to an epoch in which national states and national economies still retained a high measure of congruence, and in which states were still very much in control of domestic processes, even if the costs of adjustment to external processes became higher. In other words, international interdependence was premised on a highly internationalised economy in which there were complex connections between national economies (and societies). The original globalisation thesis, by contrast, suggested that since the 1970s, a global economy has gradually come to supplant or replace the international economy. The new world economy, so proponents of this position argued, was no longer an agglomeration of national economies, but increasingly a single, integrated global system.[2]

While internationalisation in earlier periods was mainly occurring through trade and short-term (port-folio) capital flows, the main feature of the present phase of globalisation is, in this perspective, the organisation of production and financial markets on a transnationally integrated scale. Production chains, the sequence of functions in which each stage adds value to the process of production of goods and services have been transnationalised (Dicken 1998: 7). This has occurred as a part of a 'vertical' investment strategy whereby the production process is centrally controlled but specific activities are outsourced to other countries (Gilpin 2000: 165). Through foreign direct investment, especially in as much as it concerns the acquisition of inputs and supporting services from around the world, and the formation of cross-border alliances and joint ventures, global production has become internalised in transnational corporations. Globalisation, then, implies a *qualitative* change; international production leads to "deep integration" between countries as foreign direct investment creates a

---

2   Hobsbawm (1979: 315); Madeuf and Michalet (1978); Reich (1991: 3).

more lasting linkage between countries than arms'-length trade (UNCTAD 1994: 118). A similar analysis seems to hold true for international financial markets, which apparently operate without consideration to national boundaries rendering traditional assumptions about the connections between exchange rates and trade balances, interest rates and exchange rates obsolete (Ruggie 1995: 517; O'Brian 1992). As a consequence, multiple, formerly segmented markets are fused into one (Hobsbawm 1979; Madeuf and Michalet 1978).

For most of the early theorists of globalisation (and many continue to follow their lead), the implications of such transformations in the economic structure were obvious. They argued that globalisation defines a new era in social life in which the nation-state is no longer a viable unit of social organisation. States can no longer carry out public policies effectively since their economy is only a part of global processes (Reinicke 1998: 63). Governments do no longer have any choice on policy but have to adapt to the global market place: "From now on any country [...] that wants to prosper will have to accept that it is the world economy that leads and that domestic policies will succeed only if they strengthen, or at least do not impair, the country's international economic position" (Drucker 1986: 791). In consequence, and according to this pattern of argumentation social, economic monetary policies need to be increasingly homogenised across the globe.

The origin of economic globalisation itself, however, was and is not a central issue in the globalisation debate. Many analysts seem to assume that the process is driven by technological change. Because of the ease with which knowledge, capital and management techniques can be extended around the globe, and with the internet facilitated supply-chain management across borders, the production of goods and services on a global scale has become much easier (Dicken 1998: 145). Other factors mentioned as driving forces for the movement towards a more integrated economy are the loosening of barriers to trade, and the formation of regional trading areas (Cavusgil 1993: 83). On the whole, the model of social change underlying this debate has been highly economistic and deterministic in that economic changes have been taken as independent variables, concentrating on the specification of the political *consequences* held to follow from them. More specifically, it has been suggested that the 'rise of the global market' must at the same time entail the 'demise of the sovereign state'; politics and economics have been regarded as standing in a zero-sum relationship, the gain of one side being the necessary loss of the other.

This model, it should be noted, has not been challenged by the increasing number of critics of the globalisation thesis; most seem to accept that devastating consequences for the state and its policy autonomy would indeed follow if it could be shown that the international economy has indeed been replaced by a global market (Hirst and Thompson 1999: ch. 1). But these critics aver that the process is not yet as impressive as the first one that lasted until the outbreak of the First World War. Globalisation is therefore nothing new.[3] In their overview, Glyn and Sutcliffe (1992: 79-87; Sutcliffe and Glyn 1999) point out that the increase in trade inter-connectedness has, in most cases, not yet reached the levels before 1913; the same holds true for financial markets. Foreign direct investment presents a slightly different picture; they accept that the internationalisation of capital is now higher but also insist that no dramatic consequences follow, as much of current foreign direct investment is similar to pre-1914 portfolio investment and not geared towards the control of production. Most importantly, the current world economy still fails to meet the crucial test of the 'law of one price': prices still differ according to national markets. Finally, these scholars argue that the limited nature of current

---

3 Gordon (1988); Weiss (1998: chapter 6); Wade (1996), Zysman (1996).

processes of world economic integration can also be seen with respect to the continuing compartmentalisation of labour markets, as most countries have restricted immigration since the seventies. Before 1914, immigration policy was more liberal.

For all these reasons, the critics of the globalisation thesis have come to the conclusion that the notion of a global market place is misleading. At best, they argue, it is possible to ascertain an increased level of internationalisation. The presumption of a 'global' economy is thus an enormous exaggeration.[4] For the sceptics, the extent of globalisation, and in consequence, the assumed adjustment necessities emphasised by the proponents of the globalisation thesis, are vastly overstated. Given that the world economy has only become more internationalised (rather than globalised) in recent decades, states can be expected to retain the policy autonomy in the management of their national economies; they also still have the ability to use public authority for redistributive and protective policies (Garrett 1998; Hirst and Thomson 1999).

Since the second half of the 1990s, the debate between these two schools became overshadowed by the emergence of a new paradigm claiming the 'middle ground' in the globalisation debate (Held et al. 1999). According to the so-called 'transformationalists', there is indeed a process of globalisation taking place; but the claims of the original globalisation theorists for the emergence of a totally integrated global economy and society were exaggerated, and the implications drawn by them for domestic and international politics overstated. However, from a transformationalist perspective, the response of the 'sceptics' to the claims of the 'hyperglobalisers' is just as problematic. Sceptics, in this perspective, simply fail to account for the very important transformations that have taken place and remain stuck in out-

---

4   Hirst and Thompson (1999); Weiss (1998: 167-188); Weiss (1999).

dated theories and models that have little purchase in the current world.

Transformationalists mostly agree with hyperglobalisers that the economic structure has undergone a transformation, making it more global than international, but they are more cautious about just how far this transformation has already gone. They also add a new dimension to the globalisation debate by stressing that globalisation processes have not just taken place in the economy, but in other spheres of social life as well. Globalisation is seen as a "powerful transformative force" (*ibid.*: 7); as a result of globalisation processes in the economy, culture and society, nearly all countries are now part of a larger global system. However, this does not imply that this is "evidence of global convergence or of the arrival of single world society" (*ibid.*). In particular, transformationalists emphasise that it is unclear which direction the globalisation process will take in the future.

Globalisation, therefore leads to an "emerging era of global politics", which is characterised by multi-layered networks of global and regional governance (*ibid.*: 77). The issue of global governance is becoming increasingly central, not least in the economic realm, where the state is no longer able to effectively govern a national economy that is only a subset of a larger, transnational economy. Governments already share their effective power with other agents, and in all relevant policy areas, there is intensive border-crossing co-ordination and regulation. Thus, "[c]ontemporary forms of political globalization involve a deterritorialization of political authority, although exactly how far this process has gone remains to be specified further" (*ibid.*: 81). In the emerging global system, the nature of sovereignty is therefore undergoing an important change. Sovereignty is now to be understood more as a bargaining resource as opposed to a territorially defined barrier to movements (Keohane 1995).

Migration and Globalisation Research

The emergence of the transformationalist approach to globalisation is certainly a positive development in the globalisation debate. It overcomes a very simplistic understanding of the relationship between states and markets present in some of the earlier formulations such as Ohmae's claim that the nation-state has been superseded, or O'Brian's argument that we are witnessing the 'end of geography' (Ohmae 1994; O'Brian 1992). However, all three perspectives on globalisation are problematic.

All three perspectives are committed to the same simplistic model of social change: transformations in the economy (but also in other spheres of society) are regarded as producing pressures to which "the form and functions of the state are having to adapt" (Held et al. 1999: 9). Hence, even though the transformationalists do not see a complete subordination of the state to the market as a result of globalisation, the focus of inquiry remains the same as that of the hyperglobalisers[5]: globalisation is conceptualised as an independent variable; at issue are its consequences.[6] As a consequence, an inquiry into the origin of globalisation and the politics surrounding it is no longer undertaken. Instead, globalisation is simply taken for granted and presented as an

---

5 The sceptics simply claim that there is no change in the economic field that would require an adaptation, but the underlying model of argumentation is the same: if there were a shift from internationalisation to globalisation, the consequences for the state would indeed be severe and debilitating (Weiss 1999: 64-66; cf. Hirst and Thompson 1999: ch. 1).

6 In many ways, the terms of the globalisation debate resemble the base/superstructure model of traditional Marxism, where politics is regarded as epiphenomenal; the change from hyperglobalist to transformationalist globalisation approaches in turn resembles the shift within Marxism from economic determinism to theories stressing the 'relative autonomy' of the state.

independent variable immune to political influences. It is interesting to note that the same criticism has already been applied to the interdependence theory of the 1970s, which took increasing interdependence as its independent variable, but failed to inquire into the social interests that set the conditions for growing interdependence (Kohler-Koch 1990: 112). From a critical theory perspective whereby theory is both a means for description, explanation *and* change (Bernstein 1979: 293) this argumentation is problematic because it does not allow room for manoeuvre to question and challenge the globalisation process as such but merely to deal with its consequences. What is needed is an account of the origins and the politics of globalisation itself.

This is necessary because all three perspectives ignore that there is an increasing asymmetry of allocated benefits at the heart of the functioning of the global political economy for developing countries. The central asset of developing countries in the global political economy is an abundance of labour. But while investment regulations and trade regulations have been liberalised in the last 50 years, and short-term investment flows in the last 20 years, migrants from developing countries find it difficult to enter rich industrialised countries. It is this asymmetry of access for capital and labour that creates a major impediment for the reduction of inequality (Nayyar 2002: 158). Migration then represents a paradox within globalisation. Superficially,

> [...] the resurgence in migration appears to have placed people on the same footing as capital, as being no longer territorially bound. Yet nothing could be further from the truth. In contrast with the many ways in which nation-states have removed obstacles to the circulation of capital, there has not been an extension to people of the entitlements afforded capital (Rosewarne 2001: 72).

My argument is that it is this discrepancy of access that needs to be put at the centre of globalisation theory because it shows that states are not the at the mercy of global economic flows but have some extent of policy autonomy, in contrast to the claims put forward by hyperglobalisers. It is a sign that the global economy is not the result of states giving in to increasing economic integration but points to the fact that global integration is entwined in or even preconditioned on political action.

As I will show in chapter two, migration is a laggard in the globalisation process in two ways. First, the (international) mobility of labour as a factor of production has not increased substantially over the last twenty-five years if measured relatively, and if compared with the flows of goods, services and capital. Global exports of goods represent around 29 percent of world GDP, the inflow of FDI is at about six percent of gross domestic investment but global labour migration involves only about 2.3 percent of world population (Stalker 2000: 1; cf. World Bank 1995: 53). According to Nayyar (2002: 156), the number of new immigrants per 1,000 inhabitants in the world as a whole in 1990 was lower than in 1970. It is true that if absolute figures are looked at, migration is a substantial force in the world economy: in the 1990s there were about 3 million immigrants entering western countries alone annually. Worldwide remittances were in the range of $45 billion to developing countries in the 1990s (yearly) compared to about $100 billion of annual foreign direct investment. Relatively (measured against inhabitants), however, migration flows are much lower than trade and investment flows.

Secondly and, more importantly, migration policies have become more restrictive: borders control functions of states have been strengthened, *and* access to social and labour market regulation regimes for migrants has been restricted. The latter development means that if migrants are let into a country they come under more precarious conditions and do not receive the same treatment as citizens (as they are entitled to under International Labour Organisation conventions or

under the Geneva Refugee Convention). In contrast to regimes for trade and capital flows, there are no international regimes in support for more migration. Central migration conventions are not ratified by many immigration countries, and policies at the national level aim largely at restricting and controlling the flow of people (Torpey 2000b: 32; Freeman 1998).
Saskia Sassen therefore concludes that immigration policy in western democracies "is increasingly at odds with other major policy frameworks in the international system and with the growth of global economic integration" (Sassen 1999: 7). The discrepancy between the globalisation of capital and commodities and the relative non-globalisation of migration has also been noted by Robert Gilpin: "Try telling a Mexican or North African low-skilled labourer that we now live in a global economy in which national boundaries have ceased to be important! In fact, much of the globalisation rhetoric is no more than the conceit of a rich and industrialized country" (Gilpin 2000: 295). We therefore have to conclude that while there are indeed processes of debordering of the state, there are also processes of re-bordering (Andreas 2000: 2; Klein-Beekman 1996: 454-455). Instead of focusing on one side of the coin (either disappearance or continued strengthening of the state) it is this dialectic between territorial grounding and ongoing debordering that needs to be put at the centre of research into "globalisation".
The migration restrictions that put a severe limit on factor mobility represent an anomaly in today's global economy, and it is therefore important to explain why they are there by setting them into the context of the overall tendency towards further liberalisation, in order to get a better understanding of globalisation process itself. They are an anomaly, firstly, because unfree migration runs counter to today's prevalent economic theory which argues that free factor flows are

beneficial to growth and produce efficiency gains (see for example OECD 1998a); furthermore, economic theory argues that the market and not the state is to determine the allocation of the factors of production. In a global economy we should therefore also expect a global free labour market, not a "wall around the west" (Andreas and Snyder 2000).

Secondly, this situation is also an anomaly from a historical perspective. It has become a commonplace in the literature to compare the present epoch of globalisation with the first one between the late 19th century and 1914. But one central difference between the process of economic globalisation in the nineteenth century and today is that migration played as important a role as trade and investment flows (Hirst and Thompson 1999: 26; Zolberg 1991: 311-312). Policies towards migrants were markedly different in the 19th century: immigration and emigration were almost free, at least for the migration of European people to the Americas (O'Rourke and Williamson 1999). No passports were required until the First World War (Mills 1998: 115-116; Torpey 2000a: 111). However, in the present globalisation period, the cross-border movement of people is tightly regulated and there is only a selective freedom of movement (e.g. for professionals) (Nayyar 2002: 158).

We therefore need to understand why today, migration is such an exception in the globalisation process. Any theory that purports to explain globalisation, therefore, has to account for the simultaneous occurrence of two different but closely related bordering strategies of states, one that is geared at integrating societies into a global market, and one that seeks to draw renewed boundaries for particular transborder flows (Zolberg 1989: 408). The problem then is how to explain (rather than to describe) *which* bordering strategies are applied to *what* flows. While the transformationalists recognize the relative non-globalisation but their multi-causal model of social change is unable to explain *why* states behave differently towards these globalisation flows. It is not sufficient to note that globalisation is a complex multi-causal process with differentiated impact (Held et al. 1999: 436-444). It also has to be explained *why* different aspects are regulated in such contrary ways. In other words, what is needed is an understanding of how the global political economy with its specific but discriminatory rules for capital and labour came to be constructed in the first place. Such an approach moves away from process into the *politics of globalisation* in order to understand who benefits and who looses from the present organisation of the global political economy. In the next section I will outline a theoretical perspective that allows us to uncover in how far the present discriminatory rules for the global economy are a reflection of the specific interests and power relations that underlie its making.

Globalisation as Project? The Neo-Gramscian Perspective

As the preceding section has shown, much of the debate on globalisation debate is reductionist in that it ignores the political origin of globalisation and in that it overlooks the lopsidedness of the globalisation process itself. While a more institutionalist framework such as suggested for example by Linda Weiss (1998) and Peter Evans (1997) provides a first step in the right direction, it still does not adequately address the social content and the historical specificity of what globalisation implies, and remains weak when it comes to explaining both globalisation and territorialisation. An integrated framework of analysis focusing on historical structures and the social forces involved in their making, by contrast, allows us to address the historical specificity of the present transformation and the politics behind it. This is precisely what the neo-Gramscian perspective – developed by Robert W. Cox, Stephen Gill and Kees van der Pijl– offers.[7] Politics from this perspective is not something that matters only at the 'output' side. On the contrary, politics is part of the emergence of 'globalisation' itself. Thus, globalisation may be best understood as a political project, rather than as a process that is driven by technological and market changes. As a political project, its main objective is to "institutionalise the neoliberal agenda of market reform by removing public constraints on economies" (McMichael: 2000: 110; Gill 1995a). We can understand globalisation only if we analyse not merely the political consequences of globalisation, but the politics of 'making' globalisation itself. This raises the question, for instance, as to what sort of movements and interactions we will find in a particular world economy, and how and why these (rather than others) prevail.

Most observers agree, for example, that capital mobility is a central element of the new global economy. But for Jagdish Bhagwati, the emergence of global finance and investment is not a natural extension of the free trade principle. Asking why the world accepts the increasing mobility of capital, despite the instabilities it generates, he points out: "The answer, as always reflects ideology and interests – that is, lobbies. The ideology is clearly that of the market. [...] But interests have also played a central role" (Bhagwati 1998: 11).[8] These interests,

---

7   Augelli and Murphy (1988); Cox (1987), (1996a); Gill (1990a), (1995a); Gill and Law (1988); Holman (1996); Lee (1995); Murphy (1994); Overbeek (1990); Ryner (1997); Rupert (1995), (2000); Röttger (1997); Scherrer (1999); van Apeldoorn (1998); van der Pjil (1984), (1996), (1998); Whitworth (1994); edited volumes: Gill (1993c); Overbeek (1993a); Gill and Mittelman (1997); Hettne (1995);

8   According to Bhagwati, the reason cannot be found in economic theory; for no one has so far been able to conclusively show the benefits of free

he argues, should be seen as a "power elite [...], a definite networking of like-minded luminaries among the powerful institutions – Wall Street, the Treasury Department, the State Department, the IMF, and the World Bank most prominent among them" (*ibid.*: 11). Bhagwati calls this network the "Wall Street Treasury complex", which he regards as "unable to look much beyond the interests of Wall Street, which it equates with the good of the world" (*ibid.*: 12). At least partly, globalisation is shown to be a social and political project with specific interests behind it.

But 'globalisation as project' and 'globalisation as process' should not be seen as mutually exclusive perspectives. John Gray puts forward the argument that what we call 'globalisation' should really be understood as the coming together of two distinct developments (Gray 1999: 215): On the one hand, it represents a new step in the centuries old dynamic of capitalist globalisation (and may even reach back much further); the current expansion and deepening of the world market and of transnational relations therefore follows, at least partly, a larger historical trend. Innovations in communications and information technology and in transportation are clearly important factors, which made this new step possible.

On the other hand, this process of globalisation is also decisively shaped by the attempt of those countries that first underwent a neoliberal transformation – especially the US and Great Britain – to internationalise and universalise their model of state-market relationships and to make free-market thinking dominant. For Gray, this second aspect of contemporary globalisation tells us much more about the nature of

---

  capital mobility (unlike the theory of international trade has been able to do for commodity exchange), quite apart from the risks of crisis. As Bhagwati (1998: 10) sums up: "all we have from the proponents of capital mobility is banner-waving".

the global political economy than the first aspect. He argues – similar to Weiss, Bhagwati and Evans – that many of the consequences that are attributed by both hyperglobalisers and transformationalists to the process of globalisation are in fact a result of the political construction of a global free market by the US and Great Britain (*ibid.*: 235).

Such a perspective on globalisation, as simultaneously a *project* and a *process*, has been explicitly developed by Robert W. Cox and other scholars working within the neo-Gramscian framework. For Cox globalisation is, on the one hand, a process because it "is not the consequence of a conscious decision of political leadership" but has to be seen as the "result of structural changes in capitalism, in the actions of many people [...] that cumulatively produce new relationships and patterns of behavior" (Cox 1996: 296; Gill 1995a: 405). These changes are related not simply to technological innovations, but are the result of the contradictions of the welfare state (form of state) and of embedded liberalism (world order), the decreasing profitability of investments in OECD countries during the world economic depression of the 1970s, and the increasing pressure on profits through higher wages and taxes (production relations). As Cox notes, the "crisis of the post war order has expanded the breath and depth of a global economy that exists alongside and incrementally supersedes the classical international economy" (*ibid.*: 300).

On the other hand, globalisation is also a project. For Cox, the attempts of economic actors to escape from the crisis of the post-war order through global restructuring can only succeed in providing the basis for a new model of economic development if they are embedded in a set of political and world order structures that are compatible with the global organisation of production and finance. In this context, the agency not only of states, but also of 'social forces', has been crucial in the attempt to create such a system of mutually reinforcing structures, and to bring about a 'hegemonic fit'.[9] Neoliberal ideas are a central part of this project. Thus, the measures undertaken by governments influenced by neoliberal thinking have reinforced globalising economic tendencies. That social and political agency took this neoliberal form was not given from the beginning; it emerged from social and political conflicts and represent one particular resolution (serving particular interests) of the crisis of embedded liberalism in the 1970s.[10]

In this way, the global economy of today is indeed only understandable as both a process and as a socio-political project. What Cox adds to the perspective put forward by Gray and others who focus mainly on states, is the emphasis on the agency of social forces that shape state policy in important ways. This also implies that while the United States government, American transnational corporations and private institutions have played a central role in the emergence of the neoliberal project, the latter cannot be understood simply as the reassertion of American hegemony. This historic bloc of social forces has its basis in the transnationalisation of production which took place during the

---

9   Compare Gill (1993d), (1995a), (1998); Overbeek and van der Pijl (1993).
10 Other projects were put forward for example by the new social movements (cf. Offe 1987) or by social democrats (e.g. Brandt Commission). These projects did not start their analysis of the crisis from the perspective of the First World and its economic and social problems only, but also focused on the even more pressing problems of the Third World. Instead of the subsequent adjustment of the Third World to the needs and requirements of the First through a series of structural adjustment programs, they pointed out the need for a policy in which the First World would take on board some of the concerns of the Third World. Neo-Gramscians argue that these alternative projects to deal with the organic crisis of the capitalist order since the 1970s have become or remained marginalised and the neoliberal project has taken centre stage.

period of the 'Pax Americana' (1945-1973); since then it has come to include public and private institutions and has become increasingly transnational, including elites from Europe and Japan (Gill 1990a). It is this emerging bloc of transnational interests that effectively prevented a breakdown of the multilateral system established after World War II, and made possible the co-ordinated move towards a system of global economic integration and global governance in reaction to the world economic crisis of the 1970s, instead of leading to renewed protectionism and imperialist rivalry (*ibid.*: 50).[11] This transnational historic bloc has also ensured that policy responses to the crisis of the Bretton Woods order were to some extent orchestrated, and common (or at least compatible) approaches were adopted by infusing formal governmental international organisations such as the OECD, the IMF and the World Bank with these ideas (Cox 1987: 259). From these international public (and private) fora, neoliberalism was diffused to other countries. All western (and southern) societies have since then made moves towards deregulation of prices, liberalisation of cross border exchanges (especially the capital account), and the privatisation of public enterprises, though the degree of similarity and homogeneity should not be overstated.[12]

---

11 For a similar conclusion from a liberal perspective cf. Bhagwati (1988: 73-79).
12 This does not imply a complete homogenisation of public policies and organizational structures. Like many institutionalists, neo-Gramscians stress the persistence of national differences and different institutional set-ups as a result of different historical contexts and path-dependent development (Cox 1987: 286ff). As Cerny argues, one reason for the persistence of divergence is that competitive advantage can be obtained by using specific national traditions and institutions to find a niche on the world market (Cerny 1996: 626). If looked at in this light, the divergence of state strategies and their common integration into the global

The point remains, however, that it is not globalisation itself that can be held responsible for the transformation from the Keynesian welfare state and embedded liberalism towards the 'competition state'. Instead, this shift reflects a social choice, which was itself constitutive of the nature and extent of the globalisation process that took place over the last three decades (Gill 1993d; Overbeek and van der Pijl 1993). The net effect of these developments has been to transform the state into a "transmission belt" for the "perceived exigencies of the global economy" to the national level (Cox 1996: 302). But, and this is crucial, the state itself 'participated' in this transformation by creating the conditions in which specific social forces and production processes become more prevalent than others. The agency of the state is thus crucial in the transformation from embedded liberalism to neoliberalism (Cox 1987: 399).

The central point of the neo-Gramscian perspective on globalisation is therefore that neoliberalism cannot be understood as a reaction to an external and independent process of globalisation which leaves states no other choice than to adjust to market imperatives. Rather, neoliberalism represents itself a choice, which has become more and more influential in shaping public policy and in the construction of a global 'regime of accumulation' and a related 'mode of regulation'. The ideas of neoliberalism, and the interests of neoliberal elites, have had the effect of constructing globalisation as a force that requires the subordination of politics to economics, and of the national state to the world market. This 'construction' is not only ideological; it does not simply operate in the realm of ideas. Rather, it has itself become a reality as first the United States and Great Britain and then other

---

economy go hand in hand, and should not be seen as mutually exclusive options.

state/society complexes have 'accepted'[13], and promoted the primacy of economics. Their policies to liberalise the flows of goods, services, investments and money have now created a system in which the policy options of (all) states *are* limited, though probably not to the degree suggested by the 'hyperglobalisers'. But now, as a *consequence* of the predominance of neoliberalism, "a powerful globalizing economic trend thrusts towards the achievement of a market utopia on the world scale" (Cox 1991: 335). This trend has not been stopped by the increased unilateralism of the United States fighting a war on terror. On the contrary, one of the arguments being used to justify pre-emptive actions is precisely the idea that a free global market populated by liberal democratic states is best for all.

As the idea of the dominance of the market is regarded as the most important characteristic of 'hyperglobalism' by Held and his colleagues, it is not surprising that we find Cox and Gill categorised as hyperglobalisers (Held et al. 1999: 4). But like the transformationalists, the neo-Gramscians do not regard this as inevitable and irreversible. In fact, the neo-Gramscians stress continuously the instabilities of the neoliberal market utopia: the weaknesses in its financial structure, the tensions between global accumulation and the restriction of consumption possibilities as a result of deflationary policies; and the possibility of social resistance against the subordination of more and more aspects of social life to the requirements of economic efficiency that could transform neoliberalism beyond recognition (Gill 1995a: 419; Cox 1997: 64).

In fact, the neo-Gramscian perspective *is* in many ways a transformationalist approach to globalisation. It does not posit a demise of the state, but a re-articulating of its functions. More than any other ap-

---

13 How this acceptance was manufactured see the study by Blyth (2002: 126-201).

proach, it has been concerned to show the substance (or social content) of this transformation by looking at the change of ideas, in social alliances and institutional structures as a part of historical structures. Furthermore, it avoids economic determinism by emphasising the dialectical relationship between politics and economics (Cox 1986). Instead of conceptualising the global economy as an independent variable, it sees the global economy as an expression of a specific *political project* that in turn is confronted by other political projects each competing for hegemony.

Conclusion

The question that motivates this book is whether the relative non-globalisation of migration can be explained by looking into the politics of how globalisation is made, as the neo-Gramscian perspective asks us to do. As further outlined in chapter three this requires that we look at dominant and oppositional 'historic blocs' in three different spheres: world order, forms of state and production. The central proposition put forward by the neo-Gramscians is that the current world order is dominated by globalising elites trying to cement a neoliberal historic bloc whose core project is 'globalisation'. Key ideas of this historic bloc are the fight against inflation, reducing state intervention in the economy (in specific areas) and strengthening the competitiveness of nation-states by increasing market flexibility. At the apex of these globalising elites is the United States but other globalising elite segments are willing partners. Until now, opposition to this neoliberal historic bloc is fragmented.
So far, however, the market-making elements of this political project were at the centre of the neo-Gramscian perspective. My study pur-

sues this agenda further in trying to establish whether the globalising elite is also behind efforts to regulate the movements of people by erecting and strengthening borders. This would point to important territorial elements of the neoliberal project that have thus far not been incorporated into the perspective (nor into globalisation studies more generally).

Following this proposition, the case study in chapter four will demonstrate that the selective bordering strategy for capital and labour can indeed be traced back to neoliberal elite interests. This research finding stands in marked contrast to migration research that attributes rising anti-immigrant rhetoric mostly to right-wing populist forces (see Betz 1994). As I show in this chapter, neoliberal policy designing elites at the OECD or within the framework of the Chicago School, explicitly favour the restriction of international migration flows, and advocate migration policies that do not parallel their general prescriptions for greater global integration. The contradictory nature of the present global economy, therefore, in which liberalisation and deregulation of financial and trade flows are promoted but in which restrictions on migrations have largely remained in place or have even been strengthened is also a reflection of elite preferences. This means that the selective and discriminatory opening of borders is inherent in the neoliberal globalisation project, and not an accident.

However, as we will have learned in chapter one, there are flows of migrant labour into western industrialised countries. While states in general try to reduce migration, there is a new worker migration in the form of new temporary work programmes or illegal migration. Focusing on changes in production processes, the new international division of labour, and its impact upon labour, chapter five will illustrate in two case studies that particularly this new worker migration has an important function for neoliberal strategies of labour market restructuring. As I will show in this chapter migrant labour is used to create the flexible labour market that employers in the transition to a post industrial or post-Fordist order need. But it is a special type of migrant labour that is employed in labour market restructuring, one that is in effect 'created' by the restrictive border regime: undocumented migrant labour or temporary workers. The implication is that neoliberal labour market restructuring is in part contingent on a restrictive labour migration regime.

From these results I conclude that migration has a double role in the neoliberal globalisation project: on the one hand, general free migration is not needed if there is free capital mobility since capital can go to the workers. For these reasons, the globalising elite either ignores migration totally or even rejects freedom of mobility for workers. This disinterest in free migration makes it possible to form a populist coalition for migration restrictions in order to push through more central elements of the neoliberal project. In this way the restrictive and repressive migration regime stabilises and legitimises globalisation by providing the state with a strong and active role that contrasts sharply with the state's 'inability' to promote policy changes in other, more relevant, areas. Immigrants are used as scapegoats in order to deflect the attention of the public from the need to develop more inclusive economic policies (Sutcliffe 2004: 277).

The second role of immigration is to increase the competitiveness of the national economy by increasing labour market flexibility, a central plank in the neoliberal project. This is achieved by a highly selective migration policy that one the one hand displays more openness towards skilled migrants.[14] On the other hand, the increasingly restric-

---

14 But even the skilled migrants today come into the countries first as temporary workers which makes them more vulnerable as citizens on

tiveness of migration policy creates an immigrant labour pool consisting mostly of illegal (or temporary) immigrants who are willing to accept any type of position, and especially working conditions for fear of deportation. In this way, they decrease costs for employers by accepting jobs in unsafe conditions, lower wages, and that are without social security payments. This structural need for 'undocumented' and thus flexible migrants in western economies explains why migration controls are often not very effective.

Yet, as chapter five demonstrates, this state of affairs is unstable. The specific neoliberal coalition pushing for such a specific and limited role of migrant labour is confronted by oppositional forces that are not, as critics claim, merely protectionist and nationalist but who have a different vision on global integration altogether. Whether or not, and if, to what extent this alternative vision of a global economy based on fairness and justice can be realised in the more repressive conditions after the terrorist attacks on the United States and the ensuing war against terror, is one of the central questions facing students of the global political economy today.

---

the labour market. Employers therefore receive a pool of skilled and "more flexible" labour migrants in this way.

2. INSTITUTIONAL ASYMMETRY IN THE GLOBAL ECONOMY: FREEDOM FOR CAPITAL – RESTRICTED MIGRATION

At the heart of today's global economy is the primacy accorded to considerations of economic efficiency and profitability. Global economic integration is regarded by today's policy-makers and economists as promoting efficiency gains; it is also considered to boost rational economic behaviour by firms and governments who now have to act under the pressure of 'market discipline'. In doing so, economic growth will result and global inequalities will decrease. In order to generate these benefits, countries have to reduce state intervention in the economy by liberalising trade and capital accounts, privatise state enterprises and increase the flexibility of markets more generally. According to neo-classical economic theory, commodity trade can, to some extent, be a substitute for factor mobility if trade is induced due to varying factor endowments. However, trade is only a second-best substitute for factor mobility; world production is raised more by factor mobility than by trade and specialisation (Ethier 1995: 290-293). In other words, while economic efficiency increases through the participation of countries in an international division of labour relying on trade, a functionally integrated world economy based on a global social division of labour, with global production chains made possible by factor mobility, would raise economic efficiency even more – at least in the aggregate.

In the neo-classical view, therefore, policies that restrict factor mobility put a constraint on economic efficiency and profitability, and are thus problematic from the standpoint of both the individual firm and the economy as a whole. It is for this reason that many regulations or institutional settings impeding factor mobility – such as restrictions on the capital account, state-owned industries, and tariffs – have been reduced or abolished over the last thirty years. The superseding of the international by a global economy to which these policies have led (or which they have accompanied) is based precisely on the predominance of factor movements over trade relations. For these reasons it has been suggested that a central characteristic of the global economy is just this emergence of global production and financial systems that take advantage of increased possibilities for foreign direct investment and other monetary flows. The following sections will outline the change from the embedded liberalism of the post-1945 economy to today.

Embedded Liberalism

Today's emphasis on global economic integration stands in marked contrast to what has been seen as the central economic lesson of the social upheaval of the 1930s, namely that internationalisation should take place only if there are domestic safeguards (Ruggie 1996: 37). Thus, the post-1945 economic order, even though it contained specific elements of liberalisation, cannot be characterised as a complete return to the classical liberal economic order prevalent until 1913. Instead, as John Ruggie has pointed out, it institutionalised a particular relationship between state and (world) market that may be best understood in terms of an "embedded liberalism" (Ruggie 1982). This post-war order consisted of a commitment to a liberal international trading system based on the principles of multilateralism. It also embraced the gradual abolition of all forms of exchange controls and restrictions on current account transactions.

But these measures, which aimed at the development of a universal system of free (or increasingly freer) trade, were predicated on a system of domestic safeguards and a 'double screen' to protect the domestic economy from immediate structural adjustment stemming from balance of payments deficits. This system included the pegging of currency exchange rates, and the provision of short-term assistance for deficit countries by the IMF; most crucial, however, was the imposition of capital controls (Ruggie 1996: 37-38, 110; cf. Helleiner 1994). Capital controls were necessary to ensure an independent domestic macroeconomic policy that should not be endangered by a sudden capital flight and that would allow governments to set interest rates in accordance with domestic requirements, and without reference to interest rate levels in other countries (Helleiner 1994: 164). In order to ensure this, the Articles of Agreement of the IMF laid down that member countries have to maintain currency convertibility for current transactions but not for capital flows (Sachs 1998: 103). In this way, the interventionist state was 'embedded' in the international economic order in a way that allowed for some control over the extent of integration. The post-war economic regime thus provided for some freedoms: the freedom to trade but there were restrictions on finance.

Since the collapse of the Bretton Woods system in 1971 with the unilateral retreat by the United States, the principle of multilateralism has more or less remained the dominant form of world economic organisation (even though tendencies towards greater unilateralism and regionalism clearly exist, and almost all developed states increasingly resort to bilateral treaties to regulate their trade relationships). By contrast, as will be shown in the following, the post-war domestic and international safeguards – designed to cushion adjustment pressures, make possible national economic development, and increase social stability – have been severely undermined over this period (Ruggie 1996: 35-37 and 136). The international institutions supervising the multilateral system, newly created or adapted to the new global social and political environment, have come to reflect rather different social purposes than those of the post-war period. The 'politics of liberalisation' has not only entailed a reconstitution of the relationship between the state and society with the state abandoning much of its interventionist stance towards most economic flows.

But is there also a globally integrated labour market? Efficiency gains cannot only be achieved on the basis of the mobility of capital and goods, but also through the lifting of restrictions on the mobility of labour. This is especially the case in those sectors where trade and capital mobility do not substitute for the mobility of people, which applies particularly to the service sector. Given that services have become increasingly important in the economic structures of most OECD countries, we might thus expect that there are mechanisms in place that secure the freedom of movement for people, including their right to national treatment, non-discrimination and right to settlement.

The task of the next sections is to chart the development of the global economy with regard to factor mobility since the mid-seventies. I will first show that there has been a politics of liberalisation towards financial, goods, services and trade flows in the global economy visible in such institutions as the establishment of the World Trade Organisation (WTO), the structural adjustment programs, and the move towards a regime for investment in the OECD. In the following section, I will first discuss the argument by Soysal (1994), Jacobson (1996) and Hollifield (1992) who have argued that there is also a liberal transformation of migration policies. However, I will show that this liberalisation has been limited to a specific inflow and that the new migration of the eighties and nineties is faced with an ever increasing array of restrictions on the free movement of people. I will demonstrate that the migration policies of the last 25 years – the period of 'globalisation' – have been significantly more restrictive than the public policies relating to goods, money and services.

Institutionalising Liberalism Worldwide

Governing Trade Flows

Since 1947, trade has been regulated at the international level through the General Agreement on Tariffs and Trade (GATT). The general aim of GATT was and is to liberalise trade by breaking down restrictions on imports and exports. The principal means to achieve these aims were, firstly, the introduction of the most-favoured nation principle in the GATT, under which trade advantages given by a member country to any other country must be extended unconditionally to all other GATT members; and, secondly, the idea of national treatment, under which goods and services, once in the country, are treated as favourably as domestic products concerning taxes and other regulations. Steps towards further liberalisation were negotiated among countries in successive negotiation rounds. Of these, the Uruguay Round was the latest (1986-1993) and the most extensive, covering tariffs, non-tariff measures, services, intellectual property rights, dispute settlement, trade-related investment, textiles, and agriculture. Most importantly, at the end of the round, a new organisation, the World Trade organisation (WTO) was established of which the GATT is now a part. For the first time, the trade regime is truly global because almost all Third World countries, which were formerly opposed to the central principles of GATT, have now joined the organisation. The reversal of the attitude of Third World countries that were formerly united in for a such as the G77 demanding for a New International Economic Order based on principles centrally opposite to the ones governing today, is indeed remarkable. Between 1981 and 1994, 33 countries acceded to the GATT (Cohn 2000: 228). With the impending accession of China, no major country is now outside the reach of the trade regime. In this sense, the trade regime is now truly globalised.

The Uruguay Round led to a reduction of tariffs, and prevented rising tariffs even in those countries and regions (e.g. Latin America) that were hit by economic and financial crises (Stokes 1999/2000: 90). The use of the most important protectionist instruments (such as countervailing duties, antidumping measures and safeguards) has been regulated – and thus limited – under the WTO (Ruggie 1996: 123). Voluntary export restraints have all but disappeared during the 1990s. While in 1992 Europe had 33 of these restraints, and the US 17, today they have been abolished (Stokes 1999/2000: 91). The most important and widespread embodiment of protectionist policies, the Multifibre Agreement – which negotiated fixed market shares for textile products by multilaterally co-ordinated bilateral quotas – will be phased out over the next years (Ruggie 1996: 124).

The Uruguay Round has extended the scope of the trade regime by incorporating an agreement on services, and by coming to an agreement over agriculture, investments and property rights. In agriculture, it was agreed that the value of subsidies would be reduced by 36 percent and the volume of subsidised exports by 21 percent over a six-year period (Krugman and Obstfeld 1997: 239). The actual liberalisa-

tion in services was limited, but the main achievement was the establishment of a legal framework for negotiations over services, and the recognition that services are a part of international trade (Eiteljörge 1998: 167-168). Most importantly, perhaps, the establishment of the WTO means that independent dispute settlement mechanisms have been strengthened because the consent of all member states is no longer required for a dispute settlement to be concluded. As a result the time to settle trade disputes will be shortened. Furthermore, the sanctions for norm violations have been strengthened (Zangl 1999: 11). Thus, the successful conclusion of the Uruguay Round dispelled or diluted much of the renewed protectionism that had emerged in the 1980s. Furthermore, by taking up new issues it secured a renewal and a widening of the scope of trade liberalisation.[15]
Even though the new trade round that has started in Doha in 1991 has run into difficulties, the integration of the former 'Third World' and the countries of the ex-Soviet bloc into the trade regime which signals their acceptance of free market economics stand as a major stepping stone in the development of global liberalism.

Financing Development – Debt and Global Structural Change

The development of the Euromarkets (offshore markets for dollars and other foreign currency deposits), is often portrayed as epitomising the ungovernability of financial globalisation. However, their development was tolerated or even actively promoted because both European states and the US perceived these markets as providing their interna-

---

15   For the developing countries these efforts at liberalisation come somewhat late. Most of the "new protectionism" was aimed at Third World countries (Held et al. 1999: 165), which had to earn foreign currencies especially in the 1980s in order to service their debts.

tionally active firms with capital in a period that was still characterised by domestic capital controls and controls on interest rates (Kapstein 1994: 35). Their role was strengthened by the recycling of the petrodollars after 1974 via loans to developing countries. This lending was supported by the assurance of industrial countries that they would act as lenders of last resort in times of crisis. Without this assurance, banks would not have provided many Third World countries with finance to deal with the balance of payments crisis caused by rising oil prices (Cox 1987: 301). In addition to these policy stances, official loans – via bilateral agreements and by the World Bank and the IMF – made up approximately 45 percent of the capital flows to the countries of the Third World and provided some reassurance to private banks (Kapstein 1994: 66). According to Kapstein, these assurances and pressures to continue international bank lending served to maintain the liberal economy in the seventies despite increasing calls for protectionism.

Another ingredient in the liberalising trend has been the OECD's 'Code for the Liberalisation of the Capital Account', which is now accepted by the majority of the OECD member states, and far beyond. The first code was established in 1961 and contained manifold exceptions to the proposed liberalisation efforts. For example, capital controls were seen as acceptable measures during a balance of payments crisis. "OECD member states retained the right to re-impose controls whenever conditions warranted" (Goodman and Pauly 1994: 53). However, between 1967 and 1995 the percentage of OECD countries with capital control decreased from around 70 to below 10 percent (Leblang 1997: 438). Worldwide restrictions on the current account decreased from 60 percent in 1985 to below 40 percent in 1995. In 1989 the OECD regulation governing capital movements were widened in scope. Since then, and with the impending changes in the IMF regulations (see below) we can speak of a regime change from a regime in which capital flows were allowed to be controlled, to a new era in which capital controls are outlawed by international agreement (Pauly 1995: 380).

Thus, by the end of the 1980s, one central element of the new global liberalism has been achieved: capital controls had been made outdated and unacceptable. The driving force behind this move, according to Wade and Veneroso (1998b: 35-36), was the United States, which needed the free movement of capital because of its low savings rate; in order to maintain its consumption and investment levels, the US needs inflows from the rest of the world. At the same time, as Beth Simmons (1999) notes, the US sought lost its competitive edge over Europe and sought to establish its dominance in the financial markets where its firms were more competitive.

Finally, free capital movements help to lock in more general liberal reforms of labour markets and corporate governance, modelled upon the US model. Private international capital is central in today's world economy because it is the principal external constraint on countries to maintain a policy of openness. This is achieved by shifting capital abroad if a government implements policies which are seen as problematic to economic growth and fiscal 'responsibility' (Cox 1987: 267, 305). These concerns remain relevant today, as the US exerts increasing pressure to change the 'Articles of Agreement' of the IMF to make the abolishment of capital controls a condition for membership in the Fund. By changing article one, the promotion of liberalisation of capital movements would become one of the main purposes of the Fund. Under Article VII, the Fund might be endowed with the same jurisdiction over the capital account of its members as it has over the current account. Thus, any capital account restrictions would have to be approved by the IMF (Wade and Veneroso 1998b: 34).

The most important factor for promoting further economic integration was the debt crisis in the early 1980s that also posed the greatest challenge to international economic stability that the world had faced since the Great Depression in the 1930s. With the turn to a monetarist policy and the rise of interest rates, the US shifted the burden of adjustment decisively onto Third World countries and prepared the ground for the integration of the Third World into the emerging neoliberal world order. When Mexico announced in August 1982 that it was unable to meet its payments obligations to foreign banks, the American central bank, the Treasury and other US government agencies put together a rescue package to provide bail-out money and exerted pressure on US banks to reschedule their debts to Mexico. By providing liquidity to ensure the uninterrupted operation of the international payments system, the US government and international institutions provided essential short-term crisis management (Kapstein 1994: 82, 88-89). When it was realised that the problem was not temporary, longer-term adjustment measures were developed. Both short-term stabilisation measures and longer-term structural adjustment policies contain measures to further the integration of the country's economy into the global economy (Cox 1987: 260).

By rescheduling debts and by preventing a closing off of indebted countries, the international financial institutions secured the continued functioning of the global economy. But they went beyond this. The central aim of the various structural adjustment programs was the reversal of the then prevalent import-substitution regimes that had a totally different goal than the new development consensus. The latter argues that economic growth will result if countries form a part of a global division of labour. Import substitution in contrast had aimed at developing a national industrial base from which (at a later stage) developing countries could compete in the global economy. Integral to this development strategy were, among other things, protective tariffs, exchange controls, a special import regime, cheap government credits, and the direct participation of government in certain industries (Baer 1972: 97). The outward expression of import-substituting regimes was the movement by Third World States that culminated in the demands for a New International Economic Order under which states should have the right to exercise exclusive sovereignty over their wealth and natural resources, to regulate foreign investments and to nationalise, expropriate, or transfer the ownership of foreign proprietors, with controversies to be settled by domestic law.[16]

In the 1980s, 31 countries had agreements with the international financial institutions for five or more years, and 68 countries had programmes with the IMF or the World Bank for two to four years (Stewart 1995: 6). In total, between 1978 and 1992 566 stabilisation programmes were issued by the IMF and the World Bank (Robinson 2001: 180, 185). About 50 percent of the IMF programmes contained exchange rate reforms, financial reforms and trade liberalisation (Stewart 1995: 9). With regard to the World Bank 57 percent of the structural adjustment loans from 1980-87 included trade policy measures. Other aspects concerned specific anti-inflationary measures such as a raise in interest rates, the reduction of government deficits through curbs on spending (especially for social services), a control of wage increases, and the dismantling of price controls. Most also contain provisions to increase hospitality to foreign investment, and decrease government control of its operation (Todaro 1989: 420). The implementation rate of these structural reforms was 42 percent

---

16 See the "Charter of Economic Rights and Duties of States" (GA Resolution 3281 (XXIX) December 1974), and the "Declaration on the Establishment of a New International Economic Order" (General Assembly Resolution 3201 (S-VI) May 1974).

(Mosley 1992: 32-33). Some countries adopt so-called "shadow programs" which are agreed with but not financed by the IMF, other countries adopted parts of the IMF policy prescriptions without turning to the IMF. The influence of the Fund was, therefore, much larger than the scope of the recipients suggests (Stewart 1995: 6).

The imposition of structural adjustment programs in these countries destroyed any possibility for the continuation of the 'structural conflict' between the US (and the other developed countries) and the Third World identified by Stephen Krasner (1985). It did so, most importantly, by making it increasingly costly (by limiting access to credits outside of IMF/World Bank conditionality) for Third World countries to pursue the development of the national economy, and thus the primacy of domestic production and consumption. In other words, the IMF and the World Bank, together with 'ideological recruits' in the respective countries themselves, engineered a massive policy change in the Third World (Cox 1987: 260).[17] The result was that the incompatibility of the Third World economy with the liberal international economic order was slowly abolished during the 1980s. "What Northern governments had been unable to negotiate in international trade and financial fora, they have achieved in debt rescheduling" (Dolan 1993: 266; Biersteker 1992: 106).

Regulating Global Investment

The underlying basis for the world economy is the production of goods in 'global factories' or 'global assembly lines' whereby differ-

---

17 The actual process can be quite flexible. Since it is in the interest of the financial networks to prevent the countries from open default they will be interested in accommodating some of their demands (Cox 1987: 306-307).

ent parts of the goods are produced in various geographical locations to be put together in a third country. In order to be able to use the competitive advantages of various geographical regions several support structures need to be in place. One element of these support structures is finance: for example, firms have to be able to move capital among their various production centres easily, there should be some monetary stability or predictability, and there should be currency convertibility. As the previous section has shown, structural adjustment programs ensure some aspects of these financial requirements. Another element is trade policy: e.g. there should not be a policy of national protection, and intellectual property rights have to be guaranteed. A direct regulation of global investment has thus far, however, proved to be elusive due to the resistance to the Multilateral Agreement on Investment in the 1990s. However, this does not mean that international investment does not enjoy any protection, support structure or regulation at all.

First among the support structures are export processing zones that have become a central factor in the rise of the global factory since the mid-seventies. Export processing zones are small, geographically separated areas within a developing country from which firms can export goods under a special regulatory and tax regime. They are characterised by especially favourable investment and trade conditions, allowing, for instance, firms to import goods that are needed in the manufacturing process on a duty free basis. There are special investment incentives, infrastructure and services are provided (roads, power supplies, transport facilities, cheap labour) and often 100 percent foreign ownership is allowed. These export-processing zones are often tied in with overseas 'national economies' and their regulatory institutions that enact national provisions, as is the case in US tariff policy. Under such provisions, components are exported abroad to be processed. The firm then has to pay tariff only on the value of the foreign processing, not on the complete re-imported processed product (Dicken 1998: 120). Currently there are about 200 export-processing zones in operation worldwide, most of which were created after 1971 (*ibid.*: 130-131). They employ about 1.5 million workers and are concentrated in the Caribbean and East Asia (Mittelman 2000: 42). According to Sassen (1994: 18), export-processing zones, together with the Euromarkets, tax havens and so-called global cities are strategic places of the new form of globalisation. She suggests that "[t]he central rationale for these zones is access to cheap labour for the labor-intensive stages of a firm's production process. Tax breaks and lenient workplace standards in the zones are additional incentives. These zones are a key mechanism in the internationalisation of production" (*ibid.*: 19).

Owing to the failure of the 'Multilateral Agreement on Investment', the regulation of direct investment is still characterised by fragmentation (Cohn 2000: 300). The 1947 draft of the Havana Charter, which was supposed to regulate international trade, had included some investment principles but it was not approved (UNCTAD 1994: 124). Until the mid 1970s, the regulation of direct foreign investment was mainly discussed in the United Nations, where there was an emphasis on the protection of national sovereignty and control over national wealth and natural resources, especially by recently de-colonialised countries. Negotiations for codes of conduct were initiated, but the UN Code of Conduct on TNCs was never adopted one reason being that they were seen as to costly for business (allowing for measures against transfer pricing, for example) (Cohn 2000: 303-304) but being rather short on central liberal points such as national treatment and non-discrimination.

Liberally oriented multilateral investment rules were developed by the OECD. In the 1960s, the OECD adopted two codes to liberalise investment rules (OECD 1996a: 49). For example, the 'Code on Capital Movements' was initiated in 1961 in order to encourage the removal of all restrictions on the international movement of capital (Smythe 1997: 5). However, while the codes were adopted in 1961, it was only in 1984 that an agreement was reached to make these provisions fully effective by integrating the right of establishment in the two codes (Witherell 1996: 18). These various codes "form together a coherent set of instruments to promote an open climate for international investment, free of governmental barriers" (*ibid.*). They provide for national treatment before and after establishment, repatriation of profits, dividends, rents, and the proceeds of liquidated investments, transparency of regulations, mechanisms of consultation to deal with complaints, and peer review to promote rollback of remaining restrictions. The right of member states to take measures to ensure national security are subject to scrutiny by committees. However, one major drawback of existing instruments within the OECD framework is that they do not include enforcement measures; instead, they "depend on the strength of commitment and peer group pressures" (Robertson 1996: 78). In the case of non-compliance, no sanctions are available. Thus, until the mid-1990s, there were no effective global liberal investment rules.

However, this does not mean that direct foreign investment was developing outside a regulatory framework. This was created mainly through bilateral treaties. These treaties were developed first by European countries in the 1960s to govern their relations with former colonies; by 1994, there were 570 of these bilateral investment treaties world wide (UNCTAD 1994: 124). By 1996, the European countries, the United States, Japan, and Canada had concluded 1,160 bilateral investment treaties with developing countries (Cohn 2000: 302). These treaties included the most-favoured nation and national treatment principles. Often they outlaw host country performance requirements, and include provisions for compensation in case of nationalisation (*ibid.*: 302-303).

Negotiations for a multilateral treaty on investment (MAI) were initiated by the United States and started in May 1995 with a resolution of the OECD Council at the ministerial level. The proposed treaty was supposed to contain three elements: liberalisation of investment rules, protection of investment, and effective procedures for the settlement of disputes (OECD 1996a: 3). Owing to major disagreements among the industrial countries, the opposition of developing countries, and a coalition of non-governmental organisations, the MAI negotiations were discontinued in October 1998.[18] However, since the problems are still pending, the MAI is bound to reappear in another form and forum, most probably in the WTO, which regulates investments in services (GATS), trade-related investment measures (TRIMS), and in trade-related aspects of intellectual property rights (TRIPS) (Cohn 2000: 307; Gilpin 2000: 184). The regulation of TNCs at the global level is thus not – in terms of the construction of global liberal rules – characterised by complete success, as the failure of the MAI indicates.

---

18   Many provisions of the failed MAI are already incorporated in NAFTA. Under NAFTA, member countries agreed to most favoured nation treatment and national treatment for investors. There is, furthermore, a ban on all new export performance, local content and technology transfer requirements. Existing restrictions on foreign investment have to be phased out within 10 years. NAFTA also includes binding arbitration of investment disputes and elevates TNCs as subjects in international law since "private investors who are not represented by their government may directly submit their complaints against a NAFTA government to a three -member tribunal" (Cohn 2000: 305). The decisions of this tribunal are binding.

The important point of these developments, as Radice points out, is that, 20 years ago, "even the drafting of the MAI would have been unthinkable" (Radice 1999: 8).

Having looked at central sites of the regulation of the global economy, it is possible to conclude that policies relating to domestic and global economic organisation have indeed become more liberal. Most interestingly, instead of reverting to protectionism in response to the severe economic depression of the mid-1970s and early 1980s, industrialised countries have initiated a global movement of liberal reform, led by the United States and Britain that has ensured the continued creation of a global economy for capital (King and Wood 1999). Unlike the depression in the 1930s, countries have not closed themselves off during recessionary times but on the contrary, have put policies in place that deepen economic integration. We now have in place, for the first time since the beginning of capitalist development in the 18th century a truly global capitalist society.

According to William Robinson we can even go so far as to speak of a tentative movement towards some form of global political authority. He argues that there are tendencies towards the formation of a transnational state that serves to regulate the global economy. The development of such a transnational state can be seen in all those instances where national states or international organisations pursue policies that serve the maintenance and further growth of the global economy. Instances of this transnational state can be seen in the creation of the WTO that has acquired supranational powers, the stabilisation programmes issued by the IMF and the World Bank, and national policies for trade and financial liberalisation, deregulation, and privatisation (Robinson 2001: 180, 185). According to this thesis, there are now mechanisms in place at the global level that ensure the smooth functioning of a global capitalist economy such as compensation for market failure, money creation, guarantees of property rights, and the provision of public goods (*ibid.*: 181). The question that I will turn to now is, whether such a politics of liberalisation and institutionalisation of a global space for free movement has also prevailed, over the last 25 years, with respect to the movement of people.

Migration in the Global Political Economy

In a temporal sense, migration is usually seen as involving "moves that are relatively long and relatively definitive" (Tilly 1978: 50). In as much as this takes the form of international migration, such moves, however, involve a person's "transfer from the jurisdiction of one sovereign to another" and thus raise problems of citizenship and belonging (Zolberg 1994: 153). Migration policies regulate two aspects of this transfer: firstly, who is allowed to enter a specific country; and secondly, what kind of rights should be accorded to a person having entered this state (Leitner 1995: 261; Faist 1995a: 225). As Walzer has argued: "The primary good that we distribute to one another is membership in some human community" (Walzer 1983: 31). This membership finds expression in political, civil and especially social citizenship rights (Marshall 1992: 40; Hammar 1985: 9-10). A liberal migration policy, then, implies on the one hand that persons can transfer from or to a specific country without restrictions and that residence permits are easy to obtain (or non-existent). It also entails that the circle of persons to which such entry and exit conditions apply cannot be restricted by criteria of nationality, ethnicity, gender, age, occupation, 'usefulness', etc., if a country's immigration and emigration policies are to be regarded as fully liberal. In addition, a liberal migration policy extends social, civil and political rights to all persons within the territory of a state.

These measures result in what Soysal has called "postnational citizenship", a state of affairs where national citizenship "is no longer a significant construction", and no longer confers exclusive rights and privileges. In such a regime, rights and privileges are distributed according to personhood and there is no distinction between aliens and citizens (Soysal 1994: 3, 159). The predominance of liberal migration policies would, of course, entail a fundamental reorganisation of modern society; but so does the implication of liberal public policies towards the movements of goods, capital and services. As we have seen in the preceding section, the WTO, the IMF, and bilateral investment treaties achieved the latter to a large extent: national treatment, right to entry and to settlement without discrimination are recognised 'citizenship rights' for capital in the global economy (Sassen 1996: 38-39).

However, as I will show, neither migration flows nor migration policy mirror developments in the rest of the world economy. Migration flows are lower than under the Bretton Woods System where we have had a relatively open migration system in European countries alongside a migration theory to justify it. More important, despite claims by Soysal and others to the contrary, there is no postnational constellation. Most migration policies at the international and at the national level have become more restrictive over the last 30 years.

Migration Flows: Bretton Woods and Beyond

Migration played an important part in the Bretton Woods system. In many ways, the compromise of embedded liberalism was underpinned by the ability of developed states to draw on immigrants from Third World (and poorer European) countries. More specifically, the relatively open migration system of the Bretton Woods period allowed developed countries "to procure a limited supply of *cheap and disposable alien labor* so as to facilitate the structural adjustments, [that] participation in the international economy entailed" (Zolberg 1991: 309, emphasis in the original).

The Bretton Woods migration system was also seen, rather more problematically, as positive to the development of Third World countries. As Tapinos (1993) notes, emigration was regarded as one of the responses available to individuals in cases of a failed or retarded national development process. The emigration of workers would then, indirectly, aid the development process in sending countries, because it would spread resources more efficiently, as it would satisfy excess demand for labour in industrial countries that could be met by the surplus of labour from the South. In this way, global output would grow and trickle down to the sending countries: there, unemployment would be reduced and the remittances of the migrants would increase purchasing power, and in this way support a process of local capital accumulation. In the longer term, the experience of returned migrants would transform the production system and aid the growth process. Migration was therefore supposed to be "in the interest of both North and South" (*ibid.*: 175).

It is clear, however, that these supposed effects on Third World countries were not decisive in the considerations of the governments and bureaucracies of developed countries regarding the appropriate level of openness of their immigration policies. They were guided by the benefits of immigration to First World countries, which were emphasised by liberal economists. Böhning argues that the 'leitmotif' of the Bretton Woods order "was that economic growth should not be held up in one country for lack of labour, so long as there was suitable labour available elsewhere" (Böhning 1984: 7).

The idea that immigration is an essential factor for growth was developed by W. Arthur Lewis, who argued that an abundant supply of labour is a precondition of growth and full employment. Kindleberger maintains that that this argument indeed explains why the post-war economies grew so fast (Kindleberger 1967: 3). As noted above, immigration aided the adjustment to world economic pressures. One function of immigration was to support the growth process by alleviating acute labour shortages. But a more crucial function of migrant labour within the historical structure of embedded liberalism was to minimise inflationary pressures on wages (Zolberg 1991: 308). This danger was inherent in the high-wage, corporatist and Keynesian elements of the Fordist systems based on mass production and mass consumption, and could not be banned by active manpower policies, wage control measures, or incomes policies without undermining the social compact on which 'embedded liberalism' was based.

The assumption underlying the 'importation' of foreign workers in order to support the economic development of the North was that these 'guest workers' could be sent back in times of recession, and in this way would help to absorb economic shocks (Salt 1976: 84). The possibility of these immigrants becoming permanent residents of developed countries was to be precluded by their lack of integration into the civic and political (but not social) systems of the receiving countries. While the entry conditions were relatively liberal, therefore, the extent to which immigrants participated in citizenship rights was rather low. Together, these conditions were supposed to make sure that immigrants would remain mobile economic 'factors of production' that could be deployed and redeployed according to the requirements of economic development in northern countries, without becoming citizens with rights beyond those specified contractually.

Guest worker systems existed in France, Great Britain, Belgium, Switzerland, Netherlands, Luxembourg, Sweden, Germany, and the United States. Germany's guest worker system was considered to be the most organised, while Switzerland's was probably the most effective in preventing settlement. When the system was stopped around 1975, there were about 15 million guest workers living as minority populations in Western Europe, though the number of people having participated in guest worker programmes was probably higher (Castles and Miller 1998: 72). It was estimated that in the countries of the European Union, seven percent of the labour force consisted of foreign workers. Germany with 2.5 million guest workers, representing 12 percent of the working population, France (2.3 million guest workers, 10 percent of the labour force), and Switzerland (0.6 million guest workers, 30 percent of the labour force) were the major destination countries (Salt 1976: 82). In the United States, the various schemes to import temporary labour migrants, mainly into agriculture, involved – officially – about four million persons until the mid-1960s (when the programmes were abolished), while about five million entered undocumented (Reimers 1992: 44, 49).[19]

During the 1960s and 1970s, the migration system of 'embedded liberalism' came under increasing challenge from two sides. Many Third

---

19   Besides the guest workers there were two other types of immigrants in the period between 1945 and the early 1970s (Castles and Miller 1998: 67-68). Firstly, migration from the colonies to their former colonial powers. These migration flows were important for Britain, France and the Netherlands: they involved, during the Bretton Woods period, about 541,000 people in Britain (where restrictions were imposed in 1961), approximately 830,000 in France, and about 460,000 in the Netherlands (Castles and Miller 1998: 73-74). Secondly, settler migration to the United States, Canada, and Australia continued. According to Castles and Miller (1998: 76), these settler migrations were also influenced by economic considerations on the part of receiving countries.

World countries came to the conclusion that emigration did not necessarily serve development; the resulting 'brain drain' and other factors made emigration appear an unviable development strategy (Böhning 1984: 8f). Another challenge to the Bretton Woods order came from within the industrialised countries themselves: worried about the major inflow of 'alien people', and the social conflicts to which this gave raise, governments stopped worker migration unanimously between 1964 (bracero programme was halted) and 1974 (the year most European guest worker systems were shut down). The period from the 1970s onwards is characterised by a retreat from the guest worker system and by a focus on the management of their consequences (Castles and Miller 1998: 78).

At the same time, however, new labour immigration systems were evolving in the newly industrialising and the oil-producing countries. In 1983, there were about 3.6 million migrants in the main oil producing countries (Weiner 1995: 78). In the 1990s, there were approximately 25-30 million legal labour migrants worldwide, and about 20-40 million illegal labour migrants. Since the 1970s, there has also been an increase in political motives of emigration, visible in the growth of the global refugee population. In 1980, there were about eight million refugees world wide, a number which was to grow to 15 million by 1989, and 27 million in 1995 (Castles and Miller 1998: 87). Adding up the different migration flows, then, we find that today there are about 80-100 million people who are living outside their countries of origin (Mills 1998: 97). Fifty percent of these are located in Europe, North America, and some Asian countries, while the rest are staying within developing countries. Thus, if we compare absolute levels of migration (though this perspective has to be relativised given that the global population has almost doubled in the same period), migration flows have increased over the last thirty years. Yearly net migration flows from the South to the North increased from about 200,000 to about 900,000 in the 1980s. Every year 2-3 million migrants leave the developing world, of which 50 percent head for the industrial countries (Hammar et al. 1997: 7-9). Because of the slower growth of the native population, the foreign-born share of the population in western countries has consequently been rising (World Bank 1995: 53).

Overall, however, migration, and more specifically labour migration, has to be considered a laggard in the globalisation story. If compared with the growth of trade and capital flows, migration is less important as a force of economic or social integration, as the World Bank in its survey of globalisation reports:

> Annual migratory flows from developing countries (total inflows and outflows) are no greater now, relative to population size than in the early 1970s, at about one emigrant per thousand inhabitants. The overall effect of international migration is much smaller than that of capital or trade: only about 2 percent of people born in low- and middle-income countries do not live in their country of origin (*ibid.*).

This is in stark contrast to the developments in trade and investment flows, where the 1980s and 1990s have seen massive increases (Dicken 1998: 74). According to Bloom and Brender (1993: 34), while one can indeed speak of the emergence of world economy, this had not come about because of the mobility of labour but because of "increased international trade and international relocation of jobs, facilitated by capital mobility". On the whole, therefore, labour mobility has remained constant during the period when the 'global economy' was emerging. The globalisation of the economy was achieved by transferring capital to locations in which foreign workers were employed, rather than by bringing foreign workers to the countries to which most of this production is geared (Sassen 1988).

Liberalism and Migration Policies – Towards a Postnational Constellation?

Many influential migration theorists argue that a massive movement of liberalisation of migration policies has occurred over the last two decades.[20] Soysal and Jacobson interpret the decrease in state power and the changing form of citizenship regulations as a sign that we are witnessing the emergence of a postnational constellation because the integration of immigrants "contests the foundational logic of national citizenship" (Soysal 1994: 2). The post-national state accords rights to people no longer solely on the basis of national membership but rights are increasingly distributed on the basis of a new conception of "universal personhood" (*ibid.*: 136 and 164). This, for Soysal, "is the most elemental way that the post-national model differs from the national model" (*ibid.*: 142). The distinction between the national citizen with rights and the alien without rights is thus superseded. For Soysal this development indicates the advent of a "new and more universal concept of citizenship" (*ibid.*: 1). Jacobson (1996: 40) agrees with Soysal's diagnosis of a blurring between citizens and aliens, but evaluates it more negatively because it has led to a devaluation of citizenship because immigrants no longer need to become citizens of the host states, even if they are legally entitled to it. As a result, the state is no longer the organisation that represents the community, because there is "less of a community to represent. In such circumstances, civic, economic and even political associations will decreasingly use the state's boundaries as a point of reference" (*ibid.*: 8).

A central focus of the postnational constellation argumentation is placed on the proliferation of human rights at the international level.

---

20 Jacobson (1996); Soysal (1994); Sassen (1998); and Hollifield (1992). For an overview cf. Messina (1996).

These are seen to provide "enabling scripts" for the nation state, while at the same time they challenge the legal sovereignty of the state to be the sole authority of national law (Soysal 1994: 143f). The spread of human rights is one of the triggering factors for the development of the post-national citizenship model. "In this new order of sovereignty, the larger system assumes the role of defining rules and principles, charging nation-states with the responsibility to uphold them" (*ibid.*: 144). As a result, the nature of sovereignty has changed because the existing human rights principles "constitute a binding discourse, according frameworks that render certain actions conceivable and meaningful" (*ibid.*: 43). This means that the principle of human rights is now "embedded in collective narratives". Their recognition has, in this way become "ontological", and "self-evidently necessary" (*ibid.*). Yet, if we look at the international level in a comparative way, migration is an exception in international regime formation because there is no global migration regime similar to the trade regime with binding rules, procedures and decision-making mechanisms. International cooperation on migration at the international level is fragmented; migration issues are covered by a variety of international organisations.[21] There was no global conference on migration in the 1990s unlike for other areas such as global climate change.[22]

---

21 The UN Population Division, the UN Population Fund, the ILO, the UN High Commission for Refugees (UNHCR), and the International Organization for Migration (IOM), to name but a few (Castles 1999: 6; Weiner 1995: 152).

22 At the Population Conference in Cairo in September 1994, migration was a topic among others. Migration was certainly not seen as a way to deal with population pressures (unlike in the nineteenth century), though the conference emphasised the "importance" of family reunification for documented migrants (leaving it to the sovereignty of the receiving country to define family). If immigration was not much of an issue, neither was the demand of emigration countries for an intergov-

One area where a liberal migration regime might be found is the General Agreement on Trade in Services (GATS). Here, developing countries urged for a large-scale liberalisation, but they met with resistance from the industrial countries, who were not willing to agree to the temporary stay of persons delivering services (Hauser and Schanz 1995: 196). Services in GATS are, among other things, construction or consulting jobs of nationals in a foreign country. In specific countries' lists, it is regulated that market access must not lead to discrimination of domestic workers in the included sectors. However, the migration of natural persons is specifically dealt with in an annex, which postulates that GATS is not a basis for the general free movement and settlement of people. Only those entries are to be permitted that take place in the context of the provision of services, and which are on a so-called countries' list. Visa regulations and restrictions of immigration are allowed if they do not hollow out the market access concessions (*ibid.*: 205). GATS does acknowledge that only the border-crossing of production factors makes the delivery of services possible, yet there is no obligation to actually accept such labour. The only exception to this generally restrictive rule is that states have to give temporary entry privileges for managers and professionals essential to the establishment of a commercial presence (Smith 1996: 35). The demand of developing countries to be allowed to provide services (for example in construction) was, however, not met (Ruggie 1996: 142). Thus, the liberalisation of services is limited to the movement of high-skilled workers, and restricted for low-wage and unskilled workers. One meets this pattern (liberal migration policies for highly skilled

---

ernmental conference on international migration met (Castles 1999: 7). As a compromise, a meeting of experts – instead of an intergovernmental conference – on migration issues was held in 1998 (cf. Castles 1999 for a conference report).

workers as opposed to entry restrictions for low-wage and unskilled workers) more and more.

The International Labour Organisation does not regulate the entry of migrants; it only deals with the treatment of foreign nationals that are in the country.[23] Furthermore, the labour migration regime that has developed has merely codified developments at the national level, but was not, unlike GATT, the initiator of major changes of migration policies (unlike the negotiation rounds in GATT, countries do not have to ratify individual ILO conventions). In addition, the predominant mode of regulation for labour migration have been bilateral agreements between sending and receiving states (Miller 1992: 312). These bilateral rules, however, existed only until the mid 1970s; since then the recruitment of foreign labour has either been reduced or does not take place via bilateral agreements. Instead, workers enter either illegally, or the state has established a unilateral right to enter for certain categories of workers (*ibid.*: 310). In other words, there is no international effective regime for migrant's protection at the global level.

Most marked has been the change in the international refugee regime, where the institution of territorial asylum has formed the cornerstone of refugee protection (Mills 1998: 105). In granting political asylum, or by not deporting persons that would face live-threatening conditions in their home country (principle of non-refoulement), states fulfil their obligations under the Geneva Convention.[24] However, the refu-

---

23 According to an agreement between the ILO and the United Nations in 1947, there is a division of labour between the ILO and the UN. The ILO deals with the rights and living conditions of labour migrants whereas the United Nations is concerned with the rights and living conditions of migrants as such (Hasenau 1991: 693).

24 In total 131 states have ratified either the Geneva conventions or the protocol out of 185 members of the United Nations. The autonomy of

gee regime does not impart an individual right to asylum, it is still the nation state, which determines who counts as a refugee and who does not (Levy 1999: 19). Furthermore, over the last twenty years, the refugee regime has been undermined by national policies. While many states now recognise new grounds for asylum, such as female genital mutilation, they have simultaneously undertaken concerted efforts to change the system of refugee protection via territorial asylum in favour of a regime that emphasises temporary protection or local refugee assistance (Rogers 1992: 1113). One scholar has concluded that the principle of non-entrée is replacing the principle of non-refoulement (Mills 1998: 105). One indicator in this is that more and more states do not grant political asylum but 'temporary protection'. Under temporary protection the asylum claims of refugees are not examined but they are allowed to stay within a country until the war is over and they can be sent back (*ibid.*: 107). This means, that in the case of refugees, there has been a reversal of the human rights regime and not a strengthening as Soysal and others claim.[25]

Clearly visible is the trend towards social exclusion at the global level in a new co-operation mechanism set up by the migrant receiving

---

the refugee regime from state power is however extremely limited. The UNHCR has the power to oversee the implementation of the convention (Article 8a of the Geneva Convention). States hand in reports on their implementation of the Convention but those reports are not supervised by an independent expert committee (Wolfrum 1991: 566). The UNHCR can look into single cases whether a signatory state has treated a refugee according to the Geneva Convention and can intervene (Glahn 1992: 135).

25 The success of the changes of the asylum law at the national level can be seen for the German case. The numbers of asylum application went up from appr. 57.000 in 1987 to 438,000 in 1992, the year before the change of the Constitution. In 1994, one year after the change, the figure was down to 127.000 (Beisheim et al. 1999: 125).

western industrialised countries, the so-called Intergovernmental Consultations on Asylum, Refugee and Migration Policies in Europe, North America and Australia (IGC). This is a forum of states to discuss matters of immigration control (Weiner 1995: 159-164).[26] These consultations have been established in 1985 to deal with the increase in immigration, as they felt that their interests were not taken into account by the UNHCR. These consultations cover four main subjects: "framing long-term strategies to contain mass population movements; reforming procedures for asylum claimants; current projects on East-West population movements; and certain specific South-North flows of asylum seekers" (SOPEMI 1992: 31). The main approach of these consultations is to reduce immigration with a special emphasis on improving border control.

These developments are accompanied by a conceptual change. Increasingly, migration is defined as a security problem (Rogers 1992: 1113). As a result, migration is no longer a part of the normal political agenda but is perceived as an issue of national security or as an existential threat that justifies stronger actions, outside the normal repertoire of political actors (Kostakopoulou 2000: 505, fn 12).[27] For Sandra Lavenex (1997: 20-21) the securitisation of migration has led to a

---

26 Participating states: Australia, Austria, Belgium, Canada, Denmark, Finland, France, Germany, Italy, the Netherlands, Norway, Spain, Sweden, Switzerland, the United Kingdom, and the United States. Cf. the web page www.igc.ch/.

27 For example, NATO forces are used to help Italy to deal with unwanted Albanians in the Mediterranean sea. Austria and Italy employ their military to guard the borders. A third of the Polish army is employed to track illegal migration from the east, and Switzerland has instituted the "Aktion Limes", a military infrastructure to deal with unwanted immigration. The German minister for the Interior suggests that the federal army should be employed at the border as well to guard it against illegal immigration from Poland and the Czech Republic (Nuscheler 1994: 81).

transformation of the European migration regime from one based on questions of human rights to questions of security and cultural identity. As a result of the increase in control measures, more and more migrants have to enter illegally and stay under rather precarious conditions.

Regional Integration Projects: NAFTA and European Unification

If there is any extra-discursive basis for the optimistic expectations (raised by Soysal and other liberal-constructivists) of a liberalising tendency with regard to immigration, it should be found within regional integration projects such as NAFTA and the European Union. But as the following discussion shows regional migration policies have reinforced national and global migration policies.
Migration is conspicuously absent from the North American Free Trade Agreement. Indeed, as Doris Meissner, Commissioner of the United States Immigration and Naturalisation Service (INS) has noted, both countries "have taken great pains to establish that free trade negotiations will not entail labour migration issues" (Meissner 1992: 82). In doing so, Meissner claims, both countries have missed a 'historic opportunity'. When NAFTA was originally proposed by the Mexican President Salinas, the US government agreed to it only under the condition that labour migration was not to be on the agenda (Bustamente 1994: 80).[28] This is all the more strange since the importance of Mexican immigration to the US cannot be underestimated: 10

---

28 Indeed, as to migration, the two sides could not be further apart. "In the United States, undocumented immigration is defined as a crime-related phenomenon, which requires a law enforcement solution. In Mexico, undocumented immigration is considered an economic, labour-related phenomenon" (Bustamente 1994: 81-82).

percent of the growth of the US labour supply since World War II can be attributed to Mexican immigration (Hinojosa Ojeda 1994: 231).

It has been suggested that the high incidence of undocumented immigration (mainly from Mexico) into the United States is an expression of official policy of benign neglect towards it (Martin 1994: 84). As the US Commission on Immigration Reform (1994: 88) pointed out, the US for years had tacitly accepted undocumented immigration because this was perceived to be in the interest of certain employers and the public. The Immigration and Naturalization Services, for instance, which monitors employment of immigrants, has checked only 32 out of 32,000 agricultural farms in California even though undocumented immigrants constitute about 50 percent of the labour force (Stalker 2000: 44). Thus, illegal immigration in the US is also the result of strategic 'non-decisions' (Portes and Walton 1981: 57). However, though most of the migration between the US and Mexico (as well as Canada) is not regulated by NAFTA, it is clearly a factor that decisively shaped the very emergence of this agreement. For, according to Hinojosa Ojeda, one purpose of NAFTA is precisely to prevent further (undocumented) immigration from Mexico to the US by contributing to economic development in Mexico itself (Hinojosa Ojeda 1994: 229; Alba et al. 1998: 269). In this sense, the undocumented migration from Mexico is an unofficial part of the agenda that underlies NAFTA.

It should be noted that a particular form of migration that is "complementary to investment flows" (Alba et al. 1998: 267), is in fact included in a specific chapter of NAFTA: business investors, traders, intra-company transferees, and professionals can temporarily move between the US, Mexico and Canada (SOPEMI 1998: 55). Permanent immigration is ruled out, however. According to SOPEMI, there were 27,000 NAFTA professionals entering the country in 1996, accompanied by 7,700 spouses and children. Temporary workers in total in 1996 amounted to 533,500, the largest share of which were professionals (144,500), intra-company transfers (140,500) and treaty traders, investors and dependants (138,000) (SOPEMI 1998: 182).[29] This displays a similar dichotomy as in GATS: highly skilled migration is allowed while the vast majority of migrants enters the US illegally.

General migration questions in North America have been dealt with within the Regional Conference on Migration (RCM), which includes ten countries of Central and North America, among them Mexico, Canada and the United States. This regional co-operation mechanism on migration has been initiated in 1996, two years after the Cairo Population Conference, where such regional conferences had been proposed. Thus, instead of being incorporated into the negotiation of NAFTA or the process for the Free Trade Area of the Americas, migration questions are dealt with separately (Pellerin 1999: 470-471). The central idea of the RCM is to serve as a vehicle to develop control strategies for migration flows, and to ensure that the migration that occurs is closely monitored and under control, and thus unable to disrupt the general move towards 'free trade' (*ibid*.: 481).

While NAFTA excludes a general concern for the mobility of people, the reverse is true of the European Community/European Union, which has accorded the freedom of movement a central role in its basic framework. Alongside the principle of free movement of goods, capital, and services, the Treaty of Rome established the freedom of movement for economic agents, that is to workers or to providers of services (Art. 48-51, 52-58, 59). This restriction to economic agents was gradually eased and the introduction of the European Citizenship

---

29 Non-immigrants are visitors, persons in transit or persons granted temporary residence permits. Data may be overestimated, as they include multiple entries by the same person over time (SOPEMI 1998: 182).

in 1992 under Maastricht finally detached the permission to reside from employment (Koslowski 1998: 161). Thus, concerning European citizens, member states of the European Union are indeed no longer sovereign when it comes to the regulation of entry and settlement, and with regard to European Citizens we can indeed point to one single instance where the freedom of movement has been placed on par with the freedom of movement for goods, services and capital.

But if one takes a closer look at how the freedom of movement was implemented then it becomes obvious that it was not as integral to the other three freedoms as is often asserted. According to Tapinos, European Integration is marked by a staged liberalisation process: migration barriers were removed after trade interdependence had increased prosperity of the migration sending countries (Tapinos 1993: 178; Alba et al. 1998: 266-267). It has therefore become accepted policies to extend the freedom of movement to new member states only after a period of adjustment (Philip 1994: 169, 185).

Second, the central guiding principle of immigration policy making in the European Union is that the issue of intra-community migration is to be treated separately from immigration from third countries. In other words, the institutions, principles and norms for intra-community migration differ from those for extra-community immigration (Ugur 1995: 973-974). In effect, this constitutes what Ireland has characterised as a "bifurcated policy response" (1995: 233). For intra-communitari migrants, "something approaching complete freedom of movement and a bona fide Union-level social policy have emerged" (*ibid.*: 232), and steps have been taken to develop something of a European citizenship and a common social policy (Guild 1996). All these developments do not apply to extra-communitari residents in the EU. They do not have the right to free movement and the accompanying social rights. A common policy towards extra-communitari has emerged only with regard to questions of border control. According to Philip, "the refusal of citizenship to long-term immigrants en bloc is increasingly perceived as a real barrier to their integration into the host country and to social cohesion at times of political uncertainty or difficulty" (Philip 1994: 186). Ugur (1995: 978) concludes that "it is possible to identify some indications of an emergent European identity defined against non-EU nationals". This development squarely contradicts Soysal's thesis that Western European countries are treating the former guest workers in the same manner as citizens. Clearly, with regard to the process of European integration, this is not the case. The bifurcated policy response becomes even more obvious if one looks at the role of the EU in the global asylum regime. The Schengen and Dublin Conventions have lead to a weakening of the international refugee protection regime because the individual commitment of the state to provide protection is reduced (Lavenex 1997: 19). It serves to establish, according to Lavenex, a buffer zone at the border of the EU in order to prevent refugees from access.

Thus, while the freedom of movement within the EU is indeed integral to the European integration process and impressive progress has been made in terms of the actual implementation of this freedom, the above discussed developments suggest the freedom of movement for persons is not really on par with trade liberalisation. This shows that immigration policy making within the EU reflects the dilemma posed at the outset: economic integration proceeds fast and is secured by international agreements, while policies for the free movement of people (from outside) are not liberalised to the same degree. Moreover, the little freedom of movement that is constitutionally guaranteed is limited to skilled migrants. There is thus a dichotomy in the global migration regime of today whereby vast numbers are forced to enter illegally or a temporary basis leaving their status within the country on a precarious footing whereas a few secure conditions similar or equal to citizenship.

The conclusion from this discussion is that far from providing universal, enabling scripts for the protection of migrants, states have established co-operation mechanisms at the international level that strengthen or re-enforce the sovereignty of the state to deal with migration questions. While the extent of the human rights revolution in terms of the development of norms cannot be denied, the extent of the ratification leaves much to be desired. Contrary to Soysal's claim, it is thus, possible for states to dismiss questions of human rights for migrants, and to strengthen their sovereign control at the expense of migrants. As the next section will show, a similar development holds with regard to the national level where the extension of citizenship rights to migrants has equally been limited and where it is difficult to speak of a real loss of control by states over the process of immigration and settlement.

State Policies towards Immigration and Settlement

The argument that states have lost control over their borders has to be viewed with scepticism, not least because, as Messina notes, the proponents of this thesis do not provide proof that the capacity of West European states to control immigration or immigrant policy has declined (Messina 1996: 140-141). Indeed, Gary Freeman has pointed out that the capacity and the actual control of states over immigration have been increasing rather than decreasing over time, though their extensiveness varies across nations (Freeman 1998: 93). We will gain a better understanding of whether states have lost control or not by differentiating between different types of flows.

States have managed the 'asylum crisis' of the early 1990s quite effectively by strengthening their administrative capacities, by changing laws and regulations (e.g. new visa requirements), and by improving international co-operation. The system of legal migration to the traditional immigration countries too is now controlled by quotas (Freeman 1994: 22). Illegal immigration presents a different problem requiring measures at the border, and internal controls such as employer sanctions. Here, the effectiveness of countries varies because the preconditions for effective controls are not always met. The only policy, which could be portrayed as a control failure, was the guest worker programme in Europe since the guest workers did not return as had been planned originally; many states simply allowed guest workers to stay on much longer than envisaged and did not enforce the rotation principle. Freeman concludes that the capacity of states to manage and control immigration has increased and kept up with growing migration pressures (*ibid.*: 29).[30] Looking at border control from an historical perspective, states have strengthened the administrative means to control the movements of people over the last 200 years, as John Torpey in his study of the history of the passport has pointed out (Torpey 2000a: 156).[31]

---

30 This perspective is supported by a survey the United Nations undertook in 1987 of 170 of its member countries (quoted in Bloom and Brender 1993: 23-25). The result was that none of the countries had institutionalised policies to increase the level of immigration.
31 Torpey points to the activities of the International Civil Aviation Organization where technologies of border controls (e.g. machine-readable passports and visas) are discussed and disseminated among states. Moreover, in all European states, citizens are required to carry documentation with them that proves their identity. These documents become more important with the relaxation of border controls within the European Union countries (Torpey 2000a: 156ff).

The argument of the emergence of a discourse of post-national citizenship at the national level is similarly problematic because "discourses" can change easily if they are not grounded in some form of positive law and institutions. It has been suggested that in the United States, which is usually cited as the exemplary case of post-national statehood and citizenship, "the normative foundation of a post-national citizenship may be so thin and shallow that it can easily be swept away by the tides of tribalism" (Schuck 1998: 223). The legal cases cited by Jacobson in support of his argument have since been overruled or narrowed down (*ibid.*: 98-100, and 228 fn. 29). Recent changes in rules governing access to the US-American welfare state are further testimony to more exclusionary tendencies, even in the American polity (Schuck 1998: 212; Santel and Hunger 1997: 381). The main aim of the 1996 Personal Responsibility and Work Opportunity Reconciliation Act was to sharpen the boundaries between legal permanent residents and citizens. This law decisively reverses the trend towards a post-national form of citizenship, since rights are now tied to citizenship and no longer to personhood or residence. As Santel and Hunger (1997: 382-386) note, in the future immigrants will not be entitled to Supplemental Security Income (SSI).[32] As a result, many of them will also loose access to Medicaid-Programs, which are coupled with SSI. With regard to food programs, immigrants already within the United States, as well as new immigrants, are no longer entitled to food aid. Furthermore, for the first five years of their stay, immigrants will not be entitled to Aid for Families with Dependent Children and its successor programme (Temporary Aid for Needy Families). It now largely depends on the federal states whether they will give access to these programs to immigrants.

---

32 Supplemental Security Income is a tax-financed financial support program for persons over the age of sixty-five without secure income.

Another provision of the welfare bill is that sponsors for new immigrants have to prove that they have an income above 25 percent of the official poverty line. The problem is that about 30 percent of the families sponsoring relatives in 1994 would now be unable to do so, the majority of which are Hispanics (*ibid.*: 386). It can be concluded, therefore, that the trend towards the devaluation of American citizenship has been reversed, and a revaluation has taken place (Schuck 1998: 213). Similar developments regarding the rights of refugees or migrant labourers have taken place in other countries (Santel and Hunger 1997). Thus, contrary to Soysal's and Jacobson's claim of a profound and lasting transformation of citizenship, it can be shown that this transformation has been limited, and can be (and is being) reversed.[33]

The central problem of the postnational constellation thesis is that it has generalised its findings on the basis of the analysis of one particular type of migration. Both Soysal and Hollifield assume that the experience of the guest workers tells us something about the treatment of aliens in general (Soysal 1994: 9-11; Hollifield 1992: 18). Jacobson assumes the same for illegal migration in the case of the United States, which mainly involves Mexican immigrants following a now traditional route to employment that had been initiated in the First World War (Jacobson 1996: 4). In other words, the liberalising tendencies highlighted by these authors apply merely to a limited migration inflow and its aftermath.

---

33 For these reasons, the extension of rights may be better described as "denizenship" rather than "post national citizenship" (Hammar 1990: 13). The concept of denizenship suggests that migrants have developed a measure of security (for example with regard to deportation), but also points to the limits of this development in the relationship between states, citizens, and aliens since it does not provide the full security of citizenship.

It appears that what Soysal and other conceived as the first step in the emergence of a post-national form of citizenship was, in fact, a very limited development, limited to the guest worker flow (Zolberg 1991: 317). But these developments fall short of a substantial blurring of the line between citizens and aliens. Moreover, over the same period the possibilities for legal entry have, on the whole, been severely restricted, and the instruments to prevent illegal entry have been strengthened. It is possible to speak of a veritable closure movement by industrialised states to tightly control immigration inflows so as to take in only 'desirable' aliens. But they also made sure that the rights extended to these migrants would be limited (Moch 1997: 115). The reason for this is that because of the burdensome legacy of the Bretton Woods labour migration system, the threshold for returning to a labour migration regimes has become higher (Zolberg 1991: 319).

States will now only embark upon new labour migration policies if they can ensure that the migrants will not or cannot stay or can easily be deported. Therefore, according to Salt, an important feature of today's migration flows is an increase in short-term assignments and business visits replacing more long-term migration flows. In other words, "labour migrations are becoming increasingly polarized" (Salt 1992: 1081). Receiving countries have become more selective, and are interested only in alien labour with special skills. The immigration of these workers is seen as essential to maintaining international competitiveness (as can be seen in the current scramble for information technology specialists).[34] The decrease of demand for labour in the industrialised countries and the increased immigration pressure in developing countries translates into more illegal immigration which provides the labour for low-paying services and labour intensive manufacturing.

---

34   Financial Times 12.-13.08.2000; Financial Times 19.04.2000.

The labour migration policies in Germany in the early 1990s are a good example of these trends. These policies, in contrast to the guest worker migration policies, limit the social rights of the new labour migrants. They are not integrated into the civil and social citizenship framework of the host country (Martin 1994: 194). The reason is that they are either contract workers, such as posted workers tied to a firm delivering services in Germany, trainees, seasonal, or frontier workers. The new high-skilled IT-migrant labour programme limits the duration of the stay to five years. Thus, extreme care has been taken that these new labour migrants cannot acquire denizen rights. A similar move has become more prevalent in the United States. Here, we find, on the one hand, an increasing promotion of high-skilled temporary labour migrants.[35] On the other hand, temporary and undocumented migrants fulfil a similar function on the labour market: they provide a cheap and disposable form of labour, either because they leave after the contract has been fulfilled (contract workers) or because they live under the constant threat to be deported (undocumented immigrants).

We can summarise this discussion noting that "[i]n the era of globalization, states welcome flows of capital, trade and know-how, yet frequently reject flows of people" (Castles 1999: 7). Whereas international co-operation regarding capital and trade is directed towards the aim of sustaining and expanding the scope of free movement, co-

---

35 Especially the H1B visa category (non-immigrant work visa) is of interest. This visa is given for six years, after which the alien can adjust his/her visa status to apply for permanent settlement. The US Department of Labour reports widespread misuse of these workers especially when it comes to payment. About 40 percent of these visas go to the high-technology sector (Copeland 1998: 11; 15). The employer can "test" a person, the person will agree to many condition unacceptably to domestic employees because he/she wants to immigrate in the end and needs the sponsorship of the employer; as a consequence, the overall situation of rights at the workplace often deteriorates.

operation among states on migration issues is, by contrast, geared towards the regulation and exclusion of migrants, and increasingly designed to facilitate return-migration. "The principal response to migration pressures has been for countries to develop measures to restrict entry, while at the same time seeking collaborative agreements for controlling movements" (Salt 1992: 1090).

> Many governments, especially in the industrial economies, have [...] adopted more favorable policies toward international trade by reducing tariff and non-tariff barriers to trade and by signing international or regional agreements that facilitate trade expansion. [...] However, governments have done very little to encourage international migration, and have generally tightened migration restrictions during the last forty years for a variety of economic, social, and political reasons (Bloom and Brender 1993: 35).

But this does not mean that there is a complete stop of immigration into developed countries. As Freeman argues, the restrictionist thesis is "not so much wrong as it is incomplete, misleading, and undertheorized" (Freeman 1998: 97). There are workers that are allowed into the highly developed capitalist countries and there are workers who enter illegally; but to characterise these openings as a move towards greater liberalism is problematic because the migrants do not enjoy the same rights as the native population at the workplace, as the guest workers did. They do not enjoy national treatment, nor do they have a right to settlement.

One central question for migration researchers in this context is to establish whether there are social forces at the national and the international level that try to ensure that the new migrants of the 1990s that come under much more precarious circumstances – as refugees with a temporary right to stay, temporary workers, undocumented workers and as temporarily tolerated highly-skilled guest workers – will achieve a similar recognition as citizens. We cannot assume that the existence of citizenship rights regimes for the former guest workers will lead to an automatic extension to the new immigrants since the new immigration occurs under rules and regulations devised with the 'learning process' of the 'failed' old labour migration processes in mind. A transformation of the citizenship regime for the new migrants will only come about through political struggle. But the question whether citizenship rights should be extended is not decided at the level of the international system. This question is decided within each state as states have not given up their sovereignty over immigration policy. How these questions are answered in each country shapes the development of world order with regard to migration, trade, and human rights in the years to come. This new picture of labour migration after Bretton Woods and its role in the global economy is assessed in chapter five.

Conclusion

Migration flows, and especially migration policies have to be situated in the larger context of political and economic relationships on a transnational scale (Zolberg 1991). This context is not fixed; it reflects social and international power relations and the dominance (and competition) of distinct ideas or 'social purposes'. Zolberg claims that we are experiencing, today, another 'epochal shift' in the relationship between state and societies, the national and the international. It is, therefore, to these changes that we have to relate the main findings: that the Bretton Woods order was characterised by restricted flows of capital, while migration policies were relatively liberal, whereas in the period of so-called globalisation, the liberalisation of capital controls went together with rather less liberal migration policies, when compared to the previous historical structure.

Taken together, the measures undertaken by states over the last 30 years have ensured that investors in the global economy are guaranteed their property rights globally. A new legal regime has been established that "negotiates between national sovereignty and the transnational practices of corporate economic actors" (Sassen 1998: xxvii). The result of the 'politics of liberalisation' is that the domestic and the global rights of capital – such as to market access, national treatment, non-discrimination, rights of settlement, right to shift profits – have been vastly strengthened.

The legitimisation of this project of neoliberal globalisation derives from the purported productivity and efficiency gains, which are not only supposed to raise global output, but also to benefit nations and individuals (MacEwan 1999: 35). Even more fundamentally, it draws support from its appeal to 'individual freedom' and the rhetoric of putting the state in its (limited) place. On both accounts, however, the very important limitations on the free movement of people (and on labour as a 'factor of production') seem to run against the trend of globalisation, and to put in question the justifications for the pursuit of global integration. They also tell us something about the role of the state in the global economy, which cannot be understood as a supporting structure that follows the logic of the market to a greater or lesser extent, as many Marxists and liberals seem to suggest.

Most importantly, it tells us that the national state, and national boundaries remain a very real factor in the international political economy *if states choose so.* While it is quite true that boundaries and territorial spaces have been challenged by illegal immigration, states have not reacted to this either by national or internationally co-ordinated policies of liberalisation. They have not established international regimes to facilitate and regulate global migration on a more liberal basis, but have instead reinforced instruments of exclusion: On the one hand, they have made entry more difficult, on the other hand, they have limited access to the social citizenship rights from which earlier generations of migrants were able to benefit.

The popular argument that states reacted, in the 1970s, to increasing breaches of their controls of capital movements by accepting the unavoidable and started to liberalise their economies has been challenged by Eric Helleiner (1994). He argues that (some) states could have retained or re-established control over financial flows, had they chosen to do so. That they did not pursue this option had little to do with the effectiveness of controls, and all with political choices reflecting new social purposes. That states chose to restrict migratory movements should be interpreted in the context of these transformations of social purposes and social and political power relations.

These measures have been highly effective in containing migration flows. The IMF points out in its survey of the global economy, "[l]abor markets remain highly segmented by immigration policies and by language, cultural and other barriers to the international movement of labor" (IMF 1997: 46). The migration policies adopted over the last 30 years make sure that membership in a national community remains a fundamental issue in the 'global age', and one that structures the question of 'who get what, when and how'. The interstate system is thus very far away from being a truly liberal inter-state system because citizenship still is a mechanism to tie persons to a place and it thus serves as an instrument of social closure (Brubaker 1994: 230). From a migrant's perspective, the global economy does not exist (Gilpin 2000: 295). For the majority of migrants, the neoliberal world order is made up of the territorial nation-state, not of a denationalised space.

The juxtaposition of policies towards capital and commodities flows with policies towards migration flows reveals the constructed nature of the global economy. That German investors find it easy to buy stocks or companies in the Philippines, while Philippine workers will find it much more difficult to immigrate to Germany, tells us something about the interests which have been institutionalised in the regulatory organs of this global economy, and about the politically constituted nature of the 'global economy'. Far from being an 'independent' variable that impacts upon countries, there are specific interests in favour of such a global economy. There are specific social, national and regional interests, which have profoundly shaped the way in which globalisation has taken shape.

According to Zolberg, an explanation of the specific form of contemporary globalisation, and of the different public policies with respect to different 'factors of production', "must center on the state as the principal instrument through which a variety of groups seek to achieve certain goals" (Zolberg 1991: 303). It is to these societal interests underlying the making of the 'global economy' to which we have to turn in order to understand the specific way how it was constructed. Such an explanation, which integrates forms of states, social forces, and world orders into its theoretical framework, has been proposed by the neo-Gramscian perspective. The question that will be addressed in the following chapter is to what extent the neo-Gramscian perspective offers a way to investigate the reasons for the divergence in public policies towards commodities, capital, and labour that I have described in this chapter.

3. THE NEO-GRAMSCIAN THEORY OF GLOBALISATION

The neo-Gramscian perspective (or 'transnational historical materialism', as some prefer to call it) in the discipline of international relations and international political economy interprets neoliberal globalisation as a political project by social forces, which seek to construct what Robert W. Cox terms a new 'social structure of accumulation' on a global scale, centred on the mobility of capital and a new mode of 'flexible production'. So the question is how to understand the role of migration in this project from within the neo-Gramscian perspective. Is the institutional asymmetry between the freedom for capital and unfreedom for labour in the global economy an integral part of the neoliberal globalisation project? An answer to this question is important for the further development of the perspective that has tended to project neoliberalism largely as a market-making strategy.

In order to solve this question I will, firstly, survey the theory of social transformation developed by Robert W. Cox, as well as Stephen Gill, Henk Overbeek, and Kees van der Pijl (among others) which involves an outline of their interpretation of the transformation from embedded liberalism to neoliberal globalisation as a project of a transnational class. From this overview it will emerge that in order to understand of the role of migration in the neoliberal project we will first have to establish the exact opinion of neoliberal thinkers and think tanks on migration in the present global economy since such an inquiry has not yet been undertaken. Secondly I will develop a preliminary understanding of the role of migration in the neoliberal globalisation project. It will emerge that it consists of two aspects: One the one hand, the restriction on the freedom to move for migrants by the increasing of border controls and by strengthening the internal surveillance capacity of the state serves to boost the legitimacy of the globalisation project by demonstrating the continuing capacity of the state to act. At the same time, the little immigration that is coming into western countries under the more restrictive regime (mostly illegal and temporary migrants) accelerates the adjustments in the labour markets that are needed under the new regime of flexible accumulation.

Conceptualising Hegemonic Transformations

The central concept in the neo-Gramscian framework is that of hegemony. That their conceptualisation of hegemony is rather different from the realist understanding prevalent in IR and IPE has been widely recognised. But the argument that hegemony is never simply coercive, and includes elements of consensus is not really what distinguishes neo-Gramscian from realist hegemony.[36] Instead, it is the claim that international hegemony expresses the leadership and ideas of particular social classes or class fractions within a particular country (that has become dominant), which makes the neo-Gramscian concept so different from alternative formulations. As Cox argues:

> A world hegemony is thus in its beginnings an outward expansion of the internal (national) hegemony established by a dominant social class. The economic and social institutions, the culture, the technology

---

36 The consensual elements of American hegemony, for instance, are recognised widely by scholars as diverse as Gilpin (1987), Ikenberry (1999) and Ruggie (1982).

associated with this national hegemony become patterns for emulation abroad (Cox 1993a: 61).

The implication of such an understanding of hegemony is that, at the level of world order, hegemony must not be reduced to the (power) relationships among states, as realism proposes. Hegemony is, at heart, about the creation of an international *social* order. This implies that a hegemonic country in this sense not only tries to 'dominate' international relations, as the realist perspective emphasizes but in a much deeper sense tries to restructure state/society complexes in its own image. From such a perspective, the mechanisms of world order are not simply international; as the social relations and production systems of the hegemonic state/society complex are replicated in other countries, the conditions emerge on which a transnational bloc of social forces can be formed, which exists alongside and interacts with formal interstate institutions, and processes of bilateral and multilateral co-ordination (*ibid.*: 62). As a result, the question about hegemony from a neo-Gramscian perspective is not mainly concerned with whether American 'hegemony' is declining or whether it will persist but how the *content* of US hegemony has been changing (Gill 1990a: 88; Cox 1986: 247).

For the neo-Gramscians, therefore, the study of international relations and international political economy cannot begin with states. States are not given; nor are their interests determined either by the essence of statehood, or the nature of the international system. Instead, the functions and interests of states are shaped in the process of social struggles within these states (though these struggles also reflect, especially in the case of non-hegemonic states, the rationality and values of the prevailing world order). 'National interests', in other words, are constructed in domestic conflicts that are influenced by international or transnational forces.

For the neo-Gramscians, these conflicts cannot only be understood from within in traditional Marxist terms, as the struggle between capital and labour (or, more generally, between exploiters and exploited). Instead they argue that the capitalist class is itself divided: between commodity capital, money capital and productive capital, as the Amsterdam School of transnational historical materialism – among them Overbeek (1990: 24) and van der Pijl (1984: 6) – suggests; or between nationally and internationally oriented fractions of capital, or productive and finance capital, as Cox and Gill argue (Cox 1996: 301; Gill 1990a: 50-51). These class fractions have interests which are often not compatible, each proposing different 'comprehensive concepts of control' (van der Pijl 1984: 7; Overbeek 1990: 178) which contain conflicting views on the regulation of the polity. More specifically, a concept of control or political project consists of four elements: ideas on foreign policy; a specific viewpoint on the balance of power within society; ideas on state involvement in securing capitalist accumulation; and on the organisation of inter-capitalist competition (Overbeek and van der Pijl 1993: 5).

Neo-Gramscians see the social development of the last 200 years as marked by the rise, dominance and defeat of different capitalist class fractions, which have institutionalised very different interests and social purposes through their respective projects (see Overbeek and van der Pijl 1993: 7-16 for an overview). But each class fraction could only gain and maintain dominance, if it was able to make its dominance acceptable to larger parts of society. For this, it had to gain support for its project from subordinate classes and social groups. In other words, in order to be able to represent their interests as the interests of society as a whole, the ascendant capital fractions have to forge a 'historic bloc' of social forces, which benefit from and support the project of the dominant fraction. This means that the 'concept of control' proposed by the ascendant class fraction has to become 'comprehensive', taking on board a greater plurality of interests and ideas. In this way, a comprehensive concept of control

> represents a bid for hegemony: a project for the conduct of public affair and social control that aspires to be a legitimate approximation of the general interest in the eyes of the ruling class and, at the same time, the majority of the population, for at least a specific period (van der Pijl 1984: 7).

For neo-Gramscians, there are always different and rival socio-economic projects competing for hegemony; which of them will succeed is not predetermined, since the success of class fractions in their attempt to gain hegemony, or of historic blocs in their attempts to implement their social projects, will be decisively influenced by the bargaining processes, interests, institutions, and distribution of material capabilities prevailing at the level of world order (Cox 1986).

Like hegemony at the domestic level, international hegemony reflects the interests and purposes of particular social forces, which have been able to gain hegemony at home, implemented social projects that led to a 'fit' between the organisation of society, economy and the state (in other words, created a relationship that is mutually reinforcing), and which released energies and capabilities that were then used to construct international hegemony. Here, again, this involves elements of bargaining and persuasion etc., rather than the direct imposition of power over other state/society complexes (though the coercive element remains, of course, present, especially at the margins of world order; those states which cannot threaten disruption have little bargaining power; *ibid.*: 230). The predominant state constructs a world order in which the interests of subordinate states and social forces are to some extent represented. International like domestic hegemony is a form of rule where consensus and the accommodation of subordinate interests is important (Overbeek (2000: 175).

The hegemon will provide 'public goods' that underpin world trade and production, but which public goods it provides reflects, of course, a particular understanding of the 'global interest'. International hegemony will institutionalise a specific relationship between national states and the world market, this in turn, will have great influence over the relationship between politics and economic at the domestic levels, and in this way international hegemony limits or promotes the social aspirations of some social groups rather than of others in the national context.

In one sense, then, hegemony is a situation where the ideas and interests (or the 'concept of control') of a particular capital fraction have become widely accepted, first within a state/society complex, and then internationalised through the power of the ascendant state. Hegemony in this case is a moment where there is a 'fit' between the spheres of world order, state forms, and production relations. These two aspects of hegemony are closely related: for such a fit must be consciously and actively constructed, and only if the way in which these spheres are fitted together has gained some degree of support and legitimacy can we speak of hegemony.

Historically, hegemony at the world order level has existed, in this sense, only twice: during the periods of the Pax Britannica and the Pax Americana. It is actually the very different nature of US imperialism that has led Robert Cox to insist, in a criticism of Marxist theories of imperialism, on a new conceptualisation of US power as hegemonic and not as imperialistic in order to describe the very different nature of US global power projection compared to other imperialistic powers (e.g. through international organisations) (Cox 1986: 229). These two periods were separated by a phase in which there competing projects with very different conceptions about the social and international relations of world order (this is the period of 'rival imperialisms from 1880-1945). At the centre of neo-Gramscian research is the transformation of the Pax Americana since the crisis period of the mid-seventies towards neoliberal globalisation, flexible accumulation and a more aggressive US unilateralism that will be outlined in the next section.

Crisis and Transformation: From the Pax Americana to Neoliberalism

The neo-Gramscian perspective has developed an explicit political theory of globalisation by showing that it is the project of a 'globalising elite' arising out of the internationalisation of production and finance (Cox 1987: 359; Gill 1995a: 400). Specifically, they see globalisation as originating in the break-up of the compromise in the 1960s and 1970s between productive and money capital that underpinned the post-war social order of the Pax Americana. This compromise was identified by the globalising elite as having caused the world economic crisis since the 1970s, and it is against this compromise that it developed the 'globalisation project' (Cox 1987: 267).
The period between 1945 and 1973/74 has to been a relatively stable historical structure characterised by the following features: production relations were dominated by trade unionism and mass production, state policies were guided by Keynesian macroeconomic management and corporatism while the world order in the "free world" was centred on the US. A crucial element in the US world order management were the Bretton Woods institutions that safeguarded the specific production relations and economic policies that had evolved in the post-war

era. A crucial element of the productive-money capital compromise at the international level was that trade was managed, e.g. through safeguard clauses, and short-term capital flows were restricted through capital controls (*ibid.*: 212-215). The Bretton Woods historic bloc, with its productivist ideology of corporate liberalism, "rejected the bankers' laissez-faire ideology in the financial arena in favour of a more interventionist approach that would make the financial sector serve their broader economic and political objectives" (Helleiner 1994: 164). While it did not achieve the 'euthanasia of the rentier' as Keynes had demanded, it made possible the subordination of finance capital to a project, which put priority on industrial development.

The new forms of regulation and labour relations that emerged in this period have been termed 'Fordist'. For Cox, Fordism was a 'social structure of accumulation' that made full use of the potentials of mass production, by combining a strong emphasis on state policies that promoted long-term industrial development, with policies that raised mass incomes. This included not only welfare benefits, but also legislative support for strong unions. The resulting 'tripartite' arrangements attempted to "institutionalize decision making among the most powerful group interests in those areas of public policy upon which labour relations have a bearing, e.g. prices, incomes, investment, the level of employment, and the balance of payments" (Cox 1987: 77; Rupert 1995).

Fordism was in some respects a progressive face of capitalism; the consumption of goods produced was no longer limited to the upper strata, but subordinate classes participated, and indeed their consumption was central in as far they provided the demand for the mass produced goods (Cox 1987: 310). Another characteristic of Fordism was that employment was relatively stable, and full employment became a guiding norm for government action. The standard employment relationship, secured via the struggle of trade unions for workers' rights, assumed that an employee would remain with an employer until retirement, and, more importantly, that the employment relationship would secure a middle class livelihood for the employee (Mückenberger 1989: 389).

The incorporation of trade unions, and their central role in maintaining the demand side of the mass demand/mass consumption equation, was not, as Mark Rupert (1995: 82) shows, the result of a master plan by industrial elites, but the outcome of intense conflicts, through which industrialists were forced to make concessions. Trade unions then shed their radical socialist elements, and restricted their demands to higher wages and better working conditions, instead of a complete transformation of society and economy. But this incorporation of large parts of the workers' organisations also provided the basis for the concept of control advanced by industrial capital to become 'comprehensive' and ultimately hegemonic.

It was this 'historic bloc' of social forces, which projected its concept of control from the US to the international arena and tried to establish the international and transnational support necessary to make its ideas hegemonic. Both in order to maintain domestic consensus, and to gain international hegemony, the US had to make concessions to the state-capitalist models that were popular in Europe and Japan. As a result, as we have seen, the state now acted as a mediator between a world economy and society (Cox 1987: 220-221, 223). International organisations made possible the co-ordination of national macro-economic policies and the solution of conflicts. But the European countries themselves also began to change. The production relations and models of state activity developed in the US were introduced in many countries, though the existing institutions and class relations shaped the new structures (Cox 1987: 266; Rupert 1995). The new world order was, therefore, not just an international order; it could draw increasing support from the corporate-liberal bloc in many western countries, especially as these blocs made connections and organised themselves in transatlantic private and semi-official fora (cf. van der Pijl 1984).

By the mid seventies all three elements of the post-war compromise: the Pax Americana, welfare state interventionism, and Fordist production relations had reached a crisis point (Overbeek and van der Pijl 1993: 13).). The central economic features of the crisis were inflation (partially reflecting a stronger bargaining position of labour but also the oil crisis), declining productivity (a problem because of the competition from Europe and Japan), growing unemployment, the fiscal crisis of the state, and US trade deficits (Cox 1987: 275ff). Politically, there was increased resistance to US dominance in the form of the demands from Third World countries for a New International Economic Order (NIEO), the anti-war movement and civil rights movement and the increased militancy of workers. Hence, the neo-Gramscian perspective argues that this crisis should not be seen merely as an expression of the "declining" power of the United States, as Realist analyses would maintain, but lies much deeper, expressing a problem in forms of state, the organisation of production and the declining attractiveness and acceptance of the power of the United States.

In this context, several political projects vied for national and international acceptance. In other words, what today is called neoliberalism was then only one possible resolution to this crisis (cf. Cox 1987: 251; cf. Hymer 1975: 59). Alternative programs envisaged, for example, a strengthening of the link between the state and the firm, and the massive use of state power in international economic competition. A second program called for a solution to the problems of embedded liberalism on the basis of an extension of the market through redistribution.

Instead of reconstructing the separation of politics from economics, it would have led to an increasing interpenetration, ideally in a system of democratic socialism. This approach did not look at the world economic crisis exclusively from the perspective of the advanced capitalist countries; the Brandt report pointed in the direction of global Keynesianism, and demanded an adjustment of the world economy to the needs of the Third World, rather than the adjustment of the Third World to globalised neoliberalism.

However, owing to the structural power of globalised productive and finance capital (Gill and Law 1993), neoliberal ideas became victorious by the end of the seventies. Internationalisation of production had changed the class structure of advanced capitalist countries dramatically, creating a global – but American centred – class with its own interests, ideas and institutions (OECD, World Bank, IMF, Trilateral Commission) (Cox 1996: 111) whose basic objective was to maintain a global economy, a goal that has traditionally been at the core of US imperialism but that has now become integrated in more transnational interests. Within this global elite, finance capital is dominant (reflecting the changing competitive advantage of the US) and the configuration of the new global class has changed from a productivist outlook inclined to compromises with subordinate forces to a more monetarist outlook that conforms to the interest of the rentier class (Cox 1987: 349). Finance or money capital is less accommodating towards subordinate classes because of the need to fight inflation in order to ensure high returns on the typical rentier income such as bonds and stocks. Productive capital is more tolerant of inflation since it cheapens credits (Fennema and van der Pijl 1987: 311). For Cox, it is financial markets that integrate countries fully into the world market and make sure that governments meet their commitments "within an order maintained by military strength" (1987: 360).

Neoliberalism was mostly developed in the US through economists from the Chicago School (e.g. Milton Friedman), and the predominance of US in international organisations made its spread to other countries possible. What this means is that the disintegration of the Keynesian welfare state

> was prepared by a collective effort of ideological revision undertaken through various unofficial agencies – the Trilateral Commission, the Bilderberg conferences, the Club of Rome, and other less prestigious forums – and then endorsed through more official consensus-making agencies like the OECD (*ibid.*: 282).[37]

The Trilateral Commission plays a particularly important part in the neo-Gramscian analysis of the rise of neoliberalism (Gill 1990a). It focused, initially, on the legitimisation crisis that had arisen out of the post-war 'social contract', diagnosing a "crisis of democracy" (Crozier et al. 1975), as a consequence of the "democratic surge" that had led to a rise in the exceptions for government services. As a result of this "excess of democracy", inflation had increased. The trilateral report suggested that it was now necessary to "demobilise" those groups that were pressing for new state services: "retrenchment was necessary. It was argued that a prolonged recession would lead to the demise of this governance overload" (Gill 1990a: 227; Cox 1994: 51). The discussions on 'ungovernability' as a part of the deliberations of the Trilateral Commission showed that the elites of America, Japan and Europe were well aware that "the guarantees for vulnerable social groups built into social policy during the years of expansion would not

---

37 The demise of the welfare state was implicit in the strategies proposed by these groups and organizations in order to overcome the crisis of embedded liberalism. The state was to be "bounded on one side by the need to encourage private investment by increasing profit margins, and bounded on the other by the need to avoid rekindling inflation" (Cox 1987: 283).

cede before the demands of capital accumulation without touching off a serious internal struggle" (Cox 1987: 262).

Another step in this enterprise was the so-called McCracken report by the OECD in 1977, which took stock of the situation and advocated a change of policy. According to Cox, this report has to be seen as the first official neoliberal manifesto. It presented a picture of a "narrow path to growth" as a response to the crisis of the post-war order. According to Cox, the McCracken Report emphasised the restoration of business confidence in government. It acknowledged that specific commitments such as the full-employment norm and the welfare state were no longer tenable. Included in its demands for wage restraint and budget cuts was an increased emphasis on re-establishing control over the organisation of work. Business reclaimed its ability to restructure production processes in order to integrate new technology that allowed for more flexible production. As part of this reassertion, more flexible forms of employment (part-time, temporary, and non-established workers) were also increasingly demanded (1987: 283; cf. Gill 1990a: 98-99). Thus, the standard employment relationship came under attack from within these circles as one measure to restore growth. This was implemented with the focus on monetarism and high interests rates leading to a recession at the end of the seventies in all industrialised countries, this and the ensuing attack on trade union rights led to the demise of the Keynesian welfare state and to an increase in inequality reflected in a dramatic reduction of the share of wages in national income in all industrial countries. A crucial element in this restructuring process, which would establish a new concept of control, was the acceptance of world economic competition (Gill 2003: 86). To this end, neoliberalism supports global restructuring processes that aim at an extension of markets worldwide through liberalisation, deregulation and privatisation (see Overbeek 1990: 28, Overbeek and van der Pijl 1993: 15). Despite their rejection of the state the globalising elite has embarked on a project of global state formation by establishing an effective governance framework for the global economy in terms of norms, rules, and international organisations. Central in this process have been economic institutions such as the IMF to deal with the debt crisis (and in this way reverse the Third World counter-movement based on the demands for a New International Economic Order), and the Uruguay Round of trade negotiations that established a new World Trade organisation and contributed to a further opening up of world markets. This process has culminated in a nearly complete overhaul of the IMF's policies on capital controls. Since April 1997, capital controls are only allowed in exceptional circumstances while in 1957 the IMF's Executive Board had reaffirmed the right of members to impose capital controls.

Stephen Gill summarizes these developments as a 'new constitutionalism' in order to highlight the goal of these agreements: to make sure that central economic policies are out of the reach of politics, especially left-wing politics. He sees this as a major reversal of the success of social democratic movements over the last 200 years to disentangle citizenship from economic power (Gill 1995a: 412-413). The insistence of the globalising elite on globalisation in the face of global economic crisis explains why there was no general return to protectionism or a recurrence of inter-imperialist rivalry but why, instead, we have seen further global economic integration (Gill 1990a: 50).

Based on this analysis, the neo-Gramscian perspective puts the social, cultural, economic and political implications of the movement towards the hegemony (or supremacy) of transnational capital based on rentier interests at the centre of its research agenda. There has never been a dispute within the neo-Gramscian perspective even in the eighties (when most scholars were discussing the decline of the US) that the US is the dominant power in the international system. From a neo-Gramscian perspective the real issue is the transformation of the social purposes underlying the exertion of power by the US (and other states) and the consequences for world order. One central issue here is the fact that the rule of transnational capital is not hegemonic; it is not based on compromise but is maintained by a 'politics of supremacy' that is met with widespread, and in part transformative resistance (Gill 2003: 60).

The main point of the neo-Gramscian perspective on globalisation is therefore that the move towards a global economy cannot be understood as a response to a historical, external, technologically induced and hence non-changeable process of globalisation which leaves states no other option than to adjust to market imperatives. Instead, globalisation is the result of a choice by the transnational elite that has become self-re-reinforcing over the years. While neo-Gramscians certainly concede that reductionist forms of explanations are problematic they nevertheless contend that globalisation has nothing to do with the free play of global market forces. Instead, they highlight how the global economic system is dominated by large institutional investors and by a few transnational firms. These actors are able to manipulate and influence the direction in which 'markets' move. This economic system is maintained at the political level by the power of the United States in close cooperation with other members of the Triad. In contrast to the so-called 'hyperglobalisers', however, the neo-Gramscian perspective stresses the precarious nature of the neoliberal project of global market making: the financial structure is crisis-proned, deflationary policies restrict global consumption and undermine recovery.

The US and Globalisation

For many critics of globalisation, neoliberalism is little more than Americanisation (cf. Gowan 1999). In their perspective, the last 20 years saw the reassertion of American dominance after its crisis in the 1970s. For the neo-Gramscians, the strengthening of the position of the United States in the world order is an important part of the process of globalisation, but not synonymous with it. However, they, too, point to the agency of US governments in promoting a world of capital mobility, economic competition, and limited welfare services. The US pursued these policies, clearly, because they were in its interests; but the reason why the US could expect that its policies would lead to adaptation abroad, rather than to protectionist responses, can only be understood if we consider the transatlantic and trilateral fora that secured 'ideological osmosis'. In other words, only because of the existence of transnational networks with an inherent interest in a strategy of globalised accumulation could the US (together with Great Britain) take the lead in the construction of global neoliberalism. In the absence of a 'transnational civil society' (in the neo-Gramscian sense), such a strategy would not have been viable, and would sooner or later have ended in mercantilist competition between the US and its allies/rivals (Gill 1990a: 55-56).

The strategic role of the US in the globalisation thus has to be situated in the historical context of the crisis and contradictions of embedded liberalism. Both the aims and the preconditions of the US role in the neoliberal transformation were shaped by the existence of an emerging transnational managerial class (and thus of a transnational interest), which was further strengthened as a result of the adoption of monetarist and globalising policies. But while the aims reflected the interests of specific transnational social forces, as they had been elaborated by, for instance, the Trilateral Commission, the strategy adopted by the US in the 1980s under Reagan was much more unilateralist than the Trilateral Commission has envisaged in the 1970s.[38] This was partly due to the resistance of social forces associated with embedded liberalism in the advanced capitalist states. The strength of entrenched institutions could only be broken through a confrontational strategy which produced world economic changes to which other states would find themselves forced to adapt, especially those arising out of capital mobility. It also reflected the determination of the Reagan administration not to accept the permanent decline of the US in relation to Europe and Japan, as well as in the conflict with the Soviet Union. The idea of collective tripartite leadership was in this way subordinated to American leadership until American dominance had been reasserted.

The unilateral strategy was even more pronounced with respect to the Third World, which had tried to press for a 'New International Economic Order' (NIEO). As Krasner argues, the aim of the NIEO was to "limit the market power of the North by enhancing the sovereign prerogatives of the South" (Krasner 1985: 7). In order to reverse NIEO achievements, Reagan's policies were designed to strengthen the role of the market mechanism in Third World countries (Gill 1993d: 267). This was achieved by undermining the UN institutions in which Third World countries had decisional majorities (through withholding of funds and membership suspension), and by strengthening the more market-oriented institutions, such as the IMF and the World Bank.

According to Augelli and Murphy, the US used economic force in order to reconstruct American world supremacy (Augelli and Murphy 1993: 133). The pursuit of a tighter control of the money supply drove

---

38 As different as these strategies were, both had the same aim in the economic sphere: maintaining an open world economy (Gill 1993d: 267).

up interest rates and initiated a world wide depression in 1980 (Gourevitch 1986: 210). Monetarist policies had the side effect of making debt servicing more difficult, or even outright impossible.[39] The high interest rates created the debt crisis for developing countries, which made it possible for the US (owing to its preponderance in the IMF and the World Bank) to force policy changes that emphasised openness to trade and capital flows. Thus, neoliberals were able to push through their project of market-making, and in this way they reinforced the globalisation process. Internally and externally, the United States promoted the policy reforms now seen as the new policy consensus: privatisation, deregulation, and liberalisation (Ferguson and Rogers 1986: 114-137; cf. Harrison and Bluestone 1988).

In this context, the question arises, for neo-Gramscians, whether the United States can still be regarded as hegemonic. The internationalisation of the state, which was actively supported by the US, has transformed even the US state, and integrated it into what Cox calls the 'nébuleuse'. This system of 'governance without government', which as we have seen includes both official decision-making and co-ordination agencies as well as private organs of elite consensus formation, includes the US in a central role, but cannot be understood as simply a system for the projection of 'American imperialism'. "US agencies have a dominant but not necessarily determining role; they are determining only when they rally a broad measure of support on specific policy measures" (Cox 1987: 259).

In some ways, the central role of the US limits the progress of the globalisation project. Cox argues that the main problem of 'global governance' is that the United States still has the central position in

---

39 Overbeek and van der Pijl (1993: 19) claim that Volcker was fully aware of the consequences of his policy on Third World countries and on US banks (Overbeek and van der Pijl 1993: 19).

military and economic affairs, which it uses more and more to further its own interests, and less the interests of the system as a whole (*ibid.*: 303). Thus, as Cox (1993b: 264) points out, hegemony has given way to a system of dominance or more authoritarian leadership. Indeed, in some ways, the new world order has elements of a tributary system.[40] In the face of the new global economy, the task now for counter-hegemonic social forces is to 'recapture' or 're-embed' the market in order to build a more democratic and accountable global economy. In order for this to succeed new historic blocs within and especially across national boundaries have to be built to replace the 'new constitutionalism' with an alternative multilateralism from below (Cox 1987: 307-8). However, the establishment of a progressive counter-hegemonic bloc has, according to Cox, as its precondition the ability to forge links along the lines of fragmentation of class structures just discussed (Cox 1999: 18). The problem at the moment is, according to Christoph Scherrer, that there is no convincing and encompassing

---

40 One instance of this 'tributary system' could be seen in the financing of the Gulf War, where the allies essentially paid the United States to carry out the war (Badie and Smouts 1995: 128). With regard to the financial system, the tributary nature of the governance structure is even more obvious. As Helleiner has pointed out, the United States encouraged the growth of global financial markets because it would strengthen the policy autonomy of the US government. Instead of having to deal with growing balance of payments pressures, the United States could rely on foreign investors to provide a steady inflow of capital (Helleiner 1994: 173; Gilpin 1987: 90). This was also recognized by an analyst for an American investment bank, Morgan Stanley, who pointed out that "no one has reaped more benefits from globalisation than the United States and Corporate America. [...] The greater the velocity and mobility of global capital, the more capital available to plug the nation's low level of savings and boost the liquidity of financial markets" (quoted in Gowan 1999: 3).

counter-hegemony which could replace neoliberalism (Scherrer 1999: 339).

Migration in the Neoliberal Project

The question is now how to explain the relative non-globalisation of migration regimes into the global economy which has been identified as an anomaly in the overall globalisation trend prevailing since the 1970s. From within the neo-Gramscian perspective this question is all the more pertinent because there has been a tendency to focus only on the market making aspects of the globalisation project.

One exception is Pellerin who, moving beyond the neo-Gramscian approach by following David Harvey (1982), points out that capitalism as a social system relies on both elements of mobility and fixity in order to secure further growth of profit rates (Pellerin 1999: 477). But this type of argumentation is equally problematic because it does not explain which elements in a regime of accumulation are fixed and which need to be mobile and why. It furthermore tells us nothing about the social interests behind the decision about the aspects in a regime of accumulation that are to be fixed or that are to be mobile. As the previous chapter has shown, migration policies have differed over time and it is the present curious mixture of freedom for capital but unfreedom for labour that requires an explanation.

Thus, we need to understand more precisely how migration fits into the neoliberal globalisation project. Two aspects require explanation: first, why do states restrict migration, what are the interests that press for migration restrictions? Why, as a consequence, is there no global regime for free migration? Secondly, how do we understand the present migration patterns as documented in chapter one under which mostly undocumented or temporary migrants find their way into western societies? Is it merely a control failure of states? In order to find answers to these questions we have to look at two aspects within the neo-Gramscian globalisation theory: the origin and spread of neoliberal theory and labour market restructuring.

Origin and Spread of Neoliberal Ideas

Neo-Gramscians argue that the neoliberal globalisation project has its basis in the emergence of a transnational class fraction which first emerged under the Pax Americana alongside the internationalisation of production.[41] Limited foreign direct investments during the 1950s and 1960s, especially by US TNCs, created firms that were increasingly interpenetrated (Cox 1986: 233-234). In the Bretton Woods period, these emerging transnational forces were still constrained by more nationally-oriented forces (Gill 1990a: 96); but with the crisis of embedded liberalism, the "transnational managerial class" (Cox 1986: 234), began to take a crucial role in the formulation of a new concept of control (neoliberalism), and to shape public policy in the direction of liberalisation.[42] Perhaps the most fundamental aim of this project was to strengthen the 'structural power of capital' in order to make possible the return to higher levels of profitability in the face of workers' demands for higher wages and more control in the work place (Gill 1990a: 112-115). The "extension of the geographical and economic dimensions of the market", in particular, allowed this emerging

---

41 The internationalisation of production and the resulting realignment of class forces constituted the 'diachronic' element within the Pax Americana that led to its transformation (Cox 1986: 230, 234).
42 For an extremely well-researched and detailed historical account of this process, cf. Cox and Skidmore-Hess (1999: chapters 3-5).

transnational class to gain advantage over labour organisation which were tied to national boundaries and the national (*ibid.*: 113).[43]

The crucial issue in the turn towards neoliberal globalisation is, then, the emergence of a "set of elite-based transnational alliances" that try to reshape state policies to support transnational accumulation (Glassman 1999: 673). The informal bodies through which these networks are organised, such as the Trilateral Commission, and official bodies like the OECD, are a part of this policy network securing the global economy. "These shape the discourse within which policies are defined, the terms and concepts that circumscribe what can be thought and done. They also tighten the transnational networks that links policy making from country to country" (Cox 1996: 301-312). According to Gill such forums are important "because their existence highlight the vanguard forces, and how they may serve to generate strategic consensus in order to configure what might be called the 'pyramids of privilege' in the world order structures" (Gill 1993a: 7). They determine the conditions of entry for other participants into the institutions that form the core of the "global political economy" (Gill and Law 1988). They have also led to a new level of integration of the OECD world where interests, identities and ideas are now interwoven at a more complex level (Gill 1990a: 211-212). For Gill there exist now a wider "trilateral establishment" based in the state, international production and global finance (*ibid.*: 50) that sees further transnationalisation and liberalisation of the global political economy as the core of its interests (Gill 1993d: 261).

---

43 This opposition against labour was the unifying force behind the shift to neoliberalism and world market integration. Earlier, world market integration and liberal trade (not capital) policies were promoted as a part of an anti-communist stance (Scherrer 1999: 342).

We should note however that neo-Gramscians do not claim that these elite networks control all outcomes, instead, one "should view these networks as channels of cultural synchronisation and informal policy discussion and preparation" (van der Pijl 1995: 107). Fundamentally, their aim is the spreading of ideas about the proper organisation of society, and the promotion of a process of "ideological osmosis" (Cox 1987: 256). Their role, in other words is to develop a common consciousness among the "ruling classes" or elites and to develop common approaches to common problems (van der Pijl 1998: 108).

Both Gill and van der Pijl consistently point to countervailing tendencies to such internationalist elite networks as, for example, presented by more nationalistic oriented elite networks (cf. e.g. van der Pijl 1989: 74ff; Gill 1993d: 273; Cox 1993a: 61). Thus, a central question for the neo-Gramscian perspective was and is whether these transnational forces will maintain their predominance by stabilising and maintaining the drive towards the creation of a global market, or whether alternative social forces will reassert themselves (Cox 1986: 237-239; Gill 1994a: 182).

Critical for the analysis of such transnational elite planning bodies are times of crisis "when a current concept of control unravels in the face of challenges it cannot satisfactorily deal with" (van der Pijl 1998: 118). Neoliberalism was able to provide satisfactory answers during the first political, cultural, international and economic crisis of the post-war order in the 1970s. Theoretically, neoliberalism has it origin in the economic ideas developed by Milton Friedman and Friedrich von Hayek who opposed Keynesianism basically from its inception and who wrote the central neoliberal manifestos. Their emphasis has been on "freedom" of the individual to be able to make choices and decisions without government interference. Given the emphasis of neoliberal thinkers such as Hayek and Friedman on "freedom" we should assume that they also include the freedom to move in their theoretical framework. We should also assume that crucial international bodies such as the Trilateral Commission and the OECD do likewise. This is the assumption that is investigated in chapter four.

Labour Market Changes under the Neoliberal Regime of Flexible Accumulation

According to Cox (1986: 230-234), changes in social structure of accumulation, specifically its internationalisation and the process of flexibilisation constitute the main explanation for the crisis of the Pax Americana. He (*ibid.*:233-234) goes on to distinguish between an international economy focused on exchange and a world economy that is based on transnational production where "different phases of a single process [are] carried out in different countries". In this way, Cox (1987: 270, 390) links the discussion on the new international division of labour first explicated by Fröbel et al. (1977) to the present discussion on globalisation. Fröbel and his colleagues argued that multinational corporations increasingly shifted manufacturing from the core to the periphery, and in this way supplemented the colonial division of labour under which developing countries were merely the suppliers of raw material with a division of labour within firms (Fröbel et al.: 1980; Castells 1989: 16).[44] As will become clear, however, while the discussion on the changing international division of labour focused on the move of industries to the periphery, the neo-Gramscian perspective has developed a broader view of the globalisation process by also

---

44 See Jenkins (1984); Castells (1989); Hoogvelt (1987); Mittelman (2000).

incorporation changing production relations in the centre into its analytical framework. Owing to the increasing in international competition for market shares in a shrinking world market (in the seventies) firms increasingly try to adapt production methods to cut costs either by replacing labour with machines or by using cheap labour more systematically. At the same time, production needs to adjust to the increasingly differentiated markets. All these factors led to a need to be more 'flexible' in the production of goods and services, the system of mass production established under Fordism was no longer able to cope with these pressures and had to be adjusted (Cox 1987: 321).[45] Flexibility in production thus refers to the ability of producers to respond to demand fast, being able to expand output if demand increases, and contracting output if demand reduces.

For Cox the internationalisation process is complex because there are multiple strategies that firms can use to internationalise: the employment of a (peripheral) immigrant labour force under more precarious employment conditions alongside a core labour force in the western countries, the establishment of foreign subsidiaries, joint ventures, subcontracting, leasing of patent technology and so on (*ibid.*: 247-248). The crisis of overproduction in the seventies reinforced these tendencies of internationalising of production in order to increase competitive advantage not only through greater capital intensity but also by tapping locations with lower standards (*ibid.*: 249). Central to transnational production then are the differences in factor endowments such as labour costs and environmental standards. Transnational enterprises use these differences "to minimize overall production costs" (*ibid.*: 245).

---

45 For a more elaborate discussion of these changes along similar lines see Allen (1992).

The important fact to note is that production systems today are still in a crisis of overproduction because the limits of the home markets were reached in the seventies. There were three alternatives: large firms could either continue the struggle for survival with the help of states or a radical redistribution of income could extend the market. Alternatively one could establish a new form of economic system altogether (*ibid.*: 251).[46] Neoliberalism is an expression of the first strategy because neoliberalism secures the access of firms to markets worldwide. The internationalising of production then was geared towards expanding the capacity to produce and to maintain market shares in increasingly saturated markets.

For workers the emphasis on flexibility and on integration into the global economy meant that wages are no longer functionally important for the economy in order to provide 'purchasing power' as they were under Fordism but now they are a part of production costs that need to be curtailed in order to maintain or increase competitiveness (Önder 1998: 51). This has led to an increasing restructuring of labour markets.

As a result, there is a three-tiered fragmentation of the working class occurring at the macro-social level (Cox 1999: 9; cf. 1987: 344). At the top are the highly-skilled workers which are integrated into the management process and are central to global production. This 'integrated core' relies on supporting workers whose position is more precarious, and who provide flexibility for the firm since they can be shed if there is a demand slack. Lastly, there are those who are excluded form international production: unemployed, marginalised population in poor countries, small firms, production of use value in the households or informal networks. These are supplemented by various other cleavages: public versus private sector employees, mi-

---

46   For similar suggestions see Hymer (1975: 59).

grant versus native workers, workers in the underground economies versus established workers. This fragmentation has prevented effective organisation against neoliberalism (Cox 1987: 285).

As a result the notion of core and peripheral countries has taken on a class meaning, and they indicate not only a spatial arrangement as under the old division of labour but core and peripheral workers co-exist within a firm. This manifests itself in working conditions in the industrial countries that resemble Third World conditions (as in sweatshops), and in working conditions in the periphery that resemble those of industrial countries (*ibid.*: 319-321). Thus, as a part of the restructuring of production, 'workers' are increasingly differentiated.

This analysis shows that labour markets and class structures have changed dramatically over the last 30 years in the advanced industrial countries under the influence of the neoliberal accumulation regime. The central theme of this restructuring process was flexibility as opposed to the standard employment relationship that was central to Fordism. As a result, a part of the labour force is pushed out of the standard employment relationship towards the periphery of society. This restructuring of the labour market found its reflection in migration policies. As discussed in chapter one, the Bretton Woods view of migration was that migration is beneficial to both sending and receiving countries because migrants alleviate labour shortages in the industrial countries while their remittances alleviate capital shortages in the developing countries and in this way, the two flows complement each other.[47] If we look at the legal situation of these labour migrants, scholars have rightly emphasised their different position with regard to citizens. Their stay was to be temporary, and their residence status

---

47 Pellerin (1996: 85); Tapinos (1993: 175); Zolberg (1991); Kindleberger (1967); Böhning (1984: 7).

was insecure (see Castles and Miller 1998: 72; Hammar 1985).[48] With regard to the labour market however, official regulations postulated that the wage and working conditions were to be on par with domestic workers (OECD 1978a: 29) even though the bilateral agreements that governed the guest workers were often not enforced in practice (Miller 1992: 306). With the crisis of the Pax Americana this theory of migration as a mutually beneficial phenomenon was no longer seen as applicable because the presence of foreign workers was increasingly seen as problematic in the unemployment-ridden industrial countries. In the South, where the remittances had failed to contribute to development, emigration as a development strategy was questioned too (Böhning 1984: 8f).

According to the neo-Gramscian perspective, one effect of the crisis of corporate liberalism is that it led to the development of a new international division of labour whereby trade and investment flows were seen as alternatives to migration. The underlying motive has been to impose a new core-periphery structure on labour markets in order to regain control over the work process, and the freedom to restructure production processes in order to be able to introduce new technology, and more flexible employment patterns (Overbeek and van der Pijl 1993: 15; Cox 1987: 283). The call for a new international division of labour then is on first sight the reverse expression of migration controls at the centre. Instead of sending workers to factories, the factories were sent to the workers.

The substitution of investment for migration flows can for example be seen in the United States where the stop of the guest worker program in the in 1965 (bracero program) was accompanied by a decision for

---

48   On the transformation of the guest worker systems into immigration see for example Soysal (1994); Hammar (1985); Hollifield (1992); Dohse (1981).

the establishment of the Maquiladoras in Mexico "whereby US capital could move to some regions of Mexico and benefit from propitious conditions of production and accumulation".[49] In this sense, one way to explain the presence of restrictions on labour mobility is because of substitution (Mundel 1957). This implies that instead of workers moving to capital, capital can also move to labour. And indeed, Bhagwati suggests that the general tightening of labour immigration in Europe precisely had this effect of leading to a greater outflow of multinational corporations to peripheral countries (Bhagwati 1984: 689). Following this discussion one would expect that neoliberals would be in favour of free trade, investment liberalisation but not necessarily in favour of free migration because production can be undertaken in the countries of origin of the migrants. Migration is thus not the only factor that leads to a global labour market. Trade and investment flows can substitute for migration (Overbeek 1998: 66).

The problem is however, that not all jobs can be relocated abroad where conditions are less strict but flexible labour markets in the centre are also needed. On the one hand, highly skilled migrants are needed to adjust to technological change. From this viewpoint, the competition over highly skilled immigrants is an element of the new mercantilism in the global economy (Gill and Law 1993: 109-10). On the other hand, as Overbeek (1999: 86) has argued there is a structural demand in industrialised countries for cheap and flexible immigrant labour (see also Salt 1992: 1081; Sassen 1994: 103). This demand is being met by the new immigrants whose basic characteristic is that the legal conditions of their stay are extremely precarious making them accept all kinds of 'flexible' working situations (Pellerin 1996: 89-90). Paradoxically, these new immigrants are created by the stricter control regime at the border.

---

49 Pellerin (1996: 89); see also Cox (1987: 244).

There have then been two independent trends that are reinforcing each other. On the one hand there are the still ongoing efforts to restructure production relations in order to deal with the crisis of Fordist accumulation (requiring more flexible employment patterns); and, on the other hand, immigration trends that fed these demands (Sassen 1994: 102-103). According to Pellerin, a predominant characteristics of those migrants which were allowed in is that their conditions are precarious: workers come in on a short-term, temporary or seasonal basis, asylum claimants have to wait for their approval or rejection, refugees recognised as such by the UN convention, and undocumented migrants whose existence is most precarious (Pellerin 1996: 89-90). In a sense, their status reflects the needs of the restructured labour market. The interesting fact to note is that undocumented migrant labour is a byproduct of restrictive forms of migration policies. Thus, while not specifically intended, employers are able to hire the 'flexible' labour force they need *precisely* because of the implementation of stricter migration laws. Globalisation as a political project in this case consists of dismantling or hollowing out 'protectionist' worker's legislation that strengthens the rights of workers in relation to employers. Examples of such legislation are working time, health and safety regulations, bargaining structure (firm level or corporatist bargaining structures), health insurance, a social safety net in times of unemployment, retraining and wage levels. The employment of undocumented migrants or of posted workers enables employers to surround many of these protectionist regulations. As a result, the employment conditions of other workers are affected because employers can always threaten to outsource their jobs to such firms.

Conclusion

The aim of my study is to put Neo-Gramscianism to the 'test' as a theory of globalisation. The question is whether neo-Gramscianism is able to explain the particular configuration of open and closed borders prevalent in today's global political economy? This question can only be answered if we establish that the rather restrictive migration regime that contrasts in a peculiar way with the overall emphasis on open borders for capital and goods can be traced back to the preferences of the globalising elite. This will be undertaken in the following chapter. Paradoxically, the discussion on the restructuring of labour markets has shown that more flexible labour markets can also be 'created' by the employment of immigrants under subminimal or 'flexible' conditions. This means that the type of immigrants 'needed' in order to support the restructuring process are precisely those that are created by the restrictive migration policies. Judging from this discussion there is then no incentive for neoliberal intellectuals to be in favour of free migration. Added to this has to be the fact that the new international division of labour made possible by the globalising of the economy can be a substitute for migration flows in many (though not all) sectors.

This situation will be discussed in chapter five. I will show that undocumented immigrants but also other migrants with a rather precarious position (temporary migrant workers) fulfil a crucial role in the neoliberal project of global market making, especially in those sectors that cannot be easily moved abroad (e.g. in the service sector, or sectors that have to be close to the market). This chapter will show that there are industries where there is a need for more flexible working conditions and where this need has been met largely through the employment of precariously employed migrant workers. In the US, it has been the garment industry that has been at the centre of discussion in the nineties where migrant labour has been at the forefront of a revival of the garment industry in the US (but other industries e.g. agriculture) have followed suit. Whereas in Germany the construction industry has been at the centre of the debate on the employment of migrant labour. Historically, both industries have one central fact in common: both have played a prominent role in the creation of a protected labour market in the countries involved in first place. The garment industry in the US in the thirties and the abysmal working conditions there was the prominent example for the need for more worker protection under the New Deal legislation. Similarly, the construction industry in Germany has developed the most advanced protective system for workers in the service industry that has served as a role model (seldom imitated) for other sectors. These two industries in the two countries can therefore serve as a good case study of neoliberal labour market restructuring since we are dealing with industries that are symbolic for the Fordist type of employment pattern. They also show that in each case and to a various degree there has been resistance to this neoliberal restructuring and that neoliberal predominance is has not gone unchallenged even if resistance, in the end, proved unsuccessful.

The case studies furthermore address one important point of criticism of the neo-Gramscian perspective, its concentration upon elite thinking. As André Drainville notes, structures, in the neo-Gramscian perspective, are constituted by elites and have no autonomy from them. In the contemporary process of social transformation, it is transnational elites who play the crucial role, determining structures almost as they wish. "They are not sites of struggles unto themselves, with constraints and possibilities of their own, but simple venues where one hears variations on a common (neoliberal) theme" (Drainville 1994: 114). Drainville argues that since neoliberalism is presented as "a transcendental project", the neo-Gramscian perspective "underestimates the partial, hesitant and fragmentary nature of neo-liberalism, and obscures the dynamics of its appearances as a political strategy" (*ibid.*: 116). For Drainville, neoliberalism has to be seen and looked at as two things: "a broad strategy of restructuring *and* a succession of negotiated settlements" (*ibid.*, emphasis S. Dreher).

Thus, while there is an inequality of power and influence, and while the changes of the last 20 years have increased the 'structural power' of mobile capital over labour, the neo-Gramscians have, so far, had "very little to say about political resistance to transnational neoliberalism" (*ibid.*: 121). Drainville therefore suggests that the neo-Gramscians should complement their focus on the development and imposition of 'concepts of control' with a consideration of oppositional forces and their "concepts of resistance", in order to break free from their tendency towards "elite cybernetics" (*ibid.*: 125).

For Drainville, the global should not be seen as the preserve of neoliberal elites, while oppositional forces are mostly organised at the national level. On the contrary, he suggests that concrete struggles, such as the fight against environmental degradation, for workplace safety etc., "act as bridges to the world economy" (*ibid.*: 122). These struggles, it should be noted, are not only relevant as a potential basis for the formation of counter-hegemony, but in their own right, as they will modify the geographical and social organisation of neoliberalism. Andrew Herod similarly argues that it is wrong to see the geography of capitalism solely as the result of the action of firms, as neo-classical theory implies, or transnational classes, as many Marxists seem to suggest. While recognising that the power of capitalists to shape 'landscapes' is greater than that of workers or consumers, Herod argues that we have to move towards a "political theorization of the contested nature of the production of space under capitalism" (Herod

1997: 17). Such a conception allows us to perceive how workers and consumers participate in the production of uneven development, and in the organisation of the spatial aspects of capitalist production processes.

It would be hard to deny that neo-Gramscianism has instrumentalist tendencies and is strongly elite-centric. But that is not to say that it is wrong. After all, such an approach may be exactly what is necessary to understand globalisation. Any approach will be based on methodological choices, which from other perspectives appear problematical. The real question, therefore, is what – if anything – an instrumentalist account, in the particular form presented by Cox and other transnational historical materialists, cannot explain with respect to the transformation towards global neoliberalism. As the analysis of neoliberal thinking in the following chapter will show, this type of instrumental world view yields important results. However, as the case studies in chapter five also highlight, neoliberals are not the sole actors on the political scene, and there have been serious efforts to resist neoliberal globalisation that cannot merely be seen as protectionist but point to a form of global citizenship. Even if their success until today has been limited.

4. 'EQUALITY STOPS AT THE WATER'S EDGE': NEOLIBERAL IDEAS ON MIGRATION POLICY

At the level of pure (neoclassical) economic theory, it is widely acknowledged that free factor movements increase worldwide output and efficiency (Krugman and Obstfeld 1997: 159). Policies preventing factor mobility, conversely, put a constraint on profitability. Neoliberalism derives much of its influence on public policy from its ability to refer to neoclassical economics for support of its prescriptions, which are generally aimed at helping to transform economic systems so as to promote efficiency and profitability. The neoliberal revolution that has taken place over the last three decades has seen most governments in western countries embrace these arguments to a greater or lesser degree.

There are, clearly, very important national and regional differences in the forms in which neoliberal ideas have been implemented. By contrast, as we have seen, most governments pursue a very similar restrictive policy on migration, though it has always kept some 'doors' open for particular groups of migrants. Thus, while current migration policies do not completely prevent migration, they come close to a general ban on immigration with the goal of permanent settlement (Zolberg 1991: 303). In this era of globalisation, where some have proclaimed the death of space and the obsolescence of borders as a result of the liberalisation of the flow of capital, goods, and services, there is strong interference by governments in the freedom of individuals to move.

The question that forms the starting point for this chapter is whether this development can be traced back to neoliberal preferences. As the reference to economic theory suggests, such a linkage between neoliberal ideas and interests and restrictive immigration policies of highly developed states seems at first paradoxical, given neoliberalism's embrace of economic rationality. Based on its self-representation, we would expect neoliberals to advocate free labour mobility as part of its advocacy of global economic integration. A positive answer implies that the restrictive migration policies observed in all OECD countries over the last 20 years and that has now reached a new highpoint with the increasing use of the military to deflect immigrants from landing on Western shores are part and parcel of the neoliberal globalisation project. It would also suggest that the structural reach and influence of neoliberalism is enormous. A negative answer would suggest that the influence of neoliberalism on policy making is not as huge as a lot of neo-Gramscian and neo-Marxist theorising leads us to believe.

According to the neo-Gramscian perspective, neoliberal ideas were developed first by economic theorists like Milton Friedman and von Hayek. These ideas were then taken up by transnational organisations of 'global civil society', such as the Trilateral Commission, and transmitted to more formal international organisations such as the OECD, the International Monetary Fund and the World Bank from which they were transmitted back to nation states thereby transforming them into competition states. This means we will get an idea of neoliberal thinking on migration if we look at the original economic theorists and at some of the international organisations. Since the World Bank and the International Monetary Fund operate mainly in developing countries they were not considered here, instead I looked at the Trilateral Commission and the OECD which has been established explicitly as a think tank for industrialised countries.

Neoliberal Theory and International Migration

For the classics of neoliberal theory, the aim of transformative political action was very clear: to (re-)establish a society in which individuals would be free – free to choose and free from government interference with their pursuit of privately defined goals. This freedom, they argued, was premised on private property. It is, according to Gary Teeple, therefore, essential for the neoliberal revolution to re-establish the centrality of private property rights (Teeple 1995: 76). In other words, neoliberalism is a project to "restore the power of economic elites" (Harvey 2005: 19). Private property of the means of production in a society based on free market principles establishes 'ownership' (i.e. absolute control) over factor inputs, and over the product of these factor inputs. The Keynesian welfare state limited the freedom of the capitalist to purchase factor inputs, and their use. Neoliberalism in contrast, celebrates the return of individual freedom and seeks to restrain state intervention that aims at reducing the inequality of outcomes on the market place.

The early manifesto of neoliberal thought – Milton Friedman's 'Capitalism and Freedom' (1962) – contains the now familiar neoliberal pattern of argumentation about the role of government in a free country. For Friedman, the "free man" will not look to government for an answer, but will ensure that the government will not become a "Frankenstein" that destroys individual freedom. Thus, for Friedman there are two central principles guiding the relationship between government and society. First, the "scope of government must be limited", and secondly the power of the government must not be concentrated (*ibid.*: 2-3). The latter principle is based on the assumption that individual action requires much more diversity than uniform standards prescribed by governments can provide. The central argument for

Friedman is that a system of "competitive capitalism" is a condition for political freedom. Political freedom is only possible if the market is the dominant means for the organisation of economic affairs (*ibid.*: 4).

Friedman argues that a society which regulates the economy closely, as under socialism, cannot guarantee individual freedom for two reasons. First, freedom in economic arrangements is a broader expression of the principle of freedom and is and valuable in itself. Secondly, economic freedom is necessary to achieve political freedom (*ibid.*: 8). Examples for economic unfreedom are: citizens who cannot travel to another country because of exchange controls; citizens who are compelled to spend parts of their income on a retirement contract; and citizens who cannot choose the occupation they want because of license arrangement. Each example reflects economic arrangements that concentrate power. For Friedman, economic freedom under competitive capitalism "also promotes political freedom because it separates economic power from political power and in this way enables the one to offset the other" (*ibid.*: 9). If economic activity occurs outside the reach of the government, one source of coercive power is eliminated (*ibid.*: 15).

According to Friedman there is a logical connection between competitive capitalism and political freedom because free private enterprise organises exchange for a large number of individuals with the greatest possibility of choice for these individuals. Co-ordination in such a society of individuals is achieved by voluntary exchange between private individuals (or firms). Such a society needs some authority that enforces these private contracts, and that deals with the problems stemming from monopoly situations and externalities. Government in such a society is an "umpire" that sets, interprets and enforces the rules (*ibid.*: 14-15). The advantage of a market system is that the range of issues that have to be regulated centrally are reduced and the need for government intervention too.

The state also has to regulate money. The aim of monetary authority should be to achieve a specified rate of growth in the stock of money (*ibid.*: 54); but there should be no control on foreign exchange or on foreign trade, exchange rates should be determined by the markets and should not be fixed (*ibid.*: 69-70). Fair employment practices legislation should be abolished because they reduce the freedom of the employer to hire the employees he wants (*ibid.*: 111-115). Union power should be reduced because they represent one example of monopoly in the market place leading to price increases (*ibid.*: 124). Finally, Friedman suggests that firms do not have any social responsibility "other than to make as much money for their stockholders" (*ibid.*: 133).

So what about migration? Migration laws interfere with the freedom of the individual to move to which ever place he or she chooses, and with the freedom of the employer to hire. The freedom to move would seem to be a classical liberal freedom and the restriction of the right to settle an unacceptable limitation of individual freedom, within the frame of reference of neoliberal social theory. It would also appear to be a form of intrusion into property rights, which prevents access of property holders to foreign (and perhaps cheaper) labour. Indeed, in his survey of the Chicago School, Melvin Reder (1982: 30) points out that the logical conclusion of the Chicago approach is that "equality of opportunity" has to be a requirement of worldwide productive efficiency. Thus it would be only logical that the "freedom to choose" should also imply the freedom to emigrate and immigrate at liberty.

However, this is not the case, as Reder explicitly highlights. The members of the Chicago School hardly touch upon migration. "Like most protagonists of laissez-faire, Chicago economists have not paid much attention to the issue of freedom of immigration" (*ibid.*). One representative of the School, Henry Simons (quoted in Reder 1982: 30) makes this very clear: "About immigration the less said the better". This seems to be Friedman's motto too, as 'Capitalism and Freedom' ignores migration policy completely. In a later book – 'Free to Choose' (Friedman 1979) – immigration is fleetingly mentioned but in a contradictory manner. One the one hand, he points to the free immigration laws in the US in the 19th century as a good example of limited government interference and argues that immigrants and the host country benefited from this freedom of movement (*ibid.*: 35-36). On the other hand he argues that restrictions on immigration could be "rationalized both by the needs of national defense and on the very different ground that equality stops at the water's edge" (*ibid.*: 134). Thus, while Friedman did not hesitate to advocate the removal of government restrictions in many instances with absolute certainty of their benefits, in the case of migration there is no such support.

Reder notes that Friedman (in a public discussion of 'Free to Choose') argued that the free entry of immigrants is undesirable because welfare programs provide guarantees of minimum income without consideration to productivity. This implies that free immigration would lead to substantial income transfers within the high-capital countries to gains for the immigrants, and to losses for the native population, especially the working class. As a result, "free immigration would cause rapid equalization of per capita income across countries accomplished mainly by levelling downward the income of the more affluent" (1982: 30). Henry Simons similarly suggests that proposals for free migration should be resisted:

> [w]holly free immigration [...] is neither attainable nor desirable. To insist that a free trade program is logically or practically incomplete without free migration is either disingenuous or stupid. Free trade may and should raise living standards everywhere [...] Free immigration

would level standards, perhaps without raising them anywhere (quoted in Reder 1982: 30).

For Simons (quoted in Reder 182: 30), immigration policy "must be disciplined by tough-minded realism and practical sense" and "equal treatment in immigration policy or abandonment of discrimination should likewise not be held out as purpose or hope". Gary Becker, too, supports restrictive immigration policies because open migration would "induce people in poorer countries to emigrate to the United States and other developed countries to collect generous transfer payments". While migration could still have benefits in the nineteenth century, the expansion of the welfare state makes "immigration no longer a practical policy" (quoted in Briggs 1996: 121).

Friedrich von Hayek, one of the most influential economists behind the neoliberal revolution, had nothing to say about migration in either of his main works, 'The Road to Serfdom' (1944) and 'The Constitution of Liberty' (1960). Hayek did, however, support Margaret Thatcher's restrictive immigration policies:

> While I look forward, as an ultimate ideal, to a state of affairs in which national boundaries have ceased to be obstacles to the free movement of men, I believe that within any period with which we can now be concerned, any attempt to realize it would lead to a revival of strong nationalist sentiments (quoted in Ebeling 1995: 114).

For Reder, himself a Chicago School economist, the upshot of a review of ideas on migration among the leading neoliberals is that there is a deep tension between their commitment to individual choice and the rejection of the freedom to move. As he (1982: 30) points out, the "intellectual defense of resistance to the implied redistribution of income and possible of political power requires a quite sharp reformulation of the normative principles of traditional liberalism and the associated goal of an open society". He (*ibid.*: 31) emphasises that both "freedom of opportunity and world wide efficiency of economic organization require freedom of choice in location". But it is exactly these freedoms that the Chicago School rejects for migrants on the basis of quite dubious arguments.

It should be noted that there are a number of economists who advocate the freedom of movement for migrants. They argue that, on an economic level, free factor flows, whether of capital or of labour increase overall welfare. For them, free migration is as beneficial as free capital mobility (e.g. Schultz 1978: 385). Less radical in its implications are the proposals of Julian L. Simon, and economist associated with the CATO Institute – one of the think tanks preparing the ground for the supply-side or neoliberal revolution in the United States. Simon (1989: 345) discusses the benefits of immigration and concludes that the United States should accept more immigrants by introducing policies "that discriminate on the basis of economic characteristics".

Simon maintains that international migration and international trade cannot be treated in the same framework of analysis as assumed by the Heckscher-Ohlin-Samuelson theory of factor-price equalisation because the gains from trade are unlike the gains from migration: "trade-induced shifts in prices and production benefit consumers in both countries, whereas the shifts due to international migration benefit only the migrant" (*ibid.*: 19). The clear and tangible benefits from immigration to host countries do not stem from trade-like effects but from other mechanisms (*ibid.*: 17). These benefits can best be reaped not by allowing free immigration, but by attracting more 'valuable' migrants under a quota system (ibid. : 342).

Stephen emphasises that most immigrants are indeed very valuable in economic terms. He claims that the picture of the poor immigrant is blatantly wrong; instead, immigrants are often more highly skilled and educated than the average citizens of their native countries. For these reasons, US immigration policy should aim at allowing especially those immigrants into the country that have the required skills and education. In this way America's competitive advantage over other nations that do not tolerate immigration would be increased massively (Moore 1999). Again, this is not a call for the liberalisation of migration policy but for a migration policy that takes economic considerations into account to allow for skilled migration.

Private International Fora: The Trilateral Commission

While the classical theorists of neoliberalism have exerted a strong influence on the social and political actors that advanced the neoliberal revolution, their influence was only indirect. The task of formulating strategies responding to concrete challenges, and to find some sort of elite consensus as to possible solutions, was taken up, according to transnational historical materialists, by private elite networks at the international level. Stephen Gill's work has focused on the Trilateral Commission because it was one of the central transnational bodies that sought to prevent the crisis of the Bretton Woods system from destroying the internationalisation tendencies established in the post-war period. The Trilateral Commission comprises multinational firms in production, finance and communication, as well as academics and state officials (Gill 1986: 215). To repeat, the main interest in analysing such networks is not to uncover a conspiracy of powerful people acting behind the scenes and holding the strings of puppet governments in their hands, but to examine the establishment of a new 'common sense' that frames a common approach to the definition of problems and to establish parameters for their solution (van der Pijl 1995: 107; Gill 1990a).

For the Trilateral Commission, the global migration crisis became a topic only in the 1990s with the fall of the Berlin Wall and the end of the Cold War, which for many policy makers heralded a new era of (unwanted) mass migration from Eastern Europe to Western countries. It is in this policy debate that the Trilateral Commission has intervened in 1993 with the Triangle paper No. 44: 'International Migration Challenges in a New Era' (Meissner et al. 1993). It analyses current migration flows and discusses the policies of the United States, Canada, the European Community, Japan and the International Community.

The Triangle paper suggests that Canada's approach to present migration challenges has been most successful in comparison with other countries because it has managed to establish a workable balance between self-interest and humanitarian considerations (*ibid.*: 22). In the case of the United States, the paper suggest that policies to fight illegal immigration have failed. The main measure, employer sanctions, proved to be unworkable because of the absence of a secure identity document (*ibid.*: 31-32). The report acknowledges that NAFTA will reduce migration pressures only in the long run, and will even increase migration flows in the next 10 to 20 years. The aim should be to reduce illegal immigration, but not to reduce immigration as such, in order to ease the transition (*ibid.*: 37-38).

With respect to the European countries, the report notes the urgency of the situation after the end of the Cold War, with Europe expecting more immigration movements, while at the same time anti-immigration pressures are increasing at the domestic level. After the stop of the guest worker programs, Europe perceives itself as 'closed' to immigration. However, this is a policy that – as the report points out – could not be implemented; as a result, the immigrant population has grown while tensions surrounding immigration increased (*ibid.*:

41-44). Today, immigration is seen by EU countries as an issue of high politics, and the report urges to continue with the Europeanization of migration policy as the best way to deal with the various challenges posed by migration (*ibid.*: 62). While there have been developments that might form the basis of an effective immigration management system at the European level, the outcome could also be a 'Fortress Europe' (*ibid.*: 63-64).

At the international level, the Trilateral Commission reports a marked change in the way in which refugees are dealt with. Increasingly, the system of refugee settlement by third countries is seen as no longer viable. Instead, developed countries have started to implement 'care-in-place' strategies and undertaken humanitarian interventions (*ibid.*: 75-76). It suggests that a new imperative is emerging in international relations: "the right of individuals to stay where they are" (*ibid.*: 89). The argument underlying this new imperative is that most migrations today are forced and that most individuals, if given a choice, would stay at home. It is towards this goal that policies of western countries should be directed (*ibid.*).

In fact, the Triangle report claims that state policy is already informed by considerations of the 'right to stay'. The starting point for this new policy was in the aftermath of the Gulf war when the international community for the first time authorised humanitarian intervention and the UNHCR worked within negotiated 'safety zones'. As a result there is now a linkage between the humanitarian oriented UNHCR and the military oriented approach of the Security Council, which in the long run could endanger the work of the UNHCR itself (*ibid.*: 82). A further consequence is that the in-country-of-origin strategy might replace the offer of asylum and temporary refuge (*ibid.*: 85).

The conclusion of the report is that contemporary migrations are an expression of the cultural, economic and political conditions of the present era. According to the report, the present approaches to migration flows have been rather narrow and particularistic. The report urges countries to move beyond conventional control and humanitarian measures and to make the management of migration measures a part a nation's objectives in the economic, political and security field (*ibid.*: 89). There is, then, no indication of any advocacy of an open migration system to be found in the only paper of the Trilateral Commission that deals with migration. It should also be noted that the Triangle paper on 'Globalization and Trilateral Labor Markets' does not include any role for migrant labour in its stated objective, the flexibilisation of labour markets (Thygesen et al. 1996). With respect to the treatment of refugees, it should be noted, moreover, that the new human rights interventionism appears as a practical implementation of the right of individuals to stay where they are. However, this is in clear violation of the Geneva Refugee convention that foresees resettlement of refugees abroad if a solution cannot be found (Hawthorn 1999: 150-153).

The Organisation for Economic Co-operation and Development

The OECD and the Neoliberal Project

The OECD was launched in 1961 to provide the Bretton Woods system with a "much-needed talking-shop on policy, and a clearing-house for economic information" that would "encourage a consistent way of thinking about international economic problems" and that would "help to make countries aware of the impact of their national policies on

each other" (Zolberg 1991: 314, 322).[50] Established with twenty founding members as a successor of the OEEC, it developed into a forum for transatlantic dialogue on economic problems, and into "an economic bulwark against communism" (Bowley 1997).[51]
While the 'bulwark' against communism is no longer necessary, its role as a forum on economic policy co-ordination remains. As the chairman of the OECD's annual ministerial meeting has asserted: "We don't lend money [...] We don't organize armies. But we do have this role that nobody else plays. That role [...] is to think" (Barry 1999). In concrete terms, this means that the OECD is pursuing research and provides internationally comparable statistics on economic and social matters. The main role of that research is to facilitate the exchange and dissemination of knowledge among policy-makers and to provide a place where officials can discuss ideas without having to make a formal commitment.[52] Critics, however, hold a less benign view of the OECD, describing it as the "politburo" behind the reforms of the "neoliberal international".[53]

---

50 The role of the OECD in the organisation of international relations is under-researched. Most of the information on the organisation itself had to be gleaned from newspaper articles, and self-descriptions of the organisation.
51 Belgium, Denmark, Germany, France, Greece, Great Britain, Ireland, Iceland, Italy, Canada, Luxembourg, Norway, Netherlands, Austria, Portugal, Sweden, Switzerland, Spain and Turkey. Japan joined in 1964, Finland in 1969, Australia in 1971, New Zealand in 1973, Mexico in 1994, Czech Republic in 1995, Hungary, Poland, and South Korea in 1996.
52 For example, the work of the OECD on measuring the cost of farm subsidies led to the successful conclusion of agricultural part of the Uruguay round (Norman 1994). The OECD has been used in the 1970s to develop a consensus among the industrialised countries vis-à-vis the developing countries (Smythe 1997: 4).
53 Le Monde Diplomatique (March 1998).

In contrast to other international organisations, the OECD is not endowed with sanctioning mechanisms if member countries do not adhere to recommendations. Instead, the organisation exerts 'peer pressure' through reports, meetings with national officials and ranking lists (Marks 1994; Berschens 1994). Policy prescriptions are presented in an indirect manner when reports highlight policies that worked as opposed to those that did not (cf. OECD 1993: 3). The OECD is also active in global governance by working out charters that become the basis for formal international agreements with binding rules and regulations. For example, the OECD devised methods to value intellectual capital, set up codes of conduct for transnational corporations and for the liberalisation of the capital accounts. Other initiatives are the failed Multilateral Agreement on Investment, the consultations on tax competition among industrialised countries, the suggestions for large-scale regulatory reforms and labour market reform. A new issue area is the internet, where the OECD has developed guidelines for cryptography (Hellman 1997). Concerning migration, the results of research and seminars are summarised in the yearly 'Trends in International Migration' (SOPEMI), which detail the development of migration flows and migration policies in the OECD countries. In contrast to other areas that concern the emergence of a global economy, the OECD has issued no conventions or regulations to deal with migration. This reflects the general institutional asymmetry already highlighted in chapter two.

The central task of the OECD today is the promotion of free trade and investment, and to defend globalisation (Bowley 1997; Zänker 1996). In this context, the OECD has been asked in 1997 by the member governments to summarise the benefits of globalisation, and to defend it vis-à-vis its critics. The results of this effort was a report entitled 'Open Markets Matter: The Benefits of Trade and Investment Liberalisation' (OECD 1998a), which celebrates the manifold benefits of free trade and investment. This report shows that the OECD is very conscious of the fact that "the liberalisation debate is a debate over ideas" and for these reasons has prepared the report for member governments to help them to "communicate why and how market liberalisation forms part of the answer" to many social and economic problems (*ibid.*: 14). This report is thus a crucial starting point for an inquiry into the ideas behind the drive towards a global economy.

The main message of this report is that liberalisation has clear advantages for societies because it increases competitiveness, which will translate into a more efficient production structure that "contributes to growth and rising incomes" (*ibid.*: 8). For these reasons, the report advocates the liberalisation of trade, foreign direct investment, and of the banking sector (*ibid.*: 9). However, the report notes that structural changes in OECD economies of which liberalisation is but one, adversely affects some groups in societies the concerns of which have to be taken into account. Policies to deal with these adverse effects should not lead to an increase in protection but they have to target what the OECD sees as the 'root' of the problem: rigid labour markets and problematic regulatory policies (*ibid.*: 3). In both areas, the OECD has developed initiatives such as the 'OECD Jobs Strategy' (OECD 1994a) and the 'OECD Recommendations on Regulatory Reform' (OECD 1997a and b).

However, immigration liberalisation is not regarded as a possible contribution to the solution of economic problems. The report mentions migration only once, when discussing the impact of inflows on wages, where it is pointed out that both immigration and trade flows from low-wage countries "exert only modest effects on OECD labour markets" (OECD 1998a: 52). A footnote highlights that "[w]hen considering the link between immigration and labour market performance, it is worth bearing in mind that seven out of eight immigrants who have settled in OECD countries arrive through highly regulated channels that are there to ensure that the immigration concerned also serves the needs of the host country" (*ibid.*: 64, fn. 7). Thus, immigration liberalisation is not considered part of the liberalisation agenda; the report instead emphasises the controlled nature of current immigration. The following sections look at the development of the view of the OECD on migration since the mid-seventies by focusing on various themes such as the labour market, demographic change, global development, and regional integration projects.

The Response to the Crisis of Bretton Woods System

The 'McCracken report', published by the OECD in 1977, has been described by neo-Gramscian scholars as one of the first documents to outline the neoliberal strategy adopted soon after in Britain, New Zealand and the US (though in many respects, it has to be said, it remains a 'halfway house' between embedded liberalism and neoliberalism). What was crucial was the report's emphasis on fighting inflation and consequently a focus on monetary policy (McCracken et al. 1977: 193). Its targets were wage increases and the (perceived negative) role of unions in contributing to 'unreasonable' wages and incomes policies. As the report noted, "we regret that some governments still seem to be too politically embarrassed to admit in public that, normally, anti-inflationary demand management policies lead to a temporary rise in unemployment" (*ibid.*: 186).
Concerning the labour market, the report was rather optimistic, arguing that the supply of labour will decrease and that this will take away pressures on labour markets (*ibid.*: 142). One reason was that immigration as a source of labour supply had declined, and was expected to

continue to do so. The main problem consisted, according to the McCracken report, in the decline of the flexibility of labour markets, which prevented efficient allocation of labour. The report advocated an 'eclectic' approach to reconcile efficiency and equality, including income redistribution, legislation to prevent discrimination and an increase in labour market flexibility. Furthermore, the report recommended to lower the cost of labour by decreasing the employers' social security contributions and similar levies (*ibid.*: 223).

While the McCracken report saw a need to increase labour market flexibility, migration was not seen as a way to do achieve this aim. The report accepted restrictive migration policy tendencies as given and did not try to change them; instead it aimed at achieving labour market flexibility by different methods. The McCracken report, then, already contains the new approach to migration: inflow of migrants needs to be restricted, and labour market reforms have to take different avenues, such as an attack on union power.

The McCracken report's acceptance of restrictive migration policies reflected a complete U-turn in the context of the OECD's traditional recommendations, and this turn was confirmed by the Kindleberger report of 1978 (OECD 1978a), which addressed migration issues directly. As Zolberg has documented, the OECD encouraged the use of labour migrants to alleviate shortages on the labour market as a part of the Bretton Woods compromise in the 1950s and 1960s. Labour migration was incorporated into the terms of reference of the OECD, and the promotion of the international movement of labour was "explicitly designed to complement the other nascent international regimes" for trade and capital flows (Zolberg 1991: 313). This was the result of a "coincidence of needs", as the OECD argued: "excess labour demand in one part of the area coupled with excess labour supply in the other" (OECD 1978a: 7). Labour migration thus was initiated explicitly as an "economic" policy; from this resulted relatively open immigration policies in the post-war period (*ibid.*: 9, 16 and 24).

The Kindleberger report, like the McCracken report, stands at the water-shed between embedded liberalism and neoliberalism. It summarised prevailing economic theory at that time, which held that immigration is beneficial for both the migrant who has better opportunities than at home, and the employer who can fill a job vacancy without wages and prices being pushed up. Remittances were seen as a source of foreign exchange for financing more capital-intensive economic development, and emigration provided a safety valve to export unemployment abroad. For the labour importing countries, "the availability of migrant labour, like a 'reserve army of unemployed', exerts a downward pressure on wages and prices, thereby allowing a surplus from lower cost output" (*ibid.*: 28). This was especially true in a situation where the supply of migrant labour was almost unlimited, and could be employed at relatively low wage levels. As a result, the "proceeds from increases in output were channelled to profits or returns to capital" (*ibid.*). Thus, the increase in factor mobility owing to migration was seen as leading to a rise of overall output and therefore wealth. In addition to this, it was stressed that migrant labour boosts the "efficiency of the labour markets", as migrant labour is geographically more mobile than domestic workers and can be moved to the region where labour scarcity is highest (*ibid.*: 29).

However, the report also reflected the changing circumstances of migration, which came to play an important role in the 1970s. Migration is now described as not only a movement of factors of production, but of people, which has a social component that generates externalities over time.

> Migration implies a mixing of cultures, with, at times, serious social tensions as a consequence. Over time, as migrants remain in host

countries and the process takes on a more permanent nature, larger claims on the social infrastructure arise. The children of migrants must be schooled, and medical services, housing, welfare benefits and other publicly financed services must be diverted to those whose characteristics and tastes become increasingly transformed in line with those of the host-country population. Increasing claims on public goods and services serve to reduce the net economic benefits accruing to the host country. Social tensions can completely reverse net economic profits and turn them into net social losses (*ibid.*: 29- 30).

The Kindleberger report noted the influence of these considerations on the shift towards restrictive immigration policies in the West. The presence of foreign migrant labour led to growing social tensions and authorities wanted to have a "breathing room" to enable them to integrate the migrants already in the territory (*ibid.*: 22). It also recognised the attempts of western governments to reduce the dependence on foreign labour, and to pressure firms into using more capital-intensive techniques (*ibid.*: 23).[54] Lastly, it noted that because of policy interdependence no country was able to pursue a policy of liberal immigration if all other countries restricted their immigration intake (*ibid.*: 23). Nevertheless, the Kindleberger report was remarkably critical of the shift in migration policies, which saw, after the crisis years of 1973/1974, the labour-importing countries unilaterally restricting the admission of migrants by administrative means, for example by issuing fewer work permits (*ibid.*: 20). Restrictions on immigration "are simply an obvious form of protection" as the report notes. This form of protectionism would reduce overall output and increase inefficiency in factor allocation as well as pass on the burden of unemployment to those countries that are least able to cope with it. Restrictions on immigration exported the unemployment problem from developed to

---

54 It should be noted that the sending countries, too, raised concerns since migrant labour constituted also an outflow of human capital that is needed in the sending countries (OECD 1978a: 18).

other countries (*ibid.*: 21-22). "The policy is intended to protect domestic jobs, wages, and the 'integrity' of the social transfer systems, in the face of cutbacks in demand for labour, public budgets, and medium-term growth prospects" (*ibid.*: 8).

The report concludes that the unilateral decision to stop the importation of migrant labour is against the spirit of the liberalisation of manpower movement that developed in post-war Europe (*ibid.*: 8, 44). Instead of a co-operative management of an economic crisis, industrialised countries have established competitive responses. The report urges for a new machinery of co-operation between former labour importing and exporting countries. Against these unilateral protectionist measures, the report emphasises that unemployment is a worldwide problem and recommends that OECD countries should co-operate with the sending countries in sharing these costs (*ibid.*: 33-34).

But there is no suggestion of going back to the Bretton Woods migration system. A removal of the restrictions on immigration is seen as highly unlikely. "Our view is that whatever migration takes place within the OECD area in the foreseeable future, it will be of limited scope rather than mass movement" (*ibid.*: 36).[55] It suggests that the main focus of developed countries will have to be the restructuring of their domestic labour markets and proposes the promotion of greater labour intensity of work through subsidising wages, reducing payroll taxes, or by creating employment (*ibid.*: 33). Interestingly enough, the Kindleberger report also notes that continued immigration may ease the adjustment process but that this will have to be a migration of a very different kind: "it will likely imply illegal movements and black

---

55 It was also regarded as unlikely that other areas outside the OECD area, such as the petroleum producing countries, would start importing migrant labour to such an extent as to compensate for the migration restrictions (OECD 1978a: 39).

market work of the type currently being experienced in the United States" (*ibid.*). Thus there is a tacit expectation that undocumented immigrants will provide some flexibility for labour markets; however, naturally, the 1978 report does not recommend any strategy that would make the use of illegal immigration in the flexibilisation of labour markets a part of official policy.

The report concludes by discussing the options for the migrant sending countries. In the long term, the report notes the need for development, i.e. growth, in order to absorb more labour market participants and decrease migration pressures. This growth process should be supported by western monetary assistance, capital flows or trade agreements (*ibid.*). In the short term, the report stressed the immediate need to alleviate the adjustment burden for the developing countries. While it discouraged the export of surplus labour as a crisis strategy for Third World countries, it also suggested that OECD countries should not simply impose migration restrictions in the form of administrative, market distorting measures (i.e. entry restrictions) but in the form of a tax that increased the price of migrant labour. The proceeds of that tax could then be transferred to the sending countries in order to provide them with capital resources to make up for lost remittances.

Moreover, the Kindleberger report recommended the lifting of trade restrictions on goods from developing countries in order to offset some of the costs of migration restrictions (*ibid.*: 39). Most importantly, however, it envisaged a substitution of foreign investments form migration: "Restriction will ultimately imply a change in the pattern of foreign investment. If people are no longer able to move to the jobs, the jobs can still be moved to the people" (*ibid.*: 37). The problem, according to the 1978 report, was that 'the people' benefiting from foreign direct investments would not necessarily be potential migrants, as investment follows market considerations not migration flows. This implies that capital inflows would need to take on the form of "guaranteed loans" or "outright grants" (*ibid*.: 38) in order to contribute effectively to the compensation of sending countries.

Approaches to Labour Market Restructuring

The acceptance of restrictive migration policies by the OECD characterises all the relevant reports and studies of the 1980s and 1990s. At this point in our investigation, it can thus be noted that there is clearly no immediate pressure from the OECD to liberalise the international movement of labour alongside the liberalisation of capital. But that does not mean that the OECD completely rejects the use of migrant labour in the project of neoliberal reconstruction. As we have seen, the restructuring of labour markets has become a central focus in this project, and over the 1980s and 1990s, it became even more prominent. So does the OECD recommend certain forms of migration in order to obtain the stated goal of labour market flexibilisation?

The most important document relevant to our inquiry that emerged in the 1980s was a study on the 'New Framework of Active Labour Market Policies'. The rationale for a new policy was that the diversification of jobs and markets, which, according to this study, had increased so that old-fashioned ways of job placement were outdated. In response, the focus shifted towards the promotion of an 'active society' trying to avoid dependency cycles for people in governmental programmes. In his summary of the OECD approach to labour market policy, Lönnroth (1993: 76) notes the increasing scepticism of immigration as a strategy in labour supply adjustment. While migration had earlier contributed to improved growth performance and reduced rigidities on the labour markets, it is far from certain that an inflow of immigrants will provide a permanent solution to labour shortages or structural imbalances. Immigration may create additional demand for labour, notably in the social and commercial services. The social costs of multicultural societies, stretching over second and third generations of immigrants, have to be set against the short-run economic benefits. Unemployment should neither be exported nor imported. The negative effects on sending areas' most productive and mobile labour reserves also have to be considered. The core of any labour market policy has to be reliance on domestic labour resources before any import of labour is countenanced (*ibid.*).

Immigration is thus not suggested as a way to increase labour market flexibility. This stance reappears in the 'Jobs Strategy' of the OECD, mandated in 1992. The summarising policy brief, 'The OECD Jobs Study: Facts, Analysis, Strategies', was presented at the June 1994 meeting of the OECD Council. It was followed by several volumes containing the underlying analysis and background to the strategy.[56] The impetus for this strategy was the insight that "it is an inability of OECD economies and societies to adapt rapidly and innovatively to a world of rapid structural change that is the principal cause of high and persistent unemployment" (OECD 1994b: vii). It advocates a radical restructuring of OECD societies: "No one policy pursued in isolation would have a sufficient effect. Action is required in all areas simultaneously" (*ibid.*). The basic assumption is that flexible labour markets in the US have led to higher job creation whereas the rigidity of European labour markets has meant that unemployment has been higher (*ibid.*: 61). Labour market institutions in Europe are blamed for the dismal performance of European labour markets (*ibid.*: 63).

The OECD Jobs Strategy is portrayed as a renewed effort at reform, after the first strategy devised in the early and mid-1980s had failed. The main policy mistakes are located "on the structural side and espe-

---

56 OECD (1994b and c; 1996c and d; 1997 a and b; 1998c, 1999).

cially in the labour market area", where much "was left undone" (*ibid.*: 65). According to the 1994 Strategy Paper, problems are, firstly, that there are not enough jobs and that the job potential of the service sector is not fully used. Secondly, people lack skills concerning new technologies. Thirdly, working-time arrangements are too inflexible. Furthermore, there are too many disincentives to hiring: non-wage labour costs are too high, wage differentials not wide enough, statutory minimum wages are too high and employment protection legislation is too strict. Lastly, product-market barriers have become too high as well, as a result of the lack of competition on markets.

The question whether more discretionary use of macroeconomic policy – beyond the operation of automatic stabilisers and the endogenous reaction of monetary conditions – should be made, is answered by the OECD with a clear 'no'. "This is because there is much evidence in OECD countries, particularly in Europe, of a major structural element in unemployment which requires changes in labour and product markets" (*ibid.*: 73). While the report notes that there has been a deficiency of demand because of the strict policies followed to fight inflation (*ibid.*: 66), and that there is a need for rapid and sustainable growth in order to reduce unemployment, it is suggested that macroeconomic policies cannot deal with the underlying structural element of unemployment which requires structural reforms supported by sound macroeconomic policies (*ibid.*: 73):

> In particular, greater wage flexibility, reductions in barriers to labour mobility and greater competition would make it easier for the unemployed to find jobs at the going wage, although it is noticeable that profit shares are now at historically high levels (*ibid.*).

As a response, the OECD has developed nine recommendations for better labour market performance.[57] The implementation rate of the measures seems to be quite high: All in all, 393 recommendations were developed for the OECD member countries. The review report notes that on 124 of these recommendations, no action has been taken, while 258 actions had been taken. In 192 of these cases, it suggested that more needed to be done. Only in 11 cases were opposite actions being taken (*ibid.*: 25).

One notable opposite action explicitly mentioned in the review is the introduction of the minimum wage in the construction industry in Germany as a result of the debate on posted workers. This minimum wage was introduced, according to the OECD "to prevent workers hired abroad from underbidding domestic workers" (*ibid.*: 17).[58] This suggests that the undermining of domestic wages is an explicit part of a strategy to flexibilise labour markets. This can also be seen, for instance, in the recommendation to lift employment protection legislation, e.g. by making fixed-term contracts possible. Other recommendations advocate a wider wage distribution, decentralisation of wage determination, and the use of more opt-out clauses in collective agreements.

---

57 The policy recommendations are: "set appropriate macroeconomic policies, enhance the creation and diffusion of technological know-how, increase working-time flexibility, nurture an entrepreneurial climate, increase wage and labour cost flexibility, reform employment security provisions, expand and enhance active labour market policies, improve labour force skills and competencies, and reform the unemployment and related benefit systems" (OECD 1994a). In concrete terms the OECD argues that labour market flexiblity can be increased if unemployment and other social benefits are less generous and access to early retirement and disability pensions is tightened (OECD 1998c: 15).

58 See the case study in chapter five and the context of the posted workers issue in chapter one.

The strategy paper was silent with regard to international migration (OECD 1994c: 66).[59] However, the strategy paper recommended increased co-operation among OECD countries in order to respond to migration pressures from the South, with a specific focus on effective deterrence of economic refugees and illegal immigrants. Furthermore, it was suggested that migration issues should be included in the wider trade, investment and co-operative development activities between OECD countries and sending countries (OECD 1994a).

Only temporary labour migration is more seriously assessed regarding labour market flexibility and shortages. The 1998 edition of the Trends in International Migration report (SOPEMI) contains a section on the temporary employment of foreigners in selected OECD countries. The report notes that the

> recruitment of temporary foreign workers can provide greater labour market flexibility and help alleviate sectoral labour shortages in host countries. It also promotes the movement of managerial staff and highly skilled workers. This is especially true for enterprises that wish to set up abroad. In certain cases, particularly during a period of restricted immigration, it may be a means of reducing the employment of foreigners in an irregular situation (SOPEMI 1998: 185).

---

59 According to van Dijk (1995: 223-4) the OECD distinguishes five forms of labour market flexibility: 1. External numerical flexibility implies an increase of the capability of employers to employ or dismiss people (a goal which can also be achieved by short-term or fixed contracts). 2. Increasing subcontracting and forms of self-employment to offload risks. 3. Internal numerical flexibility refers to the adjustment of working hours to the firm's needs; 4. Functional flexibility refers to the ability of workers to switch jobs within the firm. 5. Wage flexibility allows the adjustment of wages to performance, which is largely prevented by collective bargaining agreements. As he points out too (1995: 224), geographical flexibility is absent.

This report stresses that temporary labour migration "avoids the costs associated with permanent immigration regarding welfare and integration policies" (*ibid.*: 22). Temporary migration is distinguished from permanent employment by the fact that it is usually not seen as a first step to settle permanently. This makes temporary workers rather attractive because they have a fixed-term employment contract, and they must leave the country after the expiry of the contract; they are not entitled to family reunion and they are not allowed to seek other employment once the contract has expired (*ibid.*: 185). The report then discusses the various forms of temporary employment such as trainees, contract workers, students' holiday working schemes, skilled-workers (professionals), seasonal workers, entertainers and sportspersons, teachers and researchers and the specific regulations covering these forms of temporary migration.

But while the SOPEMI report notes the "generally favourable attitude towards temporary workers" (*ibid.*: 198), it does not recommend labour market flexibilisation via the employment of temporary migrants. It concludes by questioning the wisdom of relying too much on temporary foreign labour,

> both in terms of numbers, skill levels and the specific sectors involved. Is the labour recruited to meet the needs of seasonal activities or under bilateral agreements regarding 'workers on projects' absolutely indispensable? Is the social protection of temporary workers adequately ensured? One may also question whether the provisions on labour standards and equal treatment with national workers are really enforced for some categories of temporary workers. Since it is not always easy to verify that this is the case, this type of migration may be directly detrimental to enterprises and employment at local level (*ibid.*).

Thus, the report remains highly ambivalent: Noting the positive contribution to labour market flexibility, it also reflects concerns about the negative impact of temporary immigration on receiving societies, which are often voiced by trade unions and left-of-centre governments.

Policy Responses to Demographic Changes of OECD Societies

Temporary migration is also discussed in the context of the debate about the future of pension systems in OECD countries. The rising share of elderly in the population of industrial countries alongside the fall of the population in employment creates a pension crisis. There are two demographic solutions to this problem: an increase in fertility or net migration (especially of young and economically active individuals) (*ibid.*: 27).[60] According to the OECD, even if the fertility rate could be increased, the effect would only be of a gradual nature and because of this it cannot alleviate the rapid growth in the elderly population. Immigration, in contrast, would have immediate effects on the working age population. Yet, it is not recommended because immigration policy cannot really be fine-tuned to achieve precise demographic objectives, since it is difficult to control the volume and the composition of migration.

One way out would be temporary labour migration. However, "historical precedents suggest that such programmes are difficult to manage", visible in the fact that most temporary labour migrations have been transformed into permanent immigration (*ibid.*: 28). Secondly, the immigration volumes required to reduce the old-age dependency ratios would have to be extremely high. In addition, immigrants will themselves age and thus the problem would be only postponed and not be resolved (*ibid.*: 27-28). The biggest problem is that immigration

---

60 This report summarizes the findings of OECD (1991a).

policy is politically sensitive and governments may fear to engage in a debate about the need to increase immigration. A further reason is that an increase in immigration presupposes that there are enough job openings for these immigrants. At the moment, with high levels of structural unemployment, this is clearly not the case (with the exceptions of specific sectors such as information technology). The report therefore concludes that immigration cannot be used to reduce the problems stemming from an ageing population.

International Division of Labour/Migration in a Global Economy

In subsequent OECD reports that looked at the link between migration and development, the theme of 'compensation' has not been taken up again. The 1998 SOPEMI report recognises that "[i]nternational co-operation to control flows is only a partial response to the intensification of migration movements" (*ibid*: 70). However, instead of opting for a more co-operative approach between sending and receiving countries as in 1978, the report urges developing countries to adopt 'sustainable' policies in order to reduce emigration pressures. The International Conference on Migration organised by the OECD in Rome in March 1991, whose results have been published under the title 'The Changing Course of International Migration', reached similar conclusions:

> The first is that emigration is not the key to resolving the problems of underdevelopment nor the demographic and economic imbalances between developed countries, and countries which are in the process of development. The second encourages the latter with the support of the developed countries and within the framework of a new and more specific form of co-operation, to more clearly orient their economic development towards the creation of jobs and promoting a climate better able to attract foreign investment on a greater scale. Lastly, the

third invites the immigration countries to keep in mind the repercussions of all their policies, in particular their trade policies, on international migration (OECD 1993: 3).

These three conclusions basically sum up the approach to migration and development of OECD countries that is repeated (with variations) in all further publications (see for example, Soltwedel 1993: 65):

- migration from underdeveloped areas to developed areas is discouraged,
- developing countries should improve economic governance to make sure people stay at home specifically by attracting foreign investment, a suggestion that clearly is an advocacy for 'globalisation' or a new international division of labour, and lastly,
- developed countries are again urged to reconsider their trade policies (in order to allow the goods produced under the new international division of labour into western countries).

In 1993, a follow-up conference on 'Migration and International Cooperation: Challenges for OECD Countries' was organised by the OECD in Madrid. This conference concluded that trade and capital flows can reduce migration pressures only if they actually influence the factors that lead to emigration decisions. However, here too the onus was put on developing countries themselves. While OECD countries can help to develop correct policies, "this cannot substitute for effective action by developing countries" (OECD 1994d: 6). Both southern and OECD countries were encouraged to contribute to economic development by either opening their markets to commodity and capital imports from developing countries, or by implementing effective economic policies. One area for further reflection was to devise support measures for the transitional period of development at the bilateral or multilateral level. "These measures should represent an incentive strong enough to dissuade potential candidates from emigrating" (*ibid.*: 6). In the conclusion, the secretary-general of the OECD, Jean-Claude Paye points out that OECD countries are confronting a 'crisis of legitimacy' concerning migration. The reason is that the distinctions between different categories of migrants are blurred by illegal immigration and the increasing 'abuse' of asylum.

> This is causing concern and indeed hostility among the population of the host countries. If the regulations governing the entry, stay and employment of immigrants were more clearly defined, better understood by the host country's population and more effectively enforced, the integration of these immigrants would be that much easier and their contribution to the labour market that much more apparent. Thus the legitimacy of migration policies requires more effective control of flows and concerns all types of migration (Paye 1994: 304).

The implication of this statement is that strict controls of borders are a necessary precondition for the integration of legal and legitimate immigrants. This reinforces the point made in chapter two. The movement towards the liberalisation of citizenship policies that has been noted by Soysal (1994), Hollifield (1992), and Jacobson (1996) is thus intimately tied up with a politics of control. Thus, it is impossible to focus only on the trend towards the extension of citizenship rights without also discussing for example, the tighter asylum rules.

Regional Integration Processes (Staged Integration)

The clearest statement envisaging a role for migration in the process of neoliberal restructuring is to be found not in the context of the debate about the flexibilisation of labour markets or pension systems, but in a report on regional integration and NAFTA. Here the OECD report develops a 'stage theory' of economic integration, and suggests that the freedom to move can only be introduced when there has been successful economic integration and development (i.e. when there are no longer strong incentives to emigrate). The NAFTA report explicitly discussed the link between trade liberalisation and migration movements. Specifically, it asked whether the freedom of movement of persons should be included in regional integration processes, or whether it should "be considered as an important objective to be achieved only once economic convergence has reached a sufficiently high level" (SOPEMI 1998: 71). In an earlier seminar, Tapinos had presented the example of the European integration process where according to him the removal of barriers to migration succeeded the removal of barriers on goods.

> The process of European economic unification has taken place according to a timetable that is essential for an understanding of the implications for international movements of labour. The disappearance of tariff barriers and quotas on the movement of goods *preceded* the introduction of the free circulation of workers. This resulted in the development of intra-Community trade and a tendency for standards of living to come closer together, thus reducing incentives to emigrate (Tapinos 1993: 178, emphasis S. Dreher).

In the seminar on NAFTA, the participants came to a similar conclusion. According to Jean-Pierre Garson, from the OECD Directorate for Education, Employment, Labour and Social Affairs, the liberalisation of migration should be dependent on the level of integration and economic development of the countries involved. In the case of Mexico and the United States, he concludes:

> Although the absence of free movement is not an obstacle to regional economic integration, free movement should remain an objective for the longer term, when economic convergence has progressed further. In the meantime, free trade agreements should be complemented by a positive migration policy, whose primary objective would be to dis-

courage unauthorised immigration and regulate flows within the free trade area (Garson 1998; cf. Alba et al. 1998).

Garson distinguishes three levels of regional integration. The first level consists of free trade agreements without full liberalisation of factor flows (NAFTA, EU association agreements with non-member Mediterranean countries). The second level, regional blocs, integrate peripheral countries that receive budget transfers but retain barriers to labour mobility, which is the case in the relationship of the EU with certain countries in eastern and central Europe. This approach aims to reduce immigration flows while at the same time securing trade and investment integration of the countries involved. "Free trade is seen as an alternative to migration, as an instrument which may make flow regulation and control policies more credible" (Alba et al. 1998: 269). The third level is full economic and monetary integration, as in the case of the EMU, which includes full freedom of movement and establishment. The EU is also a good example that economic convergence diminishes migration flows, since labour mobility in the EU is lower than capital mobility.

> Thus, the reduction of migration flows appears not so much to be the result of institutional decisions to liberalise trade in order to stem migration with counter flows of goods and capital (NAFTA, Euro-Mediterranean agreements), as the outcome of economic development and technological catch-up brought about by regional integration (Garson 1998).

Third-level integration is "the most radical form of integration (Alba et al. 1998: 265). One reason is that adjustment mechanisms other than exchange rates have to be used thus real or structural adjustment becomes necessary in the EU. One adjustment is through labour mobility or through labour market flexibility. If there is no labour mobility and labour market flexibility in a monetary union system, unemployment could increase. If local labour markets are not flexible, 'outside' help in the form of cheap labour migrants will have to be recruited at this level of integration: "some countries will have to recruit cheaper foreign labour (new legal entrants, or illegals) rather than lowering the wages of residents (nationals and legally resident foreigners)" (*ibid.*: 265). It is important to note here that the report does not actually recommend such a strategy.

According to Garson, the emphasis on liberalisation of trade and capital movements within NAFTA, with no reference to the free movement of workers, reflects the determination to prevent the derailment of further economic and financial integration as a result of the difficulties associated with migration. It does not reflect the argument that trade liberalisation under NAFTA will lessen the incentive to emigrate because the substitution effects assumed by international trade theory are not borne out by actual developments.

> The turnaround of migration flows in some countries (Greece and Spain, for example) took place well before trade barriers had been dismantled. In the case of relations between the United States and Mexico, trade intensity is high but the reversal of migration flows has not yet begun. The turnaround when it happens will be determined not by trade, but by economic development and catch-up in training and upskilling programmes, and a massive inflow of foreign direct investment (including from emigrants abroad) to sustain growth (Garson 1998).

Concerning the creation of free trade areas, the policy conclusions are that the free movement of persons among countries with highly unequal economic development is impossible; recent trade agreements concluded by the EU with Eastern Europe and Mediterranean Countries and NAFTA are testimony to the acceptance of this idea.

Conclusion

The purpose of this chapter was to put Neo-Gramscianism to the 'test'. Neo-Gramscianism sees the global political economy as a reflection of elite choice. Following that logic, elite choice should also account for the increasingly restrictive and selective migration policies to be found in the global economy. I have established the policy preferences of the globalising elite by focusing on the economic theory of the Chicago School, and policy think tanks such as the Trilateral Commission and the OECD, as these bodies or scholars have been shown to be central to the neoliberal movement by neo-Gramscian scholars (Gill 1990a).

The results that emerge from this chapter are surprisingly clear: the neoliberal scholars and transnational elite bodies analysed here favour the closure of borders to migrants in the context of contemporary global restructuring. It is indeed ironic that the social and economic theorists who celebrate the freedom of the individual (like Friedman, von Hayek and Becker) do not advocate the abolition of one of the severest forms of government interventions: the interference in the freedom of individuals to move, and concomitantly, in the freedom of employers to hire. While we find exchange controls criticised as an example of economic unfreedom because they prevent individual travel, migration restrictions are not denounced along these lines. The freedom to 'choose' does not include the freedom to choose a country. More self-reflective members of the Chicago School, like Melvin Reder, recognise that these positions reflect a deeply political choice, which accepts economic rationality in selective cases without specifying the basis for this selectivity in systematic terms.

The discussion of the OECD has shown that the ideas on migration, labour markets and international economic integration have changed over time and develop, reflect and reinforce the prevailing hegemonic discourse. Migration under the Bretton Woods regime was clearly portrayed as beneficial for economic growth while later on only the negative aspects were emphasised and migration restrictions were seen as a way to provide a breathing space. Today, developing countries are urged to institutionalise good economic governance and make room for foreign investors. In this way, the OECD clearly promotes the idea of a new international division of labour whereby jobs are moved to the people instead of people to the jobs. As the report 'Open Markets Matter' highlighted, migration restrictions are emphasised in a reassuring note when discussing labour markets in western countries. And this theme, that migration restrictions are here to stay has now been incorporated into a "stage" theory of economic integration whereby the free flow of people is implemented only at that stage where there is no developmental difference between the areas concerned. The only exceptions seem to be undocumented migrants for which the Kindleberger Reports foresees an increase and temporary labour migration that may be able to alleviate labour shortages and be a way to go around the present restrictive labour migration regimes.

There are also, especially in the OECD reports, clear expressions of the idea that foreign direct investment should substitute for labour immigration to western countries. Instead of satisfying the need for cheap labour at home, western capital should move to the sources of cheap labour. Consequently, underdeveloped countries are 'encouraged' (and more, with the help of the IMF and the World Bank), to restructure their economies in order to make them more attractive to foreign investors. There is then a close relationship between restrictions on immigration into western countries on the one hand and the globalisation of the economy on the other hand. Both policies reflect that the compromise of embedded liberalism has entered into a crisis and a selected liberalisation policy has been adopted as a way out of the crisis.

However, we need an explanation for the continued immigration of undocumented and temporary labour migrants into OECD countries for which there are no official policy recommendations. On the contrary, they stress the costs rather than the advantages of such policies. Instead, rigidities on the labour market should be dealt with directly. The OECD Jobs Strategy recommended increasing wage disparities, reducing the role of unions, and increasing the share of part-time work cf. OECD 1994a). Immigration, it is maintained, would increase social tensions, and has to be ruled out as a solution (Soltwedel 1993; Lönnroth 1993). In short, then, neoliberals do not (officially) promote the use of migrant labour in industrial countries for labour market restructuring. Yet, as Piore (1979) has shown immigration always is a question of structural demand on the labour market. If this is the case, the question arises how to account for the persistent, if limited flows of migrant labour into western societies that have been discussed in the preceding chapters. This form of labour migration *does* provide some of the flexibility sought by employers, but it does not appear in 'official' discussions of neoliberal policies in the form of policy prescriptions.

I will argue in the next chapter that the employment of migrants under sub-standard conditions is an expression of the existence or the formation of a low-wage sector, and of the need for restructuring of labour processes brought about by the changing organisation of production relations (sub-contracting, lean production), the saturation of markets, and increased competition from low-wage countries under the new international division of labour (Cox 1987: 247-248, 321; Sassen 1988: 22). Employers will resort to the use of immigrant labour under sub-standard working conditions if other options to deal with these challenges fail (Fernández Kelly 1989: 154; Portes and Walton 1981: 55-56). With regard to the European Union, the existence of such a 'neoliberalism from below' was already highlighted by Overbeek, who argues that

> [I]t has never been the intention of EU countries to block all immigration: There is in the European economies a structural demand for cheap and irregular labor. It is therefore no wonder that a strong pro-immigration lobby exists [...] Employers and would-be employers in many small and medium-sized firms (e.g. in construction, horticulture, the garment industry) share an interest in evading immigration controls (Overbeek 1998: 86).

Paradoxically, however, this demand for a flexible migrant labour force is met by the restrictive migration regime. Undocumented migrants and temporary migrants are more bound to be exploited by employers than migrants coming in a settlers and citizens. Thus, in order to understand the politics of labour migration under neoliberalism, I will look at the national level in the following chapter, more precisely at specific sectors or industries in their national settings where such 'flexible' migrants play a role.

5. IMMIGRATION AND LABOUR MARKET RESTRUCTURING

The previous chapter has shown that neoliberalism consists of a dual bordering strategy. Prevalent in the public discussion is the intent by neoliberal forces to create a global market place. The last chapter has however highlighted that there is also another side to the neoliberal globalisation project, one that is intent on maintaining or even strengthening national borders and implicitly, national identity. This shows that there is also a strategy of re-bordering inherent in the neo-liberal project. Neoliberal forces are creating a global economy for capital but are trying to maintain a nationalist conception of citizenship. In consequence, the territorial nature of political power is maintained and to some extent, even strengthened.

The question for this chapter now is to understand how the existence of some migration flows ties in with efforts of states to create a selectively bordered global economy. As chapter one has documented there are two exceptions to the restrictive trend in migration policy: one is skilled migration. The immigration of skilled migrants is easy to explain because their importance is obvious in the race for maintaining competitiveness in a global economy. This is an argument that has silenced even the German population to such an extent that there was next to no opposition to the introduction of a 'green card' for computer experts. Skilled, knowledge-intensive labour immigration is thus a part of the market making aspect of the neoliberal project (Gill and Law 1993: 109-10). The second exception is the inflow of mostly undocumented or temporary migrants who are mostly employed in low-skilled jobs. In order to understand this continued immigration into Western countries this chapter puts these migration patterns into the context of global restructuring of industries and the creation of a new international division of labour on the one hand and the accompanying restructuring of labour markets on the other hand.

This chapter then moves from the sphere of international politics or world order and ideas to the realm of states and social forces in production relations by looking into the struggles surrounding the adoption of neoliberal labour market policies. I will sketch the restructuring of the labour market under neoliberalism in general and with specific reference to two industries: the garment industry in the United States and the construction industry in Germany. These specific industries serve as examples of the more general tendency of labour market restructuring where immigrant labour has played a crucial role. At the same time, the case studies also illustrate that the neoliberal project is not accepted without resistance. In both countries, a movement working towards a fairer global economy has grown and gained in importance though its success has been limited.

The implication of this chapter for the overall argumentation of this study is that owing to the increase in competition as a result of more global markets specific sectors or firms need a more flexible (i.e. mostly cheaper) labour force in order to be able to compete. It is not free migration that is needed but a labour force that 'accepts' lower wage and working standards. If migrants were to come in as citizens with the same social and civil rights they would remain as unemployable as much of the domestic labour force. This means that a restrictive migration regime creates the labour force that is required for further labour market flexibilisation. Only 'unfree' migration whereby migrants do not enjoy the same rights as national citizens on the labour markets provide the flexible labour pool that is needed by many employers today. The paradoxical situation is thus that while we move towards a global political economy, nationalistic conceptions of citizenship need to be strengthened in order to ensure an adequate labour supply.

The Neoliberal Approach to Labour Market Restructuring

Changes in the way goods and services are produced have been underway since the beginning of the seventies. The neo-Gramscian perspective more or less shares the general consensus within the political economy literature where this process is usually summarized as a transition form Fordism to flexible accumulation (Harvey 1990: 141-147, see also chapter 3). The term 'neoliberalism' has become prevalent to summarize political, cultural, economic and social aspects of this transition. Central to the neoliberal concept of control is the idea that rigidities in the markets have impeded growth and profits and in order for growth and profits to increase, these rigidities need to be abolished (*ibid.*: 147). On the labour market, the introduction of more flexibility has meant the development of a new structure of job hierarchies whereby primary jobs (Piore 1979) are transformed into secondary or peripheral jobs. This process of job transformation, better characterised as 'peripheralization of the labour force' (Cox 1987: 322) or 'casualization' (Broad 1995) is visible in increased part-time or temporary work, self-employment, subcontracting or in the illegal employment of undocumented workers. While there are new, well-paid jobs for highly skilled people, the new service or knowledge economy also depends on chambermaids, waiters, bartenders, janitors among others (Harrison and Bluestone 1988: 69). According to Saskia Sassen, what we are witnessing is a polarized economy, characterised by the "expansion of very high-income professional and technical jobs, a shrinking of middle income blue- and white-collar jobs, and a vast expansion of low-wage jobs" (Sassen 1988: 22). The effect of this labour market restructuring is that wages are declining or stagnating, overtime remains unpaid, health and safety regulations are not adhered to (with the consequence that accidents at the workplace increase), less workers are covered by pension and health plans, and job security increases (visible, for example in the increase in part-time work) (Mines and Avina 1992: 430). All in all, workplaces are less able to provide a middle-class life-style for a family as provided by a standard employment relationship (Mückenberger 1989) in the primary job market.

It is especially in the United States that this type of economic restructuring has made by far the biggest progress. One central avenue, especially in the United States, to bring about this restructuring of labour markets has been the employment of undocumented labour migrants (Borjas 1999: 83-84).[61] This is acknowledged by officials, e.g. the former chairman of the Federal Reserve who pointed to the flexibility of the labour market as a central reason for the high growth without inflation in the 1990s. And one main reason why labour markets in the US are flexible, according to him, is the continued inflow of immigrants.[62]

---

61 One prominent example for the type of labour market restructuring under discussion here is the Los Angeles cleaning industry. Its job structure has been completely changed by firms relying on immigrant labour. These firms were able to increase their market size because they were able to offer lower prices to customers (Dawkins 1992: 121-123). For case studies cf. Mines and Avina (1992); Mines and Martin (1984); Fernandez-Kelly (1989).
62 Baker (2000); Parkes and Tricks (2000); Utichelle (2000); Peck (2002: 215).

As a result of the growing polarization of incomes and employment conditions and of the increase in inequality in the US the 1990s have seen a massive revival of the discussion about the nature of global economic integration in the 1990s. This nationwide discussion about job restructuring and wage and labour standards in the 1990s focused mainly on the global apparel or garment industry but also highlighted deteriorating conditions at home in this industry as major public celebrities were exposed of having relied on sweatshop labour inside the US for their products.

A similar development has been observed in Europe. Under the OECD 'Jobs Initiative' the pressure is on European countries to similarly flexibilise their markets. But European Labour Markets are tightly regulated through official provisions, and prove more difficult to restructure. Here the push brought about by the creation of the Common Market in 1992 has delivered the decisive momentum for changes. In Germany, the sector most severely hit by the European liberalisation process was the construction industry, incidentally, the industry with the most advanced system of labour market regulations where trade unions and employer associations had established a tight network of institutions in contrast to other services industries in Germany (OECD 1991b: 110-111; Voswinkel, Lücking and Bode 1996). It was precisely in this sector where neoliberal forces aspired to set an example for more flexible labour markets in Germany in the early 1990s. From a neoliberal perspective, preventing minimum wages and standards in the construction industry was seen as a crucial first step towards the more general goal of further labour market flexibilisation (Hunger 2000: 86-87). These two industries, their pattern of migration employment and the ensuing policy debates will be discussed in the next two sections. The chapter focuses on these industries not just because they have been at the centre of discussion but also because they have been prominent examples under the old, Fordist labour market regime of a successful compromise regarding the problem of casual labour. The garment industry in the US was the industry whose working conditions gave rise to the New Deal Labour regulations in the 1930s whereas the construction industry in Germany has been seen as the most advanced industry in terms of labour market regulation.

Contesting the Global: Free Trade, Migration and Sweatshops in the United States

The apparel industries or garment industry produces clothes, footwear, belts, purses, luggage, gloves, scarves, ties, and household soft goods such as drapes, linens, and slipcovers. It is separate from the textile industry that fabricates cloth. Textile production differs from apparel production in that labour saving techniques can be used whereas this has proven difficult for the apparel industry. It is for this reason that the apparel industry has been at the centre of the discussion on globalisation and labour standards.
Overall, the apparel industry in the United States is marked by a decline of employment from roughly 8 percent of total employment in 1950 to 4.5 percent in 1997 while the average wage fell from 76 percent to 55 of the average total manufacturing earning in the same period (Adkisson 2002: 3). As a result, wages in the US can now compete with wages in Third World countries. Wage costs per standard minute in 1995 were 0.30 in the United States, compared with about 0.75 in Germany, and 0.55 in France. In Hong Kong and in Taiwan, as Dicken (1998: 296) notes, were the labour costs per standard minute higher than in the United States (0.33 - 0.35). While overall, employment in the apparel industry has been declining, there are some re-

gions in the US where there has been a rise of employment in the industry. In these regions there is a correlation with a rise in largely illegal immigration (Adkisson 2002: 27). This indicates that especially in areas where there is a cheap and unprotected labour force available, apparel production is still viable in the US. During this restructuring period, the apparel industry became more profitable if compared to the average of the U.S manufacturing industry, and CEO compensation rose in tandem (Rosen 2002: 221). The apparel industry thus mirrors the widening of earnings documented for the economy more general (Bernstein 2003).

These figures give a first indication of the massive restructuring processes that have taken place in the apparel industry over the last thirty years. Up to the seventies, the labour market of the apparel industry in the United States was on the whole offering primary jobs securing a middle class life-style. Of the 1.2 million workers in the apparel industry, more than fifty percent were organized in trade unions and as a result, real wages had been rising. This situation is in stark contrast to the 19th century and the early 20th century when sweatshops offering low wages and working conditions were prevalent (Howard 1997: 155).

The reason for this change in fortunes is the coming to prominence of the neoliberal hegemonic bloc in the United States that pushed for further global economic integration, and in the process reduced and transformed the role of the state in labour market regulation. In this way it created the conditions for a large pool of undocumented immigrants (Peck 2002). At the same time, as I am going to show, the neoliberal coalition is not uncontested, there are signs of a movement that push for a different growth model but their impact until now has been weak. The discussion in the United States regarding the apparel indus-

try has centred on two issues in which three positions (neoliberal, populist, cosmopolitan) were prevalent:
- Free Trade: Here, the neoliberal coalition insists on free trade to increase the ability of producers to relocate industries while opposition forces try to push for better wage and labour standards in overseas production facilities or by increasing protectionism.
- Wage and Working Standards: The neoliberal coalition tries to downplay the issue whereas populist opposition attributes it to the increase in undocumented immigration. More cosmopolitan oriented movements focus on the extension of wage and working standards to all employees, irrespective of immigration status.

Approaches to Global Restructuring in the Apparel Industry

The development of a new international division of labour has been most pronounced in the apparel industry over the last fifty years with more and more countries exporting apparel to industrial countries. As a result there were growing import pressures, "[i]n 1961, 4 percent of the clothes sold in the U.S. market were imports. [...] Today it's over 60 percent, and still climbing".[63] Initially, the apparel industries tried to suppress this competition through protectionism, the Multilateral Fibre Agreement from 1974 that is only being phased out in 2005 being the most notorious arrangement (see Aggarwal 1985; Gilpin 1987: 204ff). Protectionism did not work out and so a second strategy developed: moving production selectively to developing countries to save

---

63 Howard (1997: 156-7); see also Aggarwal (1985: 6); Rosen (2002: 7).

on labour costs. This move was facilitated by specific tariff concessions (807 now 9802). This and the Caribbean Basin Initiative allow producers to pay tariffs only on the value added abroad (Dickerson 1991: 264). In this way, official trade policy has supported the downward trend on wages by creating access to low waged workers abroad (Glasmeier et al. 1993: 29; see especially NLC 1992). There is then today an agreement that such overseas production facilities are needed and the main apparel association, the AAMA (now AAFA[64]) today has as its main goal to extend regional trade agreements, as these provide sourcing flexibility to manufacturers and thus enable them to stay competitive in a market where consumers spend more and more on imported garments.[65] The fact that recent trade initiatives such as the conclusion of the Uruguay Round in 1994, NAFTA and the Free Trade Agreement for the Americas have been accepted by Congress shows the continued dominance of the free trade agenda in the United States (Scherrer 1999).

This push of neoliberal forces towards more free trade has not gone unresisted. There are two different sets of social force opposed to the neoliberal free trade program. One is the national populist fraction and the other is the global justice movement. The former is for example represented by the Reform Party under Ross Perot. According to the Reform Party,

> The US apparel market is further opened under NAFTA to producers operating out of Mexico. Open access to US markets will speed the flight of American apparel companies out of the United States in search of low-wage Mexican labor (Perot and Choate 1993: 79-80).

---

64 The American Apparel and Footwear Association, the Fashion Association, or AAFA, was established August 14, 2000 through a merger of the American Apparel Manufacturers Association (AAMA), Footwear Industries of America (FIA) and the Fashion Association (TFA).
65 AAMA News, March/April 1998: 2; AAMA News, February 1996: 1-2.

The Reform Party demands higher labour standards abroad to "allow Mexican workers to make a decent living in Mexico" (Reform Party 1997). A further suggestion was the imposition of a 'social tariff' to stop the 'haemorrhage' of US jobs (Perot and Choate 1993: 106).

This protectionist stance is not very far away from the trade union position, and there is a danger, as Mark Rupert has documented that the trade union movement moves in too close with more nationalist populist forces (Rupert 2000: 121-122). However, the trade union movement argues that the demand for enforceable labour rights is not about protectionism but instead to create rules for the global economy and "to lift wages and conditions up rather than drive them down" (Mazur 2000: 92).

According to the AFL-CIO, "one in five full-time full-year workers in America today earns wages below the poverty level – a 50 percent increase since 1979. Therefore, the main problem for U.S. workers are low wages.[66] For the AFL-CIO, the re-emergence of large-scale sweatshop labour is the product of the "cruel new winner-take-all global economy" (AFL-CIO 1998c). This development, the AFL-CIO notes, is not the inevitable result of globalisation, but the result of conscious policy. If these are conscious policy choices, the union argues, they can be reversed by alternative trade and investment policies (AFL-CIO 1997c: 31). So far, US trade policy has concentrated power in the hand of TNCs and investment firms. It is this power-shift that is behind the wage reductions, the declining wage and labour standards, and the inability to set up effective new institutions (*ibid.*: 32).

The starting point for the unions to remedy this situation is an improvement in the 'basics': "improved wages, improved health care and

---

66 "The pay of corporate chief executive officers, which as late as 1979 equalled 40 times that of frontline workers, has ballooned to more than 200 times the pay of today's workers" (AFL-CIO 1997b: 9-10).

reform of our labor laws so that all workers – immigrants and native born – can freely join unions and protect their rights" (Mazur 1997: 8-9). The AFL-CIO like UNITE, the apparel trade union, urges employers to leave the 'low road' strategy ("pushing for competitiveness at the expense of their employers with low wages, few benefits and poor working conditions") behind, in favour of a 'high road' to competitiveness (UNITE n.d.a; AFL-CIO 1997a). It is for these reasons that the labour movement is among the most outspoken opponents for more free trade (as visible in the 'battle of Seattle' where the labour unions came out in full force).

The labour movement is sceptical regarding codes of conduct that have been at the centre of the discussion in the 1990s. This is in part a debate on government versus governance. Government is the hierarchical imposition of rules by a sovereign authority, governance is the negotiation of rules between the governed and the governors (Lake 1999: 33). In order to deal with the global reach of multinational corporations able to exploit 'comparative advantages' world wide 'codes of conduct' as new governance mechanisms gained in prominence in the 1990s. Their advantage is that they cut across borders and help to level the playing field between export processing zones where wage and labour standards are often even below the standards valid within the host country of the zone and the United States. In contrast to national public legislation, codes of conduct operate at an intermediate level; they are essentially private or semi-public initiatives at the industry and firm level (Altvater 1999: 329). This means they are as strong as multinational corporations want them to be unless there is an incentive for them to cooperate with stricter measures (e.g. forced by public pressures, withdrawals of orders of large purchasers e.g. universities).

Under pressure from public opinion more and more firms and associations now profess to adhere to some form of code of conduct. But the response of the apparel association AAMA illustrates the difference introduced above between global government and global governance. The organisation rejects the inclusion of environmental and labour standards within the WTO, since this would undermine the credibility of the trade organisation (AAMA 1998a; cf. AAMA 1999). It would also mean that these standards would actually be observed because the rate of compliance with WTO rules is much higher than with those developed by the International Labour Organisation. Therefore, in order to pre-empt the development of global government, the organisation developed its own private governance framework: The World Wide Responsible Apparel Production (WRAP) Program (which represents a real improvement on the Statement of Responsibility of the AAMA.[67]) The WRAP Program is factory-based; the independent WRAP Certification Agency will approve outside monitors, which will certify whether a factory is in compliance with the WRAP principles (AAMA 1998b).

The move from government to governance is criticised by the trade union movement because too many uncertainties surround it. One be-

---

67   The statement adopted by the AAMA simply reads: "Members of the American Apparel Manufacturers Association (AAMA) are committed to the fair and rational practice of business in the United States and abroad. Basic to this commitment is the fair and equitable treatment of employees in wages, working conditions, and benefits. In no case do we support the use of child labor, prison labor, discrimination based on age, race, national origin, gender, or religion, the violation of legal or moral rights of employees, nor destruction or harm to the environment. The AAMA has established this Code of Responsibility as a guideline for all member companies for their own facilities and for the facilities where the production is contracted" (AAMA n.d.).

ing whether monitors are really independent.[68] A second problem is the level of wages to which private codes of conducts are committed. Very often, national minimum wages in countries hosting export processing zones are below what is actually required, instead unions push for what they call a 'living wage'. The apparel trade union, UNITE points out that wage equalisation predicted by economic theory cannot happen because worker's rights are systematically suppressed in many countries and especially in offshore and free trade zone production facilities. Because the laws protecting worker's rights are weak and there are no internationally agreed labour standards, a 'downward spiral' has resulted, "workers [are] forced to compete with each other on the basis of ever more miserable working conditions" (Howard 1997: 163). Codes of conducts do not deal with the fact that many countries outlaw union activities. For these reasons, while private actions are welcome, public action by the state ensuring that trade unions can organise workers is better.[69] UNITE therefore, calls for an international comprehensive monitoring system for labour standards that are included within trade agreements, a public arrangement rather than the voluntary private code of conducts (UNITE 1998). The trade union movement in cooperation with the student movement against sweatshops has therefore set up its own code of conduct with the Worker Rights consortium that has been joined by 128 universities.[70] The main difference between the union supported code of conduct and others is that it acts on the basis of complaints by workers whereas under the code of conduct proposed by the imitative of the Clinton Administrations through the Fair Labour Organisations or by the ap-

---

68   UNITE press release (16.07.1996).
69   UNITE press release (16.07.1996).
70   Workers Rights Consortium http://www.workersrights.org/as.asp (accessed September 2004).

parel producers (WRAP) workers have no input into the monitoring process.

Maintaining Wage and Working Standards in the US

Sweatshops have reappeared in the United States since the mid-1980s. Drawing on (but not caused by! Borjas 1999: 83-84) a renewed momentum in immigration after the passing of the Immigration and Nationality Act in 1965 (Jones 1992: 266).[71] In addition to renewed legal immigration, the 1970s saw an increase in illegal immigration. These undocumented immigrants were drawn in by a specific demand for people to fill in positions in industries under pressure from import competition that needed a more flexible workforce (Piore 1979: 163; Fernández Kelly 1989: 154). There are no reliable figures on the extent of the sweatshop problem but according to research by the GAO (General Accounting Office) sweatshops exist, their numbers have increased in the 1980s, and largely employ, often undocumented, immigrants (GAO 1988: 34; GAO 1994).

It has been suggested that the high incidence of undocumented immigration (mainly from Mexico) into the United States is an expression of an official policy of benign neglect towards it (Martin 1994: 84). This policy exists alongside more public emphasis on increased control since the mid-eighties. As the US Commission on Immigration Reform (1994: 88) pointed out, the US for years had tacitly accepted undocumented immigration because this was perceived to be in the

---

71 The General Accounting Office defines a sweatshop operator as "an employer that violates more than one federal or state labor law governing minimum wage and overtime, child labor, industrial homework, occupational safety and health, workers' compensation, or industry registration" (GAO 1994: 1).

interest of certain employers and the public. One expression of this official policy of benign neglect that increases the ability of employers to hire undocumented workers is that the United States deliberately does not effectively guard its borders. This can be seen in the fact that the staffing levels in the US for the border with Mexico are lower than at the German border with Poland (Vogel 2000: 403-404).

Furthermore, once inside the country, immigration and worksite law are not effectively monitored. This means that employers face few risks when hiring undocumented aliens (Borjas 1999: 204-205; Vogel 2000). The Immigration and Naturalization Service has monitored only 32 out of 32.000 agricultural farms in California even though undocumented immigrants constitute about 50 percent of the labour force (Stalker 2000: 44). Apart from immigration controls such as these or the employer sanctions introduced in 1986, the remainder of the internal worksite control regime consists of the Fair Labor Standards Act (1938) (FLSA), which sets standards for minimum wages and overtime pay and prohibits child labour; and the Occupational Safety and Health Act (OSHA) (1970), which sets standards for working conditions; But these wage and labour standards provisions are also not really enforced properly. The Department of Labour (DOL) had 800 inspectors to monitor 2 million workplaces of which 22.000 are in the apparel industry alone. The OSHA Administration within the DOL had 1.100 officers while the INS had approximately 1.150 officers in 1988.[72] "With these limited resources going to enforcement of labor laws, nobody should be surprised that workplace standards throughout the economy have deteriorated" (Howard 1997: 164).

---

72 This number was increased through the 1996 immigration law (IIRAIRA). The INS received 1,200 additional investigators and support personnel to investigate human smuggling, employer sanctions violations and visa over-stayers (Fragomen 1997: 443).

These figures reflect the cuts in the extent (and personnel) of worksite enforcement during the Reagan and Bush administrations in the 1980s and early 1990s (Ferguson and Rogers 1986: 133-134).

As a result of the non-existing control regime there is now a huge low-wage sector in the United States relying on undocumented immigrants (Nevins 2000: 105; Borjas 1999: 203-204). In the mid-1990s, the number of undocumented immigrants in the United States was estimated at four to five million, a historical high. They are concentrated in five states: California, Texas, New York, Florida and Illinois (50 percent in California) (Passel 1998: 193). We find secondary or low-wage and low-standards jobs that mostly employ immigrant labour in many sectors, including furniture making, poultry production, meatpacking, cleaning firms, high-tech IT firms, apparel industry, and in seasonal employment such as agriculture and construction (Dawkins et al. 1992: 122-123; Sassen 1988: 22-23; 39-40). The apparel industry is most prominent in the public discussion over the employment of undocumented migrants because it is the largest employer of undocumented immigrants (White House 1995).

The neoliberal coalition that seeks to sustain the status quo is made up of employers and human rights organisations. The employers in the coalition are only active if they need immigrants for their specific purposes, otherwise they support the general tendency for more restrictive laws. The National Manufacturers Association epitomises this bifurcated response to immigration. In 1995 and 1996, during the discussion of the new immigration law, the NAM was part of a broad coalition that sought – successfully – to prevent specific passages of the law that would have further restricted legal immigration, at the same time it joined in the general consensus to "make illegal immigration and border enforcement the first order of priority" (NAM 1995). Regarding the enforcement of wage and labour standards the neoliberal coalition objects to the strengthening of the existing regime or works to undermine it. The AAMA for example opposed the imitative by the Department of Labour to brand firms as sweatshop firms on its trendsetter list (the department had to discontinue this list after apparel firms protested) (AAMA 1998c). Neoliberal forces also put the blame squarely on the shoulders on the very agencies the coalition has worked to undermine. After all, as the National Retail Federation put it, "enforcing US labor law is the job of the US Department of Labor" (NRF d).

The human rights organisations (American Civil Liberties Union (ACLU), the Mexican-American Legal Defence Fund (MALDEF) and the National Immigration Forum (NIF) try to prevent restrictive immigration legislation and measures that discriminate against immigrants, and by doing so, succeed in upholding a political regime that allows for exploitative workplace conditions. This is a manifestation of the new configuration in immigration politics first documented by Bach that ensures unrestricted growth of immigration (1992: 158). For example, regarding the 1996 Immigration Act the ACLU simply set out to criticise the border control measures, employer sanctions and the move towards a national identity card (ACLU 1996f) but their generally immigrant-friendly stance ("immigrants create more jobs than they fill" and they "pay more taxes than they cost in services" (ACLU 1997a) does not push them towards a fight for better working conditions for these immigrants (or workers more generally) at workplaces in America. Similarly the National Immigration Forum (NIF) claims credit for the defeat of certain propositions in the 1996 immigration bill that would have helped to strengthen worksite enforcement (NIF 1997: 3-4). The NIF did not, however, make any suggestions as to how to deal with low wages and low standards in industrial sectors where immigrant labour is dominant. Instead, the NIF makes suggestions how to reduce emigration pressures through trade accords, international aid, debt relief, conflict prevention and resolution, family planning, and community development are suggested to reduce push factors (NIF 1996: 11). According to the NIF, immigration strengthens America's tradition of a melting pot in which diverse nations can come together to live, and increases the competitiveness of the US (NIF 1997: 1-2; NIF 1996: 12).

> Immigrant labor allows many goods and services to be produced more cheaply and provides the workforce for some businesses that would not otherwise exist. For example, immigration has helped build and maintain America's textile and agricultural industries. [...] Immigrants may have contributed to a decline in wages of native-born high-school dropouts, though the overall effects are quite minor (NIF 1998a).

This statement clearly shows that NIF, like other actors in the neoliberal coalition, is unconcerned by declining wage and labour standards in the United States that have been extensively documented by neutral sources (e.g. GAO 1988; 1994).

The Mexican-American Legal Defense Fund (MALDEF), an immigrants rights organisation, joins in the condemnation of employer sanctions that have failed to effectively prevent undocumented immigration (MALDEF 1993: 373, see Fix 1991), and have furthermore had unintended consequences like increased discrimination on the labour market.[73] Employer sanctions have this effect because they have introduced an additional level of illegality on undocumented immigrant workers. As a result, traditional legal remedies are no longer available for undocumented immigrant workers and "employers freely threaten documented workers with hiring undocumented workers if

---

73 According to a study by the GAO 19 percent of employers discriminated on the basis of national origin and citizenship (MALDEF 1993: 364-365).

they complain about low wages or working conditions (MALDEF 1993: 369). MALDEF, however, does not question the need to fight illegal immigration and suggests among other measures to promote trade and investment programs to fight the root causes of migration (*ibid.*: 380). Yet, MALDEF does not deal with the criticism by trade unions of how present economic integration has been carried out. In this way, MALDEF supports the creation of an unregulated global economy and therefore has to be considered as a part of the neoliberal forces in the United States.

This neoliberal coalition is opposed by a right wing populist opposition on the one hand and by trade unions and student activists on the other hand. Exemplary for the first category is the Federation for Immigration Reform (FAIR), one of the central anti-immigrant organisations in the United States in the 1990s. The organisation wants to stop immigration into the United States mainly because it has changed the ethnic make-up of the country quite radically (FAIR 1997a). For FAIR, the present level of immigration "is far above historical levels and is not consistent with our immigration tradition" (FAIR 1997c: 16, emphasis in original). The organisations uses every available argument against immigration to attain this goal of zero immigration. Wage and labour standards are therefore one of its concerns but its main activity lies in reducing access to the US (FAIR 1992: i). Similar criticism though with a less racist slant than in part inherent in the FAIR position has come from the Reform Party who also insists that there are too many immigrants coming into the United States. This has led to a situation where US companies can hire foreign workers at reduced rates who then replace US workers (Reform Party 1997). Illegal immigrants, in particular, have reduced the real wages of US workers and have led to a displacement of workers "in some fields". In the light of this assessment the party advocates a reduction of immigration, employer sanctions and a restructuring of guest worker programs to make sure that workers are not displaced and wage levels reduced (*ibid.*).

A more progressive argument to deal with undocumented immigration and sweatshop labour has been put forward by the trade union movement. Their argument is first of all that the low-wage and low standards sector is not caused by undocumented immigrants but by the prevalence of neoliberal ideas about the role of the state in regulating labour markets (AFL-CIO 1995 a/b/c/d/e). Trade unions are in favour of keeping the tradition of immigration into the United States alive, there is now a (recent) consensus that employer sanctions have a negative impact on the ability of unions to organise immigrant workers and there is a consensus that better wage and standards enforcement in the United States is needed (Mazur 1997: 30; UNITE 1999).[74] According to the union all other efforts at worksite enforcement that focused on the immigrants have failed, instead the

> long-term solution to undocumented immigration is to remove the incentive for employers to hire undocumented workers. This can be achieved by effective, targeted and aggressive enforcement of our various labor protection laws – with respect to both the undocumented and the documented (UNITE 1999).

In this context what is needed, according to the union is to provide more resources to the Department of Labour (DOL), to stop the cooperation between the Immigration Naturalization Service and the DOL. This would imply that worksite enforcement of labour standards is delinked from enforcement of immigration laws. There should be more protection for complainants and witnesses, and, most impor-

---

74 In a dramatic policy shift, the AFL-CIO joined in the rejection of employer sanctions in 2000 (it had been one of the driving forces behind the introduction of the sanctions in 1986 (Haus 1995).

tantly, the employer sanctions provision must be repealed (Mazur 1997: 9). Employer sanctions have made the organisation of immigrants much more difficult because employers can use this provision to threaten workers with dismissal, for example, if they decide to join a union or resist an increase in their workload (Mazur 1997: 9, 30). Furthermore, undocumented workers can no longer sue their employer for re-instatement and back pay, as a labour court cannot re-instate undocumented workers because of the employer sanctions provision (AFL-CIO 1992: 437).

A recent development is the move by retailers such as Wal-Mart to develop their own private labels, effectively turning them into apparel producers. This has led to a gap in the legislation covering apparel manufacturers because the garment proviso does not apply to retailers. The garment proviso in the National Labour Relations Act allows trade unions to boycott contractors in order to put pressure on their subcontractors (secondary boycott). But as it does not apply to retailers, the power of unions to regulate the wage and labour standards of the subcontractors to retailers is undercut (Proper 1997: 184). There is then between the retailer and its garment subcontractor no joint liability as exists between the garment manufacturer and its subcontractor (Howard 1997: 155-159). Another gap has appeared with the move of manufacturers abroad that invalidates the 1965 US Supreme Court decision 'Textile Workers vs. Darlington Mfg.' stating that firms closing shops to move to non-unionized areas violated U.S. labour laws. However, there is no such protection if firms move abroad (Scheuerman 2001: 360).

The main protagonists here are the retailers such as Wal-Mart and the National Retail Federation (NRF) the largest retail organisation in the United States who predictably oppose retailer responsibility. It has come to recognize that it has to deal with the issue of sweatshops. But its main attitude is that the issue has been blown out of proportion. The NRF suggests that "America's retailers are committed to selling products that are made in a fair and ethical manner" (NRF a). According to the Federation, the real problem is public perception. No retailer would buy knowingly from a sweatshop. In other words, the Retail Federation more or less rejects retailer liability and in order to fight the negative public perception of retailers has set up a foundation informing the public about retailing and issued a non-monitored code of conduct.[75] According to the President of UNITE, Jay Mazur, this shows that

> [...] retailers are trying to shift the enforcement responsibility to the DoL. Their demand for DoL to increase enforcement of wage-and-hour laws' is hypocritical coming from major cheerleaders for the Republican majority's budget onslaught, [...] The Department of Labor lost 23 percent of its enforcement agents during the Reagan-Bush years; today congressional Republicans call for additional cuts (Cooper 1995b).

In stark contrast to this attitude is the demand by UNITE the apparel trade union in its 'Partnership for Responsibility' for retailer and manufacturer liability as suggested by the proposed Stop Sweatshops Act (HR 23/S 626 (UNITE n.d. b).[76]

---

75 The statement of principles, which has been signed by 250 retailers, repeats the commitment to legal compliance and ethical business which should also extend to suppliers. The NRF supports law enforcement and co-operates with authorities in this respect. The NRF also supports educational efforts (NRFc).
76 UNITE, press release (16.07.1996).

The Policy Debate in the 1990s

With the incoming Clinton administration in 1992 the tone in the United States changed slightly and an active labour secretary (Robert Reich) ensured that the overall climate became amenable to develop some form of governance framework to combat 'sweatshops' in the country. The onset of the public debate was a highly publicised discovery in 1995 of a sweatshop operation in El Monte in California that was used by the administration to put pressure on the industry. More direct actions to combat sweatshop had already been taken and were reinforced, with a specific focus on garment manufacturers. As a part of the strategy to deter illegal immigration, the Department of Labour intensified its investigations in industries with patterns of labour law violations, e.g. by using the 'hot goods' clause in the monitoring of interstate trade that allowed federal authority to confiscate assets that are the fruits of unfair competition (Clinton 1995). One initiative was the Targeted Industries Partnership Program (TIPP) under which conducted over five years, from 1993 to 1997 sweeps of over 3.000 sewing shops in LA.

In August 1996, the so-called 'White House Apparel Industry Partnership' (AIP) which developed a 'Workplace Code of Conduct' and a 'Fair Labour Association' (FLA) in 1998 was set up by the Clinton administration. The FLA would oversee compliance and certify which monitors would examine factories. Companies that do not comply with the code would be punished (Greenhouse, 1998). The Apparel Industry Partnership and the Fair Labour Association are based on voluntary co-operation on the part of firms whether they agree to public monitoring of their worksites. The Fair Labour Association has however not been accepted by the major players in the debate. As discussed above, the Apparel Industry has developed its own 'code of conduct' with the World Wide Responsible Apparel Manufacturing Program while the trade unions and the student movement against sweatshops have set-up the 'Workers Rights Consortium'. This fragmentation of the governance structure ensures that little progress is made on the ground, especially as all these initiatives are directed against sweatshops abroad. Thus far there is no national legislation on sweatshops. The garment proviso has not yet been extended to retailers and the sanctions on employers remain in place.

Mainly with regard to immigration has the state acted more decisively in the United States. The Clinton administration made (illegal) immigration to one of its central concerns from the beginning.[77] In the Presidential Report on the problem, focus was on border and worksite enforcement to ensure that it is decreasingly possible for firms to hire undocumented workers willing to work at "subminimum wages, dangerous workplaces, long hours, and other poor working conditions because they are desperate for work and are in a weak position to on their rights" (Clinton 1994: 35). The Illegal Immigration Reform and Immigrant Responsibility Act made the enforcement of employer sanctions more effective by reducing the number of documents which establish employment eligibility from 29 to six (Section 247a of the Immigration and Nationality; INS 1997). The 1996 law strengthens border control increases sanctions for illegal crossing of borders and illegal stay and deportation procedures are extended.

This means that with the exception of the slight raise in minimum wages, no measures have been taken that would reduce the secondary labour market. Such measures would include the effective monitoring of health and safety standards and the unimpeded unionisation of immigrant workers among other things (Piore 1979: 184-188). Unionisation drives are countered by employers with the threat of relocation to

---

[77] The Wall Street Journal (29.06.1993).

Mexico or impeded by employer sanctions (Rupert 2000: 32-41).[78] In this way, the neoliberal coalition succeeded in keeping the social arrangements in place that have led to the creation of a substantial low-wage and low-standards sector fed by undocumented immigrants. Internationally, the aim of the social-reformist coalition to strengthen public standards in international trade agreements has not met with much success, except at the oratorical level. In contrast, there has been a proliferation of voluntary monitoring agreements (FLA, WRC, and WRAPP) that are considered as ineffective by trade union activists In the end, therefore, the conditions that created the basis for sweatshops were neither mended nor regulated in such a way that immigrant workers would be integrated into national wage and working condition frameworks. In this sense, we can conclude that the tacit acceptance of immigrant workers that do not enjoy the same wage and workplace standards as national citizens (either because they are undocumented or because they are temporary) has become an important element on the US labour market that ensures its increasing flexibility. At the same time, we have to note that the trade unions in tandem with other labour activists have developed an alternative vision of a global social economy that contrasts starkly with the neoliberal vision of unhindered growth at all costs (Bach 1992: 162-163). This is a cosmopolitan view of how a global society should be regulated in a way to take into account concerns of social and environmental justice. This perspective is guided by the ideal of effective human rights secured by a legal status, and better employment standards for all workers. Nationally, such a stance results in the opposition to immigration restric-

---

78 Between 1993 and 1995, approximately 50 percent of all union certification elections were accompanied by threats to relocate production abroad (Rupert 2000: 37). Regarding employer sanctions see the comments made by MALDEF and UNITE in the preceeding section.

tions and in an effort to steer the discussion more on employment and social conditions of the immigrants once they are in the country and to improve the mechanisms to protect them. Internationally, this stance leads trade unions and social movements to try to create a 'floor' for the global economy as a whole by trying to secure higher wage and working standards in production facilities abroad. The following section shows that similar processes can be observed with regard to the labour market in Germany.

Restructuring German Capitalism: Temporary Workers in the New European Division of Labour

As the nation-state has lost some of its powers to effectively regulate social and economic processes, it has been suggested that macro-regions, such as the European Union, may be able to regain some of it. However, as Wolfgang Streeck has argued, the process of European integration has been mainly concerned with the construction of a common market while the social and economic disruptions that such a market-making project brings with it were not really dealt with because European Integration is geared towards the creation of a competition state (Streeck 1999: 44-46). Streeck's portrait highlights the victory of a specific set of social forces underlying the process of European integration, as authors from within the neo-Gramscian perspective have demonstrated. According to van Apeldoorn, the neoliberal victory was only gained in the 1980s and early 1990s with the renewal of the single market project and the creation of a monetary union (van Apeldoorn 1998: 31).

The single market initiative put an end to the estrangement of business from the European Union. Business groups had criticised the stagflation induced, according to them, by rigidities in product and labour markets (Streeck 1999: 69-71; Grahl and Teague 1989: 34, 39). One central policy document concerning labour market policies that shows how these positions have found their way directly into EU policy documents is the 1993 'White Paper on Growth, Competitiveness, and Employment' (European Commission 1993). One central concern expressed in the paper was the need for increasing flexibility and the paper recommended a reduction of wage costs and of the costs associated with hiring or maintaining workers. This was meant to reduce unemployment (*ibid.*: Part B, Chapter 1, 1.4.). Greater 'flexibility' as to minimum wages, and reduced social welfare contributions were also recommended. The Commission recognised that these measures could create a class of working poor and that costly compensatory measures would have to be taken to prevent this. However, like the OECD Jobs Study, it presented no substantial strategies to this effect (*ibid.*: Part B, Chapter 8, 8.2). The 1993 White paper thus forms part of the background that helps us to understand the general climate of discussion at the beginning of the 1990s because most of its themes, competitiveness, flexibility and wage costs reappear in national policy debates regarding labour market regulation.

There is no European social policy that would prevent the undermining of national social policy by the creation of the Common Market (Talani 2004: 165). One policy area where this absence has created dramatic repercussions for national labour markets is the regulation of services in the EU with specific reference to the posting of workers. The posting of workers is different from the freedom of movement for workers, one of the central freedoms of the common market. The central difference concerns the regulations under which posted workers are covered that is very different from the regulations that apply to migrant workers. According to EU regulations, the migrant worker should be treated like a domestic worker. However, a posted worker is not a migrant but is detached by a firm to another country in order to carry out a contract, and returns to the home country after the contract. In terms of wages and social security he remains thus part of the regulatory framework of his home state. If service providers from low-wage countries carry out services in high-wage countries by using posted workers, domestic workers in high-wage countries would find it increasingly hard to compete on the job market if the posted workers earn lower wages in their home countries and continue to do so while providing services abroad (Deutsche Bundesregierung 1995). Given the substantial wage differentials in the European Union – while the average hourly pay is 2,5 ECU in Greece and 3,0 in Portugal, it is 10,97 ECU in Germany – processes of 'crowding out' or, as the trade unions argued, 'social dumping', appeared. The European Commission was aware that the Single Market Program would increase downward pressures in the services industry, specifically construction and transportation (Falkner 1993: 273).

The social regulation of the Common Market Project (1992) began in December 1989 with the European Charter of Social Rights for Employees and the Social Action Programme of the European Commission. As a part of the latter, the Commission provided a directive on the problems of the regulations under which posted workers were to be covered in 1991 but a directive was only passed in 1996, after five years of intensive negotiations (Eichhorst 1998: 240-251). The problem, then, was that a social policy in the sense of a correction of markets with a view to guaranteeing "a minimum standard of living regardless of market condition and productive contribution" (Streeck 1999: 131) was largely absent in the 1992 market-making initiative. This case study of the posted workers is of central importance because the posted workers directive and its national implementation processes shows the difficulties in the making of social policy in transnational markets – with no effective supranational state (*ibid.*: 64). Furthermore, it was one of the crucial instances where the question of whether a country like Germany can maintain its welfare state and system of collective bargaining is was fought over and decided.

One of the core features of German capitalism is (at least until recently) that competition takes place over product quality, rather than over their price (see Streeck 1999 for a detailed discussion). One result of the German model is that (compared to Great Britain, the United States and Japan) wages in Germany are higher; in particular, a specific low-wage sector is not part of the institutional structure. Wage inequality in Germany is low; Furthermore, low wages in Germany are relatively higher than in other countries, and have increased during the 1980s (*ibid.*: 13-15). Despite this, German capitalism has been competitive on the world markets, visible in constantly high exports of manufactured goods, and balance of trade surpluses with many countries.

Institutions that contributed to such an outcome were, among others, tightly regulated labour markets. German labour markets are governed by agreements negotiated between employers associations and industrial unions. The degree of union organisation in Germany remained stable in the 1980s, whereas it decreased in Great Britain, Japan and the United States. Collective agreements covered 82 percent of employees in 1980 and 1990, while their reach decreased in Great Britain, Japan and in the United States during this decade. Moreover, there is not much variation in the coverage of the collective agreements between sectors, unlike in the US, Japan and Great Britain (*ibid.*: 21). In this situation, competition through undercutting prices is difficult because wage scales are centrally negotiated.

It is the survival of this system of German capitalism that is at stake in the debate about posted workers, and, as the outcome of the debate and subsequent developments show, the survival is not guaranteed. German capitalism has had to succumb to the pressures for labour market flexibilisation that have emanated from the US system allowing for the exploitation of comparative advantages based more on cost, and less on quality. The debate on this question has been and still is intense in Germany and in international organisations. The OECD suggests that Germany (and other countries) should follow the US model of more flexible labour markets in order to stimulate job creation. It is not surprising therefore that the OECD singled out the German legislation to regulated the problem of posted workers in its 'Jobs Study' as the one example of a 'contrary action'. The OECD thus followed the employer's interpretation of the legislation on posted workers that projected it as an introduction of a binding minimum wage. The OECD was highly critical of this legislation, for the same reason as German employers were opposed to it, because the legislation has the aim "to prevent workers hired abroad from underbidding domestic workers" (OECD 1998c: 17). For these reasons, the OECD regarded the posted workers legislation as contradicting the goal of establishing a "more efficient structure of relative wages, including a widening of the wage distribution, wages more in line with skill levels, reduced use of administrative extensions, or increased use of opt-out clauses in collective agreements" (*ibid.*).[79] In other words, from the neoliberal

---

79 Within Germany, the themes of the OECD Jobs Study have been taken up, for example, by the 'Future Commission' set up by Bavaria and Saxony (Kommission 1996; 1997a and b; see the discussion in Offe and Fuchs 1997; Kistler and Schönwälder 1998). They were opposed by an "alternative" future commission from the social democratic side (Senatsverwaltung 1998). The central point of contention in this debate was whether the US model of labour market flexibilisation should be

perspective, posted workers were an important step in creating low-wage labour markets in Germany (Santel and Hunger 1997: 391).

The fact that the issue arose in the construction industry should not come as a surprise because the construction industry was seen by employers as the prime example of what was wrong with German capitalism as such: wages are too high and there are too many regulations. From the trade union perspective, the regulations for the construction industry however, are a prime example of how a labour market that lends itself to casual labour can be regulated in a way to ensure a middle class standard of living for the workers. They see this as the 'high road' to competitiveness.

The social regulations of the construction labour market arose out of the distinctive labour process that firstly, allows for an 'industrialisation' of only a limited parts of the construction process. Construction still relies on artisan work (and thus on skills associated with individuals). However, work is highly seasonal in character, making conditions of employment rather unstable, and the continuous change of location involved let the nature of employment appear as deficient if compared to the "standard employment relation" (Voswinkel et al. 1996: 18). This means that the construction industry faces inherent difficulties recruiting sufficient workers and it explains why it has been characterised by a high degree of guest worker employment (Mückenberger 1989; Faist 1997: 235-236).

In order to deal with these problems the employers and the trade union have set up an elaborate system of social funds (Sozialkassen), a form of insurance scheme for holidays, training among others.[80] These are

---

followed or whether Germany should find its own way out of the 'structural trap'.
80 One problem arising from foreign service provision is that foreign service providers do not contribute to these additional social funds. If more

regularly negotiated between the trade union, the IG Bauen-Agrar-Umwelt (IG BAU) and the two employers associations: the Zentralverband des deutschen Baugewerbes (ZDB) and the Hauptverband der deutschen Bauindustrie (HDB). The state plays an important role in regulating industrial relations through bad weather payments and subsidies of construction projects during the winter while public construction projects constitute a large share of overall demand for construction projects (Voswinkel et al. 1996: 111). Furthermore, the state is involved by issuing a declaration of general binding for the system of additional social funds (Eichhorst 1998: 196).

However, the political discussions and developments discussed above and the more general changes in industrial transformation (cf. Allen 1992) have meant that these regulations are under attack. As a result of the drive towards flexible accumulation (or post-Fordism) the actual construction process is loosing its value in contrast to organisation and mediation processes, such as marketing, logistics and financial knowledge (Voswinkel et al. 1996: 121). The possibility for the rationalisation of production processes in response to the crisis is limited, because of the linear methods of production (many working processes can only be started, after the preceding ones are finished). This implies that the highest efficiency gain can be achieved not through the introduction of machinery or by pre-fabricated production,

---

and more services are provided by foreign firms, then this system of additional social funds will no longer be viable and either has to be extended to the European level (rather unlikely because the systems of additional social funds differ vastly from country to country), or it has to be reduced in scope - if it is not demolished altogether. The slogan of "low-wage sector" in Germany then implies a concern that goes beyond wages and includes the general set-up of labour market regulation (cf. Köbele and Sahl 1993).

but only through an efficient organisation of the building process itself. The latter has occurred through an integration and disintegration process, which involved, on the one hand, the appearance of the general building constructor (Generalunternehmer), and the systematic use of subcontractors on the other (Syben 1999: 110-112; Voswinkel et al. 1996: 121). In the traditional organisation, the constructor concluded contracts with the different firms necessary to build a facility, while the architect supervised the actual building process. This makes the construction of a building a time-consuming task for the constructor. By contrast, a general building constructor offers finished construction projects (turn-key projects). A further step in the integration process is for the construction firm not only to organise the construction process itself, but to become involved in the planning phase of a project too (Generalübernehmermodell; Syben 1999: 124-128). Between 1971 and 1995 the share of subcontracting in total turnaround rose from 11.7 to 25.3 percent in Germany (IG BAU 1994-1996: 10).[81]

It is this process of integration and disintegration of the production process, which provided the entry point for foreign service providers into the German construction market in the 1990s. The restructuring of the industry was tied up with the creation of an international division of labour: firms from low-wage countries bring in their competitive advantages in the form of lower wages and social security provisions, and firms in high-wage countries can lower their costs by subcontracting with firms from low-wage countries.[82] This shows that the employment of posted workers reflects the restructuring of an industry from Fordist to flexible accumulation since their presence permits the

---

81 The data stems from research of the ifo-institute.
82 Hunger (2000: 36-59); IG BAU (1994-1996); Bosch and Zühlke-Robinet (2000: 204).

emergence of labour market segmentation specific to it: core workers, securely integrated into the firm, and a number of (foreign) peripheral workers in flexible working arrangements (Harvey 1990: 151). Most developed is this pattern of concentration and fragmentation in the construction industry in Great Britain where 50 percent of the construction firms are one person businesses, and 82 percent of all construction firms have less than four employees in 1990 (Eichhorst 1998: 77).

In the beginning of the 1990s, the German construction industry had entered its biggest crisis since 1945. While some of the problems can be attributed to the above-mentioned structural changes in the organisation of work in the industry, the political decision at the level of the European Union in the early 1990s to liberalise services without any social regulations was one of the major reasons for exacerbating the crisis (Stahl and Sang 1996: 652-654). As a result, at the beginning of the 1990s, the numbers of posted workers employed in Germany increased dramatically. Portugal, for example, detached 706 workers in 1988 but 19,583 in 1994 (Hunger 2000: 37).[83] Between 10 and 15 percent of the total Portuguese labour force in this sector worked in Germany during that year (Faist 1997: 235). According to Eichhorst, in 1994/95 there were approximately 150,000 to 200,000 posted workers in Germany, while the same number of domestic construction workers were unemployed. It is estimated that between 200,000 and 500,000 foreign workers were employed on the German construction labour market in the mid-1990s under various flexible contract schemes. The construction industry itself employed about 1.5 million workers in the main trades. Thus, foreign workers under sub-standard conditions

---

83 The calculation is based on the issued E 101 certificates that confirm that an employee is covered by social security in the sending country. The majority of these certificates were issued to construction workers.

comprised up to one third of the labour market in the construction industry (Eichhorst 1998: 46, 56). The structural change this imposed on the construction industry, and on the labour market in this and other sectors, was thus massive and occurred within a very short time span. The fear was that the employment of this specific kind of migrant labour could create precedents for the casualization of the labour market as a whole (Faist 1995a: 245). At issue, then, was not only the situation of workers in the construction industry, but the general regulation of labour markets in Germany.

In this situation the federal government, dominated by the Christian-democratic parties (CDU/CSU in a coalition with the liberal party (FDP), proposed a law to prevent an undermining of national wage and labour standards. The law was highly contested within the coalition with the CDU/CSU (controlling the labour ministry) in favour of a law and the liberal party (controlling the economics ministry) fiercely opposed to one. The Christian Democratic labour minister argued that a social market economy is not a wild west economy and that markets needed a certain amount of governance.[84] On the other side, the FDP who argued that labour markets in Germany were too inflexible and characterised by an institutional sclerosis, which it held responsible for the high unemployment levels existing since the 1970s. The speaker for economic policy, Otto (Graf) Lambsdorff consequently argued that the cartel that dominated the wage bargaining process in Germany had to be broken and that the prevention of the posted workers law would be a first step in this direction.[85] In other words, for the neoliberal coalition, the discussion over posted workers

---

84 Norbert Blüm in Deutscher Bundestag, Plenarprotokoll 13/58, 28.09.1995 page 4919.
85 Lambsdorff in Handelsblatt (27.07.1996; quoted in Hunger 2000: 86-87).

was seen as one central way to increase labour market flexibility in Germany as a whole by breaking the power of the unions to bargain wage and labour standards.

The central proposition of the proposed posted workers law was to guarantee a minimum wage for posted workers. It did so by stipulating that wage agreements that had been declared as generally binding also extend to posted workers. But this meant that such a declaration of general binding had to be achieved in the first place because the committee that decided upon these declarations includes neoliberal social forces that were able to veto such a declaration and agreed to it only after extreme modifications to the wage agreement. As a result of this experience, there the central opposition of trade unions in Germany to a minimum wage legislation (that undermines the bargaining power of trade unions) is slowly diminishing because without a centrally enforced minimum wage there is no limit to the fall in wages, as the example of the construction industry has shown.

Creating a European Common Market

The neoliberal fraction (BDA, FDP, Gesamttextil, Gesamtmetall, economic think tanks) resisted the posted workers law proposed by the government because it implied a continuation and further strengthening of the German system of 'social capitalism' that – in the neoliberal perspective – had become outdated and needed to be flexibilised. The normative argument underlying the neoliberal coalition, in contrast, was one based on the idea of economic efficiency. In the end everybody would better off because there is a new international division of labour in the construction industry whereby firms from low-cost countries carry out some of the low-skilled construction work, and firms from high-wage countries are responsible for the high-skilled component of a project. One argument repeated by all neoliberal actors was that the posted workers legislation is a protectionist measure and as a result of it the high prices of building in Germany would be maintained.[86] The upward pressure on already high wages and high construction prices were two major economic reasons for rejecting the posted workers legislation. They thus wanted the construction industry to face the same import competition from low-cost countries as other industrial sectors have had to for over thirty years (Gesamttextil 1996: 3). From this perspective, the use of posted workers does not constitute social dumping but the legitimate and legal use of competitive advantages by these firms whereas the posted workers legislation would be considered as a massive case of protectionism inviting retaliation from foreign countries (Gesamttextil 1995; BDA 1995b: 2-3). One prominent critic of the proposed posted workers legislation was the president of the metal employers association (Gesamtmetall), Dieter Kirchner, who was also a member of the body deciding upon the declaration of general binding. Kirchner conceded that the posted workers legislation would actually be in the logic of the German collective agreement system and would maintain the centralised bargaining of collective agreements;[87] but he claimed that this system was itself outdated, and had to be hollowed out. Kirchner argued that the old, unsustainably high wage level could not be stabilised through legislation, and that German employers had to use every single opportunity to undermine collective agreements, whether through special wage rates for women, beginners, foreigners or long-term unemployed

---

86 The positive effect of the employment of cheaper foreign workers could be seen in Berlin. Despite the construction boom induced by unification, the prices for building shells did not increase substantially (Wochenpost 06.04.1995).
87 Handelsblatt (24.07.1995).

persons. The proposed minimum wage was higher than in other sectors and would create upward pressures. Employers wanted the widening of wage disparities, and for this reason did not want to support what Kirchner denounced as a 'Reichseinheits-Mindestlohn' (national minimum wage) for the construction industry. For Kirchner, it was clear that "the barricade formed by the system of collective agreements in Germany will not outlive the present crisis".

The main proponent of the neoliberal coalition was the Bundesvereinigung der Deutschen Arbeitgeberverbände (BDA), the central German employers association. The BDA was opposed to a national posted workers law. If such a regulation were at all necessary, then it should be implemented at the European and not at the national level (BDA 1995b: 10). The BDA did not see a need for a regulation, as the rules and regulations applying to posted workers were already laid down, and were by no means uncertain: posted workers are protected by the public law of the country where the work is undertaken and whose safety and health regulations therefore apply to them. The existence of wage differentials (including social overhead) is part of the logic of the competitive system environment created by the Common Market (BDA 1992a: 6).

> This logic consists in the recognition that there are different wage and other social levels in the member states; but this fact will be solved with the continued efficacy of the Common Market, and these differences will be levelled owing to huge transfer payments (Deutscher Bundestag 1995b: 46).

It claimed, therefore, that "[t]hose who disagree with this, do not accept the logic of the common market" (*ibid.*: 58). The BDA assumed that the difference in wage levels between Portugal and Germany would disappear. Any attempt to abolish wage differentials would constitute a protectionist barrier to states with lower wage costs (BDA 1992 a: 7). The BDA's support for services liberalisation and the use of temporary migrants to lower the costs of construction has to be contrasted with its generally restrictive stance on immigration issues visible during the debate on political asylum in the early 1990s (BDA 1992a). According to the BDA, migration pressures represented one more example of the burden that Eastern Europe and Third World countries already placed on industrialised states. It argued that the institution of political asylum was being abused, and it called for a tightening of access to the procedure, along the lines that were adopted in parliament (BDA 1992b: 17-19). This was an expression of a generally sceptical attitude towards immigration:

> Germany is not an immigration country. The mere fact of massive immigration does not justify the use of this term. As a densely populated industrial country, the Republic never has undertaken an immigration policy in the classical meaning of this term. At present and in the near future there is no need for additional immigration (BDA 1992a: 21).

But while an immigration policy in the 'classical' sense of the term was rejected by the BDA, the BDA specifically welcomed temporary labour migrants because they represent "an interesting instrument to flexibilise the labour market" while at the same time insisting that their presence remained temporary (*ibid.*: 24). This contradictory stance, overall negative attitude towards legal immigration and a more '(neo)liberal' position towards temporary labour migration highlights again the central finding of my study: it is within neoliberalism itself that we have to look for the sources of the selective and discriminatory border regime that is characteristic of neoliberalism.

The coalition in favour of a social Europe was supported, at the political level by the opposition in Parliament: the Green Party and the Social Democratic Party whose initiatives closely mirrored those of the trade union movement (SPD 1995; Bündnis 90/Die Grünen 1995). The social-reformist coalition aimed at transforming the market-making bias of the European Union into a more social and rights-oriented direction. Their argument was that the employment of posted workers undermines national wage and labour standards, and creates adjustment costs that, ultimately, might lead to a rejection of the process of European integration. For them, the employment of workers under sub-standard conditions is not considered to be a form of legitimate competition, but should be outlawed.

These groups recognised that the European integration process cannot be turned back; their aim was therefore to preserve gains made at the national level in terms of wage levels and working standards by pushing for some form of European standard. Thus, one common factor of this coalition was that all organisations favoured a regulation of the posted workers problem at the European level. Only when this failed again, for the third time, in December 1994, they started to demand a national regulation (cf. Eichhorst 1998: 105-108). The pro-regulation camp wanted to deal with the problem by granting all national regulations referring to paid holidays, accident prevention, and especially wage levels, to posted workers from the start of their work in Germany. The central slogan of this camp was: "Gleicher Lohn für gleiche Arbeit am gleichen Ort" (Equal pay for equal work at the same place). The starting point for this camp consequently was that "low wages should not be the foundation for competition" in the Common Market.[88]

The current practice of posting challenges the core feature of our welfare state and of our system of industrial autonomy. No state should be a bystander if the national legislative regulations and collective agreements are denigrated in this manner. Since the non-discrimination of migrant workers is anchored in European law pertaining to the freedom of movement, it has to be made applicable to posted workers as well.[89]

The main trade union representation (DGB) repeatedly stressed that the freedom of movement within Europe explicitly outlawed discrimination between foreign and domestic workers, and demanded that this rule should be extended to posted workers as well.[90] The DGB thus saw the employment of posted workers in the context of migrant labour while employers had categorised the issue under the liberalisation of services. For the trade unions in contrast, unlimited competition with regard to social standards threatens all workers in Europe and in the end may endanger European integration itself.[91] "If we want to attain a high degree of social protection in the European Community – a goal which has been agreed upon in the Treaty of Maastricht – then economic integration has to proceed alongside a harmonisation and improvement of working and living conditions of workers" (DGB 1995c: 5-6). The main point for the construction trade union (IG-BAU) was that the present mode of European integration through social dumping would cause anti-European sentiments, and

---

88 DGB press release (20.03.1995).
89 DGB press release (29.06.1995).
90 DGB press release (13.03.1996).
91 DGB press release (22.03.1996) which summarised a joint declaration of the DGB with Portuguese trade unions before a meeting of the Council of Ministers, where the posted workers directive was to be discussed.

that, therefore, the demands of the trade unions could not be considered 'anti-European'; rather, they were presented as a way to create and maintain the acceptance for the process of European integration among workers. The construction union argued that "Europe can only be built together with workers and not against them" (IG BAU 1995a: 12).

The central trade union organisation, the DGB, regarded the debate about posted workers as particularly important, as it spotlighted the absence of a European social policy. It showed the problematical consequences of differences in wages and working conditions across boundaries within a single market framework. A social policy was seen as urgently needed to ensure that the differences in living and working conditions would not lead to a downward spiral in the high-wage countries. The crucial point of the posted workers directive and of the legislation in Germany was that both aimed to set minimum standards. The passing of the posted workers directive in tandem with a German law was thus regarded as an important case in the attempt to develop a genuine European social policy. For the IG BAU president, Bruno Köbele, the "construction sector had become a test case for the introduction of a low-wage sector in Germany."[92]

If the situation endured, the DGB foresaw segmented labour markets and a "threat to social peace on construction sites."[93] In a parliamentary hearing, the construction trade union IG BAU emphasised that the situation had become "explosive", and that many construction workers were no longer prepared to accept the employment of foreign temporary migrants under sub-standard conditions alongside a domestic core team (Deutscher Bundestag 1995a: 31).

---

92 Handelsblatt (14.10.1994).
93 DGB press release (24.10.1995).

The stance of the trade unions in the posted workers case cannot be interpreted as general sign that the trade union movement was opposed to immigration as such. Both trade unions repeatedly emphasised that they merely disapproved of the fact that posted workers were not employed under the same conditions as domestic workers, which was one of the conditions under which trade unions accepted the employment of migrant labour in the first place. The generally rather open attitude towards immigration can also be seen in the resistance of the trade unions to the change of Art.16 of the German Basic Law that guaranteed individual access to the asylum procedure.[94]

The basic aim of the trade unions was thus to achieve a regulation, preferably at the European level, which ensured that posted workers are employed under the same conditions as domestic workers. Effectively, this implied that posted workers should be covered by the same collective agreements as domestic workers. Thus, for example, all eight wage groups should be applicable to posted workers too. The unions wanted to prevent that only the lowest wage level would be applied to posted workers (see DGB 1995b: 3-4; IG BAU 1995a: 9-10). Furthermore, the trade unions movement was in favour of a law that would cover all sectors rather than just the construction industry.[95] The organisations argued that postings are not restricted to the construction industry but occur also in other sectors, and that therefore any regulation should refer to the problematic of posting in general (Deutscher Bundestag 1995a: 32). The DGB argued, moreover, that

---

94 In this case the DGB participated in mass rallies to protest against the changes in the asylum law and supported the work of pro asyl, a refugee rights organisation set up with the support of trade unions and welfare organisations (see Dreher 2005).
95 DGB press release (09.08.1995).

any regulation should not be of a limited duration and that there should be effective control mechanisms in place (DGB 1995a: 22).

An important aspect of this case is that the coalition of social groups demanding a posted workers law went beyond the trade unions, and included the most important employers associations in the construction industry. Owing to the regulatory problems involved, the HDB initially favoured a time limit on the regulation and saw it only as a transitory means to facilitate the structural change in the industry (Deutscher Bundestag 1995a: 48). The other employers association in the sector, the Zentralverband des deutschen Baugewerbes and the Zentralverband des deutschen Handwerks agreed with the assessment of the trade unions that the posting of workers constituted a major problem for the industry, and that either (and preferably) a European, or a national regulation was necessary to create a level playing field for competition (ZDB 1995a; ZDH 1995a). The emphasis of the employers was more on the distortion of competition and on the problems for small and medium size enterprises, which were increasingly being forced out of business owing to the competition with firms employing low-wage workers from other EU countries while other arguments also played a role such as the increasing scepticism regarding European Integration (HDB 1995a: 13).

Policy Outcomes

The posted workers law that was finally passed in March 1996 represented a compromise between the social-reformist coalition and the neoliberal fraction. The social-reformist coalition achieved a law that extends collective agreements, concluded by trade unions and employers organisation, to posted workers. However, in order for this law to become effective, a declaration of general binding was needed.

In this way, the neoliberal coalition has secured a veto position since the three employers associations (alongside three trade unions and the labour minister) are represented in the committee that decides on the declaration of general binding. Such a declaration was achieved only in November 1996 because the BDA, repeatedly refused to agree to declarations of general binding. This procedure, meanwhile, has been reformed, and the minister of labour can now decide unilaterally on a declaration of general binding (though only for cases falling under the posted workers law). Furthermore, the general contractor is now liable for wages and working conditions of subcontractors.[96] Thus, with the change of government in 1998, the social-reformist coalition has gained some ground. However, the length of time it took for the issue to be regulated (six years) had the effect that an international division of labour in the service sector was established, and companies have come to rely on cheaper foreign-service providers. Furthermore, the difficulties in implementing the law (Eichhorst 1998: 224) point to a situation similar to the United States, where a control structure for labour market monitoring is in place that does not have sufficient resources to actually implement national laws. Most problematic is the fact that the law is only effective if there is a declaration of general binding. In most of the ancillary trades, there is no such tradition of declaring collective wage agreements generally binding and, in consequence, only two ancillary trades are covered by the law (Hunger 2000: 111). With regard to the European directive, the situation is not encouraging either because the directive does not establish harmonised rules, instead the political process in the member states largely determines whether and how posting will be regulated (Faist 1997: 236). As the situation of the ancillary trades highlights, the result is

---

96   Schwäbische Zeitung (01.08.2000).

that the unregulated situation and thus the segmentation of labour markets may remain.

Conclusion

This chapter has discussed the restructuring of the garment industry in the United States and the construction industry in Germany that contributed to the undermining of a relatively standard employment relationship achieved in the fifties and sixties despite the atypical employment patterns characterised by subcontracting, outsourcing and seasonal variability. Today, both industries that have been at the forefront in the fight for standard employment patterns and the creation of primary job markets have been targeted by massive restructuring processes. One element in this restructuring pattern was the hiring of migrant labour under substandard conditions. These migrant workers are either, as in the US case, undocumented workers, or they posted workers (as in Germany). In either way, their main characteristic is that they, in contrast to the guest workers, are not part of the social policy regime of the host state, not to mention the citizenship regime of the host state.

These developments have to be seen in the overall context of the neoliberal project of global market-making because the aim of firms when hiring this sort of 'flexible labour' is to better be able to adjust to market pressures and to increase profit rates. The goal is to create low-wage and low-standards sectors with 'flexible' working arrangements in order to facilitate the integration into the global economy (Borjas 1999: 63). The creation and maintenance of such a low wages and low standards segment within the construction and the garment industry then reflects the general tendency within the global restructuring process that is typical of flexible accumulation. As the case studies have shown there are also specific interests that make this happen. Employers who resist better enforcement of wage and labour standards (United States) or who refuse to establish such standards in the first place (Germany). At the same time the case studies have also shown that there is within the neoliberal coalition a certain nationalistic element that aims to reinforce citizenship regulations (e.g. regarding asylum) as a way of showing it commitment to the specific nation state (see also Dreher 2005).

The case studies have also highlighted that there is an opposition to neoliberal ideas about global market making and regulation. This opposition now goes beyond national borders in two ways. First, it is strictly opposed to the restrictive neoliberal immigration regime and advocates more liberal immigration rules. It also shifts the focus away from immigrants to general labour market governance as a whole, irrespective of the immigrant status of the worker. Secondly, there is a clear understanding that firm and effective international rules are needed to create a more humane level-playing field in the global (or European) economy. This more cosmopolitan or reformist approach to global governance shows that for these social forces, rights can no longer tied to citizenship but to human beings as persons irrespective of where these persons are living. It is thus possible to glimpse elements of a more global understanding of citizenship in these positions, a fact that will be taken up again in the concluding chapter.

6. GLOBAL CITIZENSHIP AND TERRITORIALITY IN A GLOBAL POLITICAL ECONOMY

The primary purpose of this inquiry has been to contribute to the evaluation of neo-Gramscianism as a theory of globalisation. Specifically, the question was whether the observed non-globalisation with regard to migration that finds its expression in the low degree of liberalisation of migration policies and its consequences – the increase in temporary and undocumented migration – constitute a part of the neoliberal political project of creating a globally integrated economy. Since most neo-Gramscian research has concentrated on the elements that have brought about an increase in global economic integration – a focus that has led to the (incorrect) categorisation of the perspective as 'hyperglobalisers' (Held et al. 1999: 7) – the present study has sought to counterbalance this tendency by focusing on the territorial elements within the neoliberal concept of control. I have achieved this by looking at the preferences of the globalising elite regarding migration policies (chapter four) and its representatives at the national level in the case studies (chapter five), showing that the continued importance of territoriality (the emphasis on migration control) can be traced back to the preferences of the globalising elite itself.

This outcome has two implications. First, it stands in stark contrast to migration research that attributes the increase in migration restrictions and xenophobism in the Western World largely to right wing populist parties (see e.g., Castles and Davidson 2000: 145; Betz 1994); instead, we now know that the neoliberal globalising elite itself is not pursuing liberal migration politics. As I will explain below, it transpires that migration restrictions seem to be central to the neoliberal project because they provide an avenue for building a hegemonic bloc: In order to maintain popular backing for the project of neoliberal restructuring, neoliberal forces rely on a conservative and often xenophobic 'politics of support'. Specific migration flows are permitted if they contribute to clearly specified aims and yield clear economic benefits; but such policies are narrowly circumscribed by the need to maintain electoral support that expresses a preference for the strict control of further immigration.

The second implication is that a political project perspective on globalisation as presented by the neo-Gramscian approach is able – in opposition to liberal globalisation research – to demonstrate that the political and social construction of the global space favours specific social interests. It has focused on how the transnational, but predominantly US-based, globalising elite has succeeded in maintaining and even spectacularly increasing the momentum towards a global economy in the face of the crisis of the welfare state and the increasing assertion of Third World Power. A general retreat into protectionism and isolationism (as for example advocated by Krasner 1985: 302) has been avoided; instead, global economic integration has deepened under US guidance. However, this globalising elite subscribes to an extremely uneven and contradictory view of global economic integration, one that allows for further economic integration with respect to capital and goods on the one hand, and on the other hand erects new barriers for the migration of people. A global economic system has been constituted in which particular forms of movement (and particular types of 'freedom') have been institutionalised, while others have been restricted.

Until the mid-nineties, this form of neoliberal globalisation has been a 'revolution from above'; the social forces underpinning this transformation are dominant rather than hegemonic, their predominance is not sustained by far-reaching consensus. This can be seen in the fact that neoliberal globalisation still is more about breaking up the institutions tied to the Fordist accumulation pattern than to forging a new, stable historic bloc that would incorporate the interests of subordinate social forces. In this sense, neoliberalism is much more elitist than any other concept of control institutionalised since the formation of laissez-faire liberalism in the mid-19th century. But the limits of this project, and of a unilateral elite strategy, have been reached. Neoliberal globalisation is today faced by an emerging counter-movement, not just on the streets of Seattle and Genoa, but also one that draws on the resources of an increasingly internationally-oriented trade union movement. In addition, there are also other, more destructive social forces opposed to globalisation that are fed by the increasing inequality created by neoliberal globalisation (Rapley 2004: 107ff). The global political economy has never been on a more precarious footing than at present.

In this concluding chapter I want to summarize the central insights regarding the role of migration in the constitution of a global political economy. The next section will start out by highlighting how migration has been instrumentalised within the neoliberal project to increase the reach of the global economy (by increasing labour market flexibility through the employment of undocumented immigrants). I will also show how resistance to neoliberalism is, in turn, aspiring to change the basic parameters of the neoliberal concept of control regarding migration policy (by developing global forms of citizenship). However, as I will point out in the following section, we also need to understand the causes and the implications for the global economy of the fact that migration controls de facto strengthen the territorial power of the state. This discussion will show that the continued importance of territoriality points to specific problems in the neo-Gramscian perspective.

The normative conclusion from the present research is that the neoliberal globalisation approach clearly recognizes that there are limits to economic integration. Migration controls (whose importance has continued to grow with the war on terror) are a clear sign that a global economy as such is not a sustainable space and therefore requires elements of territoriality. There is then an inherent contradiction within neoliberalism itself. However, it is entirely unacceptable from a human rights point of view why these limits should be set only for one set of globalisation flow (migrants) and not for others (finance, trade, investment). Migration controls are a reminder that a more cosmopolitan form of governance of the world economy is necessary.

Globalising Citizenship?

Migration is a crucial case of non-globalisation. As I have argued in chapter one, the developments in both migration policies and migration flows do not show the same degree of liberalisation and transnationalisation as do trade and financial flows. On the contrary, while trade, finance, and investment flows have increased over the last three decades when compared with the immediate post-war period (when the international order foresaw only a limited extent of integration (Ruggie 1982)), we find the opposite tendency with respect to migration. Immigration regimes in the OECD world have become more restrictive in the 'global age' than they were in the post-war period, through a variety of measures that create inequality of access to national citizenship regimes: temporary workers programmes, restricting access to services offered to citizens, and reducing the number of immigrants allowed into the country. The limitations on asylum are the most extreme manifestation of the tendency towards closure.

I have also argued that, while there have been clear movements towards extending citizenship rights to former 'guest workers', Soysal's (1994) conclusion that the line dividing citizens from non-citizens is dissolving is misleading. The (hesitant) integration of former guest workers by expanding their access to citizenship has not led to the dissolution of national citizenship regimes more generally. This is clearly observed in the case of the most vulnerable of the new migration streams in the eighties: refugees. The increase in the number of refugees in the eighties was not met by liberalisation or even by the maintenance of the liberal Geneva refugee convention; instead, all Western states restricted the right to asylum dramatically. Secondly, new labour migration in the 1990s mostly takes place without the migrant workers acquiring the same level of social and civil citizenship rights as the guest workers did in the sixties, either because they have entered the country undocumented or because they have acquired only temporary work permits (or come in as posted workers, as in the case study on Germany). As a result, the status of these immigrants is precarious and they are easily dismissible from their jobs only to be sent back to their countries of origin. This reduction in citizenship rights for recent immigrants is, as I have argued, a crucial element of the neoliberal migration regime.

However, the very non-globality of migration policies and the inequality of access to citizenship regimes that these policies create, make them a central element in the constitution and further extension of the global market place. The inequality of access to citizenship regimes increases the competitiveness of national labour markets by contributing to the creation of a pool of 'flexible' labour. Observers of current labour migration processes have pointed out that labour immigration has become polarized with some legal forms of immigration that cover mostly skilled migrants, while most other immigrants come in under extremely precarious conditions (refugees, temporary migrants, illegals) (Salt 1992: 1081). These two migration flows complement the needs of the job market in advanced industrial countries where the standard employment relationship is being replaced by more 'flexible arrangements' with only a minority of employees enjoying full job security and entitlements. As a result of this restructuring, migration complements the process of segmentation in national labour markets with that have seen the creation of differential access to entitlements, employment security, industrial rights, and even civil and political rights (Rosewarne 2001: 81). In these ways, migration is crucial for the restructuring of labour markets under the neoliberal regime of flexible accumulation because migrants provide both core and peripheral labour, where necessary. These migration policies are also supportive of neoliberalism more generally because states no longer need to invest resources in the reproduction of domestic labour since necessary labour can be imported from abroad instead of being trained and educated at home.

As I have shown in the case studies, however, there is an opposition movement against the neoliberal migration and labour market regime that is creating the basis for a truly 'global citizenship'. This opposition was most first visible in the fight against the tightening of asylum regulations beginning in the eighties and culminating, for example in Germany in the early nineties when the constitution was amended to make Germany part of the more restrictive European asylum and refugee regime. During this period, trade unions and social movements (unsuccessfully) fought employer associations and political parties in order to maintain the more liberal German asylum regime. Similar processes of resistance could be observed in the US (see Dreher 2005). The central contribution of this oppositional movement lies in the development of our understanding of what global citizenship has to mean when it is applied to concrete processes within the global political economy (see Held 2002; Falk 1994). Citizenship refers to the rights and duties of a person that come with the membership in a state. A central element of citizenship rights is that they are independent of market outcomes, in a sense, they also should mitigate the effect of inequality in the economy. In order to achieve this, citizenship rights have slowly interfered with market outcomes to ensure that status in a society is not just determined by the market (Dahrendorf 1994: 13 – a process that is now reversed by neoliberalism). Global citizenship in turn means that the operations of international institutions and global governance are based on democratic principles (Falk 1994); but it must not stop there. It also has to mean that, within the global economy, firms engaged in globalised production and services need to become much more accountable for their decisions on what, where, and how to produce (Held 2002). The very notion of the global has to become more politicised, a move in direct opposition to neoliberalism. Global citizenship in effect is needed in order to recover some of the ground lost regarding social citizenship at the national level – without being another word for protectionism.

Two concrete steps towards the development of global citizenship have emerged in chapter five that put an interesting twist on the debate on global citizenship. They both stem from the same problem: in the global economy, the production of goods or services is organized across different territories but at the same time the end product is the result of a single production chain where workers in different parts of the world "cooperate" for the production of one good or service. It is therefore necessary to focus on the production chain as such when it comes to increasing workers' rights, and it is this global production chain that constitutes the basis for demands for "global citizenship" rights. These two steps concern first, the insight that immigration regulations are the wrong way to deal with labour market problems, and second, the need for consumers buying foreign products to be informed about the conditions under which they are produced.

Regarding the regulation of immigration and labour markets, the concern here is to reduce the build-up and maintenance of a secondary or peripheral labour market that comes into existence through the use of immigrant labour under substandard conditions (Piore 1979), a process amply documented in the two case studies. This reduction can be achieved if immigrant workers are guaranteed the same rights as national citizens as not doing so would mean that there can be no effective struggle to increase (or maintain) wage and labour standards. This demand is similar in status to the internationally recognised and generally accepted requirement that foreign investors receive national treatment and that there is no distinction between foreign and national capital.

The recognition of the need for equal treatment of national and immigrant workers, and, in consequence, the need to ignore the immigrant status of a worker is one of the central changes in trade unions' attitudes towards migrant workers in the United States. In concrete terms, national treatment means that immigrant workers and national workers are treated equally; more specifically, it implies that there are effective complaint procedures against substandard working conditions that immigrant workers can use without fear of deportation. It also means that enforcement of public law through state agencies ignores the workers' immigrant status.

The most interesting finding here has been the case of those US trade unions that were in favour of sanctions on employers who hired undocumented workers in the eighties. After some experience with this provision, trade unions concluded in the nineties that employer sanctions divide workers in the workplace when it comes to industrial struggles for better wage and working conditions for all workers because employers used the sanctions provision as a tool to intimidate immigrant workers (Haus 1995). For many industries (e.g., the cleaning industry in Los Angeles) this meant that the unionisation of immigrant workers had become nearly impossible. As a result, the trade union movements (in both the US and in Germany) developed a surprisingly liberal approach towards immigration in which immigrants cannot be used to undermine national social workplace standards. Now, the central approach for dealing with the labour market consequences of immigration is no longer to focus on immigrants as such but on the need to maintain workplace standards more generally, irrespective of immigration status. At the same time, as trade unions and social movements have become more liberal, employer associations have become more restrictive regarding immigration and working standards. Instructive here is the case of the German employer association that is vehemently opposed to further legal immigration on the one hand, while it fully supports immigration regimes that give fewer rights to immigrant workers on the other. Furthermore, this stance is accompanied by a vigorous resistance to an increase in minimum wage and other labour market standards.

A second step in terms of the recognition of global citizenship is that the fight for enhanced wage and working standards in a global economy can no longer be fought in the domestic sphere alone. This struggle needs to be tied in with developing ways and means to make sure that workers abroad are also able to improve standards in their own countries and to allow consumers to make an informed choice when buying foreign products.

There are two ways to achieve this: one is to make sure that international public law is created and effectively enforced. The discussion here centres on the integration of wage and working standards in the trade regime governed by the World Trade Organisation. This is a discussion that has so far not produced any results at the global level. The posted workers directive is one way the European Union is creating public law at the international level. But the European directive also shows the problems and pitfalls in doing so because the directive does not make all national wage and working standards binding for posted workers but focuses on national public standards. For countries where wages are negotiated between trade unions and employers, such as Germany, this means that a second, national process is needed to ensure that posted workers are paid the same wages as national workers. And, as we have seen, this outcome is not guaranteed; with the result that labour markets in the construction industry are now segmented (Hunger 2000: 136).

The second way to develop a level playing field in terms of wage and labour standards is to establish private governance mechanisms. Three initiatives came out of the US in this context in the 1990s: the Workers' Rights Consortium (WRC), mainly supported by trade unions and student movements against sweatshops, the Fair Labour Association (FLA), created under the Clinton Administration as an autonomous body, and the World Wide Responsible Apparel Production Principles and Certification Program (WRAP), created by the apparel manufacturers themselves.[97]

---

97 For a more recent overview over both US and European initiatives see Merk (2005).

The aim of the Workers' Rights Consortium is to support and verify licensee compliance with production codes of conduct established by universities. It has established its own code of conduct, and it acts on specific complaints from workers. So far, 114 colleges and universities have become members of the WRC and there are also many corporate members now (see www. workersrights. org). The Fair Labour Association (FLA) emerged as a result of the discussions of the Apparel Industry Partnership process organised by the Clinton Administration in August 1996 at the White House (see www.fairlabor org) and aims to improve working conditions in factories in the US and abroad. In order to achieve this aim, the FLA has established a code of conduct and an independent monitoring system. It includes the International Labor Rights Fund, the Lawyers' Committee for Human Rights, apparel and footwear manufacturers, and the National Consumers' League. Until now 141 colleges and universities have affiliated themselves with the FLA to have their suppliers monitored. The World Wide Responsible Apparel Production Principles and Certification Program (WRAP) was initiated in 1998 with the publication of the Principles and launched officially in June 2000 by the American Apparel Manufacturer Association (AAMA) that has since merged with the Fashion Association and the Footwear Industries of America to form the American Apparel and Footwear Association in August 2000.

The three initiatives have in common that the producer has to comply with local laws. All three outlaw child labour, prison labour, indentured labour, and bonded labour. The respective codes also include a rejection of discrimination, harassment, and abuse of workers, and guarantee the freedom association and bargaining. In terms of human rights, they are remarkably similar. However, there are substantial differences. For example, the trade union supported WRC contains many more favourable regulations regarding working hours. Another difference concerns the wage level. Both FLA and WRAP stipulate that at least the minimum total compensation as required by local law should be paid, whereas the trade union supported WRC introduces the concept of a living wage that should provide for the basic needs of an average family unit of employees. This is a necessary provision because in many places the wages paid to workers are not enough to cover necessary expenses. For example, workers in Haiti have to spend almost their entire daily earnings to pay for transport to the factory and food for the day (Krupat 1997: 63). The concept of a living wage is thus a necessary corrective to the national minimum wage when it is set too low.

The central difference in the three approaches is in the way compliance with the code is ensured. FLA and WRAP issue certificates to "clean" producers, whereas WRC works mainly on the basis of the "fire alarm" method. They conduct independent investigations but these are to be triggered by the concrete complaints of workers who report violations of the code of conduct. Under the WRAP scheme of the textile association, the workers in the factories have no chance to complain about working conditions once the monitoring agency has left the premises. In the FLA, there is a "Third Party Complaint Procedure" that allows the initiation of a "Complaint of Alleged Non-compliance" against a company and lodge it with the FLA who will have to investigate.[98] In contrast, the institutions that operate under the WRC Verification Agency are human rights and religious organisations. These organisations report non-compliance directly to the WRC and perform spot investigations. In contrast to FLA and WRC, WRAP is not tied to universities as consumers of apparel products. The com-

---

98 Charter Document, Fair Labor Association, Amended Agreement, June 1999, Title X.

pany that wishes to obtain a certificate from WRAP has to apply and pay a fee and will then be monitored by private firms. If the outcome of the monitoring is positive, a certificate, valid for one year, will be issued. The company may or may not receive an unannounced visit by independent monitors. According to WRAP, the advantage of a factory-based certification system is that it eliminates the duplication of monitoring efforts when different corporate customers monitor the same factory in an uncoordinated way. There is no third party complaint procedure, nor is there a secure channel for workers to blow the whistle on employers that do not adhere to the Code. For a given factory, then, there may be only one announced visit by the independent monitoring agency and for the rest of the certification year the company can continue to produce as before. The WRAP and, to some extent, the FLA operate on a voluntaristic basis. It is quite unclear whether they actually introduce hard and legally enforceable status rights and obligations. Critics of the process claim that companies can easily avoid compliance with the codes. The "fire alarm" method of the WRC seems to be the only way to guarantee effective compliance. This seems to be the reason why firms try to boycott it and put pressure on universities joining the WRC, for example by withdrawing donations.

This discussion of three concrete examples of global governance mechanisms shows that there are massive differences among the various approaches that have a dramatic impact on the workers in factories overseas and therefore on the degree of realisation of global citizenship. It is hotly debated what the content of the actual standards to be enforced should be, how the compliance of these standards should be monitored, and who should be involved in the governance process, i.e., in the setting and monitoring of standards. This shows that the slogan of "global governance" is not a panacea to solve all globalisation problems but is as contested as the globalisation process itself. Nevertheless, it is possible to claim that the development of codes of conduct and of a governance system to monitor them have to be seen as real progress in the creation of a global economy guided more by cosmopolitan standards (Held 2003), especially since these initiatives are still in the infancy stage and the situation changes daily. For example, in order to reduce the confusion generated by the multiplicity of codes of conduct six organisations have set up the "Joint Initiative on Corporate Accountability and Workers' Rights".[99] In the first phase of the project, these organisations are working in Turkey together with local counterparts to develop a common approach that could be extended to other countries.

Developments such as this show that there is a serious and ever more effective aspect of the anti-globalisation movement that actively tries to change the conditions of global production on the ground world wide. But as the case studies show, action is needed across the whole production chain to deal with wage and labour standards issues at home and abroad. Working conditions in the countries of origin need to be improved and at home it is crucial to move away from the focus on immigration issues when dealing with wage and working standards but instead to make sure that existing standards are enforced. Employer sanctions and the deportation of workers without work permits are not measures that will increase transparency and trust at the workplace. At the same time, a more transparent, flexible and open approach to immigration is needed.

---

99 For further information see Joint Initiative on Corporate Accountability and Workers Rights at www.jo-in.org (accessed December 2005).

Migration and Territoriality

The general thrust of the globalisation literature for much of the 1990s has been that globalisation weakens the territorial basis of the state. In contrast, the present research shows that the increase in globalisation for production and finance resulting in the (near) disappearance of the distinction between national and foreign capital goes hand in hand with a strengthening of the territoriality principle for the new migrants (asylum seekers, refugees, temporary workers, and undocumented migrants). These migrants experience a decrease in citizenship rights while global capital now enjoys more or less the same rights as national capital. This is a highly paradoxical policy stance because in economic theory it is generally agreed that the freedom of movement for the factors of production contributes much more to increased efficiency and output than world trade (Ethier 1995: 290-293).

This is the paradox that started the present inquiry. It is, in a sense, dissolved by the project perspective on globalisation that the neo-Gramscian approach has put forward. We no longer have a paradox because the globalising elite has a selective globalisation project: The neoliberal ideology propounded by the globalising elite does indeed involve a project that changes the territorial organisation of social life but, paradoxically, also seeks to maintain the very shape of territoriality by upholding national conceptions of citizenship. Neoliberalism, in contrast to the way it is presented in public debate, is not an objective economic theory but in reality, a theory for specific social forces that serves a particular purpose (Cox 1986).

The role of migration restrictions in the neoliberal project is to sharply delineate who belongs and who does not. Despite their insistence on the need for global economic integration, neoliberals envisage a world which remains based on exclusive political communities, however much individuals located in different countries 'interact' with each other across borders, for example in the production of goods and services. What the inquiry has left open so far are the reasons for the opposition by neoliberals to free migration, and what this implies for the continued importance of territoriality in the global economy.

Migration restrictions first have to be seen in a functional light. For Robinson, present capital/labour relationships are characterised by the structural power capital has acquired over labour – a power that allows it to institutionalise a new relationship based on the "global casualisation of labour" (Robinson 2001: 170). Casualization of labour concretely means that wages and working standards are declining and the production of goods becomes cheaper as a consequence. This policy of making labour cheaper is stated quite bluntly in official policy papers. As I have highlighted in chapter five, the OECD opposed the German legislation to regulate posted workers because it aimed "to prevent workers hired abroad from underbidding domestic workers" (OECD 1998c: 17). The posted workers law in Germany was indeed in direct opposition to the OECD idea of labour market regulation. Robinson gives another, even more explicit quote from the Director of the International Monetary Fund in 1984, who discusses the declining returns on capital investment in manufacturing, which he attributes mainly to the increase in wages. He then openly states that there is a need "for a gradual reduction in the rate increase in real wages over the medium term if we are to restore adequate investment incentives" (Robinson 2004: 108). The German employers' association (BDA) is equally outspoken regarding the use of labour migrants in Germany. On the one hand, the BDA shares the general conservative opinion that "Germany is not an immigration country", and that "in the near future there is no need for additional immigration" (BDA 1992a: 21). However, the BDA welcomes temporary labour migrants because they are "an interesting instrument to flexibilise the labour market" (BDA 1992a: 24). Open borders but closed societies form two sides of the same coin of the neoliberal project of global market making. According to Robinson, we have to see this as an expression of the power of globally mobile capital which, by strictly regulating access to national labour markets, is able to regulate the conditions for the global supply of labour (2004: 106). We must therefore focus more on migration controls as being part of labour control in general.

A second functional explanation for migration controls is the role of "learning". This learning comes in two ways. On the one hand, the neoliberal globalising elite has 'learned' from the mistakes of earlier migration processes and has come to the conclusion that migration movements can be substituted with capital movements. It is therefore no coincidence that one of the central elements of the neoliberal agenda has been to insist on the liberalisation of the capital account. The goal was to compensate for the need to restrict immigrant inflow.

A second learning process seems to have happened with regard to the presence of migrants in western societies. Judging from the analysis of OECD documents, the present origin of migration restrictions alongside the move to introduce liberalism on a global scale have to be seen in the context of the failed guest worker programs of the fifties and sixties in European countries, and the bracero programme in the US. Initially, the OECD encouraged the use of labour migrants to alleviate shortages in the labour market as a part of the Bretton Woods compromise in the fifties and sixties, and the promotion of the international movement of labour was to complement the other regimes for trade and capital flows (Zolberg 1991: 313). This was the result of a "coincidence of needs", as the OECD argued: "excess labour demand in one part of the area coupled with excess labour supply in the other"

(OECD 1978: 7). Labour migration in that period then was initiated explicitly as an 'economic' policy.

However, this economism in migration policy had to be reassessed in the light of the economic crisis of the early seventies, an undertaking carried out by the so-called Kindleberger Report (OECD 1978). While the report restates the economic reasoning behind free migration, the central portrait of migration itself has undergone a major shift. In the report it is now described not only as a movement of factors of production, but also of people. As such, it has a social component that generates externalities over time which reduce the benefits and increase the costs. The conclusions of the report reflect today's consensus on migration and global economic integration. It recognizes that guest worker programmes cannot be revived and that this impossibility will result in increased illegal immigration. Ultimately, the report recommends that the division of labour needs to be adjusted. "If people are no longer able to move to the jobs, the jobs can still be moved to the people" (OECD 1978: 37). The substitution of investment for migration flows can for example be seen in the US where the discontinuation of the guest worker program (bracero program) in 1965 coincided with the decision to establish the free economic zones in Mexico (Pellerin 1996: 89). According to Bhagwati, the general tightening of labour immigration in Europe likewise led to a greater outflow of multinational corporations to peripheral countries (1984: 689). Globalising elites then seem to have 'learned' and consequently integrated into their preferences the fact that the economic policy of importing labour resulted in higher costs than benefits. Furthermore, immigrant labour is not really needed because much work can be outsourced globally. Added to this comes the insight from the case studies that those industries which still need immigrant workers are able to procure these through illegal and/or temporary immigration, and in order to increase the supply of such workers, immigration had to be made more difficult.

The real reason for migration restrictions, however, seems to be a certain sense of national entitlement. Milton Friedman argues quite clearly that "equality stops at the water's edge" (1979: 134), meaning that there is no obligation towards distributing the wealth accumulated in one's own country, even if, as it is the case today, over forty percent of this wealth now stems from accumulation abroad (Gowan 2004: 14). At the core of neoliberalism is a reduction of the welfare state and the citizenship rights accompanying it. If migration were free, then the young and the old would come as well and place an increased burden on the welfare state. The OECD has come to a similar conclusion.

> Migration implies a mixing of cultures, with, at times, serious social tensions as a consequence. Over time, as migrants remain in host countries and the process takes on a more permanent nature, larger claims on the social infrastructure arise. The children of migrants must be schooled, and medical services, housing, welfare benefits and other publicly financed services must be diverted to those whose characteristics and tastes become increasingly transformed in line with those of the host-country population. Increasing claims on public goods and services serve to reduce the net economic benefits accruing to the host country. Social tensions can completely reverse net economic profits and turn them into net social losses (OECD 1978a: 29-30).

In other words, immigrants that come in undocumented or on a temporary basis are welcome because they put a lower strain on welfare state services while, as soon the arrangement becomes more permanent, immigration is no longer cost-effective.

Legitimacy of Neoliberalism

This ties in with the problem of the legitimacy of the state in the face of the neoliberal project of global market building. Border controls create a sense of identity and legitimacy in a state which is unable to protect its population in economic terms. According to Rosewarne (2001: 83), borders "have been an integral element in the efforts of the state to promote territorial and social integrity. To remove those controls could well undermine the political cohesion upon which the authority of the state rests". Boundaries thus remain crucial in the global economy in order to secure social cohesion and to enable disciplinary sanctions on unruly elements. As Goff argues, to some extent these boundaries become "invisible" or "conceptual", substituting for the permeability of borders to capital and goods (2000: 533). But the fundamental purpose of these boundaries – "demarcating distinct political communities" – is reinforced by very visible limits on the movement of people (*ibid.*).

Drainville (1995), too, suggests that the globalisation of the world economy has made the territorial state more rather than less important. Its role is still to secure global accumulation and, in order to do so, it has to make compromises at the national level. The restrictions on immigration are one such compromise that is made possible, furthermore, by the fact that restrictions on immigration only place a burden on the immigrant while they simultaneously increase profits for the employer. Their functional usefulness therefore makes it possible for the neoliberal globalising elite to be fundamentally illiberal regarding migrants and their rights.

The generation of legitimacy for global accumulation and for supporting the integration of the national economy into the global market thus remains a crucial task of the state. In this sense, the state has to structure its participation in the global economy in such a way that it can maintain some degree of legitimacy, through measures of both inclusion and exclusion. As Hirst and Thompson (1999: 257) note, the nation state remains the only organisation that can legitimately speak for a mass of people.

> While the state's claim to exclusive control of its territory has been reduced by international markets and new communication media, it still retains one central role that ensures a large measure of territorial control: the regulation of populations. People are less mobile than money, goods or ideas, and in a sense they remain 'nationalised', dependent on passports, visas, residence and labour qualification. The democratic state's role as the possessor of a territory is that it regulates its population, and this gives it a definite and unique legitimacy internationally in that it can speak for that population.

However, this also means that nation states *need* to speak for their people in order to retain this legitimacy; they cannot simply speak for global elites. Phil Cerny argues:

> The state retains a certain hold over national consciousness and constitutional legitimacy, and its residual functions (the 'competition state') are still central both to the globalisation process and to carrying out a range of crucial political, economic, and social tasks (1996: 136).

Migration restrictions then highlight the more general tendency within neoliberalism that a free economy needs a strong national state to make it possible (Gamble 1994: 35). The contrary developments regarding migration and capital are but another instance in this more general tendency to establish a free market economy with the help of a strong territorial national state.

One of the central explanations for migration restrictions then is the need for legitimacy. Despite globalisation, elections are still very much national affairs, and globalisation (specifically the idea of free trade resulting in the export of jobs overseas) is not really popular with the electorate and could lead to a revival of nationalism bringing the downfall of globalisation more generally (Messina 1996: 137). Neo-Gramscians have argued that this fusion of liberal and conservative elements is necessary as a "politics of support" in order to implement the central elements of the neoliberal reform programme (Overbeek and van der Pijl 1993: 15). Migration policy can provide the state with an opportunity to demonstrate its ability to act in the name of the people even in an era of globalisation where the state's power seems to be so limited. According to Cox, this is one of the central indicators that the understanding of sovereignty of the state has undergone a shift away from power over the economy, as was the case in the fifties and sixties, and towards the affirmation of identity (1996: 306).

The maintenance of territorial national states is then an integral part of the neoliberal project, and quite possibly beyond, as a structural feature of capitalist accumulation. The territorial state is necessary to control the labour force by granting access to the labour market, in the form of visas and citizenship. The paradoxical insight from the case studies was that strict migration controls create the very labour force needed for the neoliberal restructuring of specific sectors of the labour market. This shows that further globalisation and territorialisation are therefore dependent on each other. In this sense, territoriality, the organisation of the state system in multiple states instead of one world state, has been integrated as a functional element in capitalist accumulation. Multiple states (or regions) are needed for labour control in order to uphold differentiated labour and citizenship or entitlement regimes, to provide legitimacy and enforce property rights for a global market (Wood 2003: 136-7).

Neo-Gramscianism as a Theory of Globalisation

The conclusion to my investigation into the role of migration in the neoliberal project that follows from the discussion in the last two sections then is that migration has a twofold role: first, restrictive migration policies legitimise the neoliberal project of global market making. They do this by creating one area where states can still display their sovereignty that has been undermined by the global market. In this way the more important aspects of the neoliberal project (free markets for capital and good) can be maintained while an important concession can be made to the electorate. Secondly, and at the same time, restrictive migration policies support the neoliberal project of market making by increasing the supply of a specific type of labour. The specific type of labour is made up of undocumented or temporary immigrants that constitute a more 'flexible' labour force often not bound by the rules of the country where they work. This means that the restrictive migration regime helps to create the flexible labour force needed for neoliberal restructuring. The two aspects therefore feed into each other. The question now is what these two results mean for neo-Gramscian globalisation theory.

In his post mortem on globalization theory, Rosenberg (2005) argues that the claims by the globalisation theories have turned out to be premature. First, a profound transformation in the organisation of human life has not taken place as claimed by the majority of globalisation theories. Second, globalisation theories extrapolated on the extraordinary changes after the end of the Cold War in 1998 (Rosenberg 2005: 42). One of the central points of the neo-Gramscian perspective, however, is that the 1990s were not really the crucial turning point for the reorganisation of social life associated with neoliberalism but the 1970s. Secondly, the transformation the neo-Gramscians were mostly concerned with was the nature of US power exertion and the accompanying restructuring of state/society complexes, production relations, and world order under neoliberal guidance. The central claim was that "globalisation" is the expression of a specific political project pushed through by a specific set of social forces (the globalising US-centred neoliberal elite) and opposed by counter-hegemonic forces. The Neo-Gramscian globalisation theory is thus much more limited in scope than the theories criticized by Rosenberg. It focuses on the parallel processes of neoliberal restructuring at the level of production (1), state (2), and world order (3) (Rupert 2000: 16).

(1) Specifically, the perspective argues that we are observing a restructuring of production relations both spatially and socially. The standard employment relationship has made room for a core/periphery model of labour employment, in which only a minority of workers is able to make a decent and secure living. At the same time, the national economy is now but one anchoring point in a larger, global division of labour where different elements of the production process are performed in the most competitive geographical location, joined together in a commodity chain. Furthermore, production as such has become devalued by the rise to prominence of finance capital, which also has brought with it a more authoritarian and remote relationship to labour. Finance is derivative of production but, since the seventies, it has become autonomous from it because financial flows are no longer related to flows in the productive economy. These changes have had an enormous impact on state/society relations and on the way the international political economy functions.

These changes have reinforced the power of a globalising elite reaching across the globe through ownership patterns and financial interests and it is this elite that is intent on the maintenance and further extension of this global economy. According to Gill, a study of the Trilateral Commission shows that integration among OECD countries has taken on a very "organic" character because of the acceptance and integration of transnational social and political forces which try to influence foreign policy towards other countries according to their own interests (1990a: 210). These transnational social forces have become more organised and ordered over the last twenty years and have established complex alliance structures. As a consequence, a more complex "intermeshing" of interests, identities, and ideas has occurred (Gill 1990a: 211-2). Gill argues that there is a wider "trilateral establishment" within which a transnational capitalist class faction – which consists of politicians, civil servants, and the executive members of transnational corporations in finance and production – is developing. "At the apex of such a bloc are the elements in the state and in capital which are linked to dynamic, international production and finance" (Gill 1990a: 50). This emerging "transnational historic bloc" sees its interests and ideas as a further liberalisation and transnationalisation of global political economy (Gill 1993d: 261).

(2) With their ability to pour money into economies in an instant and to withdraw it equally fast, the power of financial interest groups has been the main agent of change in state/society relationships, from welfare state to competition state through the transnationalisation of the state (even though, of course, the extent and degree of these changes have varied across countries). The welfare state under Fordism formulated policies that promoted long-term industrial development accompanied by policies that raised mass incomes. This included not only welfare benefits, but also legislative support for strong unions. This institutional structure allowed the (more or less) consensual formulation of policies on prices, incomes, investments, levels of employment, and balance of payments. The transnationalisation of the state means that the power and mobility of global capital have a decisive

impact on state policies. Often, such policies are fixed internationally, in regional and global trade and economic integration agreements that lock in neoliberal policies of privatisation, deregulation, and liberalisation. Stephen Gill has rightly characterized this process as a new global constitutionalism (2003: 131). The latest element of this new constitutionalism was visible in the defeated new constitution of the European Union, unlike any other constitution in that it contained quite detailed economic policies which are usually decided by an elected government. By including such provisions in the EU constitution, elected governments would have been able to only pursue neoliberal policies. For example, Part III included provisions such as the principle that "free and undistorted competition" is the prime instrument for the allocation of resources. Articles 116-156 outlawed restrictions on capital movements, a provision that would effectively block the introduction of a tax on speculative capital movements (the constitution can only be changed if all 25 member states agree to an amendment) (Cassen 2005: 39).

The victory of the transnational state in the form of the competition state has led to the abandonment of the principle of full employment while the fight against inflation took priority in order to increase profit rates. The rise of the competition state is a sign that there is indeed a new axis of influence which consists of an international linked policy network integrating the key central agencies of government and big business (such as in the Trilateral Commission) and that this new set of social forces has been successful in securing the restructuring of state policies to support transnational accumulation (Glassman 1999: 673).

(3) A world order under capitalism is characterised by a dual nature: on the one hand, we have to consider the balance of power in the interstate system, and on the other, the changes in the global economy

(Cox 1987: 107). The central change in the interstate system is that the US has lost its hegemony but has to rely on an increasingly repressive policy in order to maintain its predominance. Cox argues that the main problem of "global governance" after the end of the Cold War in 1989 is that the US still has a central position in military and economic affairs, which it uses more and more to further its own interests and less the interests of the system as a whole (Cox 1987: 303). For Cox, however, hegemony has given way to a system of dominance or more authoritarian leadership.

> The United States does not pay its way in the world, while its structural power, resting increasingly on its military strength, continues to bias the global system in its favour. This is a far cry from the post World War II world in which the United States provided the resources for recovery, and the model of productivity for the rest of the world. What was a system of hegemonic leadership has become a tributary system (Cox 1993b: 263-264).

One instance of this was seen in the financing of the Gulf War in the early nineties, where the allies essentially paid the US to carry out the war. With regard to the financial system, the tributary nature of the governance structure is even more obvious. As Helleiner has pointed out, the US encouraged the growth of global financial markets because that would strengthen the policy autonomy of the US government. Instead of having to deal with growing balance of payments pressures, the US is able to rely on foreign investors to do so and to provide the necessary finance (Helleiner 1994: 173; Gowan 1999). This has led to a situation where the accumulated external debt of the US is $2.2 trillion, an amount nearly equal to the one owed by the Third World (including India, China and Brazil): $2.5 trillion. While the developing world in total is paying about $300 billion a year in debt service, the US only pays $20 billion. This deficit is financed by the surplus countries (e.g. Japan, China) and by capital flight from developing countries (Greenhill and Pettifor 2002).

The problem at the moment then is that there is still a system of territorialized states in which seemingly national interests (especially those of powerful states) play a role but that co-exists with partially globalised economy. In other words, while traditional competition among territorial states is still a relevant process in international relations, there is also a transnational coalition, based on the globalising neoliberal elite, supporting further global economic integration or globalisation (Cox 1994: 53-57). Competition among territorial states and the move towards a transnational state constitute two relevant processes in international politics with an as yet uncertain outcome, as is the academic debate. On the one hand, there is William Robinson (2001) who pushes aspects of neo-Gramscianism to their logical conclusion with his argument that we are witnessing the emergence of a transnational state based on a transnational class, whereas others such as Peter Gowan (2004) emphasize the continued national interests of the US elite that finds their expression in US foreign policy.

Robinson assumes that US hegemony is declining and that we are experiencing "the early stages of the creation of a transnational hegemony" (2001: 167). This transnational hegemony is built on the transnational class and on the transnational state. The transnational class comes into being because "class fractions from different countries are fusing together into new capitalist groups within transnational space" (*ibid.*: 165). They are involved in global production and manage the global circuits of accumulation. These activities have led to the development of an "objective class existence and identity", according to Robinson (*ibid.*). In order to govern the global circuits of accumulation, these groups are in the process of developing a transnational state. At the moment, this state is more of a network of governance processes than a state in the traditional sense with a real power centre. The transnational state "comprises those institutions and practices in global society that maintain, defend and advance the emergent hegemony of a global bourgeoisie and its project of constructing a new global capitalist historical bloc" (*ibid.*: 166-7). This network is made up of two different institutional structures: the transformed nation states which "serve as transmission belts and filtering devices for the imposition of the transnational agenda" (*ibid.*: 188), and the international fora and institutions such as the International Monetary Fund, the Bank for International Settlements, and the World Trade Organisation.

At the other end of the spectrum stands Gowan's insistence that globalisation is really an extension of US power with the more or less willing cooperation (but also resistance) of other core capitalist states. It allows the US state/society complex to interpenetrate and transform national spaces through US capital. At the same time, it makes the continuous functioning of US capitalism possible since US capitalism has now become dependent on internationalisation. Approximately 40 percent of the streams of value of US corporations are now realized abroad (Gowan 2004: 14). A large portion of US power now depends on the dominance of the financial sector through the imposition of the US dollar as centre currency. This interpenetration and transformation of US capitalism with other state/society complexes, added to the ability of the US to transform the rules of the game ensure the continuation of the US protectorate system (Gowan 1999: IX; 2003: 13-14). In this sense, the US was and is, according to Gowan, a "sovereign power" because it defines who counts as a friend and who as an enemy. It is able to impose on its "protectorate" states central elements of American style capitalism on its allies, and to decide which norms to adhere to and which rules to break (2003: 2). The central aim of the

US now is to extend and adapt this system to the requirements of an age dominated by the rise of Asia and the corresponding shift of power to other areas (2004).

These two seemingly opposite ends of the debate cannot be resolved by empirical research, establishing the truth content of one over the other. Rather, it seems that there is a contradiction between the requirements of a global space on the one hand, and the arrangements of power structures or centres on the other (see also Lacher 2005). The crucial problem is that the US is now dependent on the present functioning of the global economy, especially in the financial area, which makes reform impossible. At the same time, the unwillingness of the US to reform creates incentives to establish alternatives which, in turn, push for a strengthening of the power struggle.

Studying the role of migration clearly shows another way this interrelationship between globalization and territoriality is played out. On the one hand, global migration certainly increases globalisation. Given the form it takes (mostly undocumented or temporary labour), it furthermore supports the spread of neoliberalism because it undermines national regimes of citizenship rights regarding labour standards. It is in this context that the struggle against neoliberalism has also created the basis for new forms of global citizenship as the case studies have shown. On the other hand, since the current migration regime is focused on either reducing or at least controlling immigration flows, it simultaneously territorializes the global economy. Migration policy has emerged as one of the central ways to maintain national conceptions of citizenship and of the territorial state. The idea of the state as a welfare provider, which is being undermined by neoliberal policies, is giving way to the state as an identity provider. Re-nationalisation or the renewed emphasis on territoriality regarding citizenship rights does not prevent the further spread of global economic integration but, on the contrary, makes further integration possible.

The neo-Gramscian perspective is at a crossroads. Its original starting point was the insight that the United States is a different kind of imperial power and that the only way to understand this difference was to apply Gramsci's understanding of hegemony on the way the US interacts with the rest of the world. Hegemony is understood here, not only in the sense that the US was out to achieve consensus on how to rule the world, but instead, as the spread of a social order which allows the central power to reproduce and increase its supremacy worldwide by creating a world that mirrors it. The central point of this perspective, long before anyone else in the discipline of international relations understood it, was to point out that this hegemony changed dramatically with the destruction of the Bretton Woods system in 1971 and took on a more aggressive character. At the same time, the core of hegemony was no longer one of production but a system of global finance. US hegemony was not declining but changing in nature.

The central problem of the neo-Gramscian perspective is that it does not really take further its specific understanding of the social forces pushing for the creation of a global market as such, and specifically, of the role of US power in it. While the continued relevance of territoriality is mentioned as an element of opposition to neoliberal globalisation, there is no conceptual basis to understand the co-dependency of globalisation and territoriality. Central concepts such as "dominance" or "new constitutionalism" do not allow room for an inquiry into what is in effect the central contradiction of the global market today: that it is indeed global, but its spread is uneven and that there is, even though there is a need for it, no global authority to govern it. Instead, territorial states that are interested in safeguarding their own interests within an unevenly developed global economy compete among themselves to secure national advantages (Lacher 2006). It is this contradiction that ultimately needs to be resolved if a new, stable regime of accumulation is to come into being.

The conclusion of this study regarding the neo-Gramscian globalisation theory is thus twofold. On the one hand, the neo-Gramscian perspective faces the problem of developing an adequate understanding of the structural changes within capitalism. This would require an adequate conceptualisation of the enduring territorial dimension of political organisation that has been shown to be of such importance in the present research. While the neo-Gramscian perspective emphasises transnational elements, the interrelationship between state and global economy (or, more precisely, the political constitution of the global economy through states), cannot be grasped adequately. The reason, ultimately, is that transnational historical materialism does not include a theory of territoriality and of capitalist development. It can recognise the empirical importance of borders, but does not build on a systematic theory of the state (preferring to deal with more concrete "forms of state").

In order to better understand the nature of globalisation, and its limits and contradictions, neo-Gramscianism needs a more sophisticated understanding of the relationship between the national and the global, and of the structural relationship between the nation state and the world market. Thus, while the neo-Gramscian approach can recognise the agency that leads to the reassertion of state borders with respect to people, it is much more questionable whether it can incorporate the far-reaching implications of the persistent tie between statehood, territoriality, and citizenship into its conceptualisation of globalisation. In the end, the reason for these limitations lies in not recognising that the globalising classes do not reinvent the world from scratch, nor have they replaced a global with a national form of social organisation; the agency of these classes is not simply limited by resistance from other social forces, but takes place within a structural framework, not least that of bounded political communities, which forms the unavoidable backdrop to all attempts to create a global civilisation. Thus, what neo-Gramscianism really needs is to put the agency of the globalising elite into the context of a more general theory of capitalism as a social system. For, as Simon Bromley notes, "no amount of discussion of such themes as 'hegemony', 'historic blocs' and 'transnational capital' adds up to a theory of the modern state system or of the world market" (1995: 232).

On the other hand, however, the focus of the neo-Gramscian globalisation theory on political projects or concepts of control on the one hand and on its – albeit neglected (Drainville 1994) – counterpart on the other, the close examination of the oppositional forces that resist domination and hold the key to a (hopefully more progressive) transformation of capitalist social relations, remains one of the central strong points of the neo-Gramscian perspective that distinguish it favourably from other approaches within historical materialism. This focus on political project made the identification of the dark side of liberalism today possible that only concedes open borders to capital not to people. This insight highlights that the global economy is not a force from nature but a socially constructed space with specific interests and power relations to back it up and that it requires the development of a counter power to change the now prevailing configuration of social and political arrangements. There is, however, a need to recognize more precisely the limits of such an approach and to more closely anchor neo-Gramscian research and concepts within the larger body of historical materialist research.

Closed Borders – Open Societies? Normative Implications

The co-dependency between globalisation and territoriality creates its own inherent normative contradictions within the neoliberal project. Along with the continuing trade protectionism of developed countries towards many products from the Third World, the neoliberal migration system has to be seen as the Achilles' heel of global neoliberalism because it is such an glaring exception to the neoclassical doctrine of the freedom for factors of production (Briggs 1996: 122). More important, the continued existence of migration controls ensure that global inequality is here to stay. According to Samir Amin, "the progressive unification of the commodities and capital markets alone, without being accompanied by gigantic migration of populations, has absolutely no chance of equalizing the economic conditions in which different peoples live" (quoted in Sutcliffe 1993: 102).

Neoliberalism, of course, is not a project to create global equality, but claims to be able to increase efficiency and aggregate wealth if its prescriptions are followed, especially those concerning the global integration of the economy. It does, however, posit that "social welfare is maximized when government regulation is minimized and, in particular, national boundaries should be fully open to commercial intercourse" (McEwan 1999: 35). But if the argument is that open markets contribute to growth, then, as McEwan suggests, "the question must immediately arise: why regulate labour markets by preventing the movement of labour across boundaries?" (1999: 35).

It might seem that the answer to this question is obvious: free migration is neither feasible nor desirable, as it would lead to negative social consequences. But the same could be (and is being) said about free capital mobility. Thus, if we admit the importance of social considerations in the construction of the new global order, rather than allowing it to be guided purely by the pursuit of economic efficiency and growth, then why should we only accept the problems associated with free migration to constitute a reason for the "self-protection of society" against the violence of the global market? If there is one limit to the free market, then why not others? Alternatively, why should it be ruled out that a global form of regulation can be established as the cosmopolitan framework challenges us to do (Held 2002)? As McEwan (1999: 35) argues, migration controls show that neoliberals allow social and political considerations to override the market. If this is accepted for migrants, why not allow the same questions and concerns for capital whose cross border movements can be equally disruptive?

The new global order is not simply integrated by transnational actions and the transborder effects of rational individuals' domestic actions, but constituted by social choices and social power, which make certain forms of actions possible and rational, while preventing others. The new global economy is, in other words, a socially constructed space. It has therefore to be considered as a space that can, in turn, be altered by political action and counter-action. The inherent contradiction between the rhetoric of globalisation and the reality of migration is one opening for social forces seeking to change the prevailing power configuration and the institutions that are attached to it. Whether and to what extent such transformative action emerges, which direction it takes and whether it becomes successful is one of the most important problems of the global political economy today.

BIBLIOGRAPHY

AAMA – American Apparel Manufacturers Association (www.americanapparel.org).

AAMA (n.d.) *AAMA Statement of Responsibility*, Arlington.

AAMA (1996) Statement of Larry Martin, President, *Fashion Industry Forum*, 16th July 1996, www.gatekeeper.dol.gov/dol/opa/public/forum/martin.txt (accessed March 1997).

AAMA (1998a) *Statement of the American Apparel Manufacturers Association. Submitted to the Office of the US Trade Representative.* Stephen Lamar. Director of Government Relations, www.americanapparel.org/ News_FTR_USTR.html (accessed July 1999).

AAMA (1998b) *Worldwide Responsible Apparel Production (WRAP) Program. An Initiative Aimed at Improving Apparel Industry Working Conditions Worldwide*, Arlington.

AAMA (1998c) Letter to the Office of International Economic Affairs. Bureau of International Labor Affairs. U.S. Department of Labor, www.americanapparel.org/ News_FTR_DOL.html (accessed July 1999).

AAMA (1998d) Testimony, Larry K. Martin, President of the American Apparel Manufacturers Association before the Oversight and Investigations Subcommittee of the House Education and Workforce Committee, *Monitoring and Compliance Activities by the US Apparel Industry*, 25th September 1998.

AAMA (1999) Statement Submitted to the Chairman, Free Trade Area of the Americas, Committee of Government Representatives, *On Civil Society*, 31st March 1999, www.americanapparel. org/AAMA_ Industry_News.html (accessed July 1999).

ABLI – American Business for Legal Immigration.

ABLI (n.d.a) *What is ABLI?*, Washington.

ABLI (n.d.b) *Facts. H1B Visas*, Washington.

ACLU – American Civil Liberties Union (www.aclu.org).

ACLU (n.d.a) *Guardian of Liberty: American Civil Liberties Union*, Briefing Paper No. 1, New York.

ACLU (n.d.b) *The Bill of Rights: A Brief History*, Briefing Paper No. 9, New York.

ACLU (n.d.c) *The Rights of Employees'*, Briefing Paper No. 12, New York.

ACLU (1993a) Statement and Supplemental Statement of Lucas Guttentag, Director, Immigrants' Rights Project, ACLU and Antonio Maciel, Staff Attorney, United States. House. Committee on the Judiciary. Subcommittee on International Law, Immigration, and Refugees. *Employer Sanctions:* Hearing, 16th June 1993.

ACLU (1993b) Statement by Antonio J. Califa, *Terrorism, Asylum Issues, and U.S. Immigration Policy*, United States. Senate. Committee on the Judiciary. Subcommittee on Immigration and Refugee Affairs, Hearing 5th May 1993, Washington.

ACLU (1993c) Prepared Statement of Antonio J. Califa, Legislative Council, *Asylum and Inspections Reform*. United States. House. Committee on the Judiciary. Subcommittee on International Law, Immigration, and Refugees, Hearing 27th April 1993, Washington.

ACLU (1994a) Policy Guide of ACLU, Policy No. 325, *Admission of Immigrants*, New York.

ACLU (1994b) Policy Guide of ACLU, Policy No. 326, *Admissions of Non-Immigrants (Students, Business Visitors, Visitors etc.)*, New York.

ACLU (1994c) *Immigrants and the Economy*, New York.

ACLU (1995) Statement by Deborah Lewis, *Legislative Council on the Civil Liberties Implications of Welfare Reform*. United States. House. Committee on Ways and Means, Subcommittee on Human Resources Hearing, 6th February 1995, Washington.

ACLU (1996a) *National Identification Cards "Why Does the ACLU Oppose a National I.D. Card System?"*, New York.

ACLU (1996b) *Workplace Rights*, New York.

ACLU (1996c) *Clinton Administration Rushes to Dismiss Immigration Lawsuits*, Press Release 24.10.1996, New York.

ACLU (1996d) *Immigration Measure Moves Towards Passage*, Press Release 24.09.1996, New York.

ACLU (1996e) Letter to a Senator, 24.04.1996, Washington. www.aclu.org/congress/discuss.html (accessed July 1998).

ACLU (1996f) *ACLU Denounces President and Congress for Attack on the Basic Rights of Immigrants*, Press Release 03.10.1996, New York.

ACLU (1996g) *National ID on the Horizon?*, Press Release 02.05.1996, New York.

ACLU (1997a) *The Rights of Immigrants*, Briefing Paper No. 20 (Autumn 1997 update), New York.

ACLU (1997b) *Campaign Finance Reform and Legal Immigrants*, ACLU in Congress, www.aclu.org/congress/l010797a.html (accessed July 1998).

ACLU (1998) *Immigrants and Health Care*, New York.

Adkisson, Richard V. (2002) 'Immigration and Regional Comparative Advantage in the Apparel Industry', *The International Trade Journal* 16 (1):1-31.

AFL-CIO – American Federation of Labor – Council of Industrial Organizations (www.afl.cio.org).

AFL-CIO (n.d.) *The Union Label*, Service Trades Department, www.unionlabel.org/ (accessed July 1998).

AFL-CIO/Los Angeles (1992), Immigration Committee, Los Angeles County Federation of Labor, *The Impact of the Immigration Reform and Control Act on Organized Labor in Los Angeles*, Report 03.03.1992, Report attached to the Statement of John J. Sweeney, International President, Service Employees Union. United States. House Subcommittee on International Law, Immigration, and Refugees. Committee on the Judiciary. 103rd Congress, Hearing on Employer Sanctions, 16th June 1993, Washington.

AFL-CIO (1995a) *Immigration and the American Dream*. Executive Council. Adopted Policy Statements, 23.02.1995, Bal Harbour.

AFL-CIO (1995b) Prepared Statement of Markley Roberts, Assistant Director, Economic Research, United States. House. Subcommittee on Immigration and Claims. Committee on the Judiciary. 104th Congress. *Legal Immigration Reform Proposals*. Hearing 17th May 1995, Washington.

AFL-CIO (1995c) Statement of the American Federation of Labor and Congress of Industrial Organizations. United States. House. Committee on the Judiciary. Subcommittee on Immigration and Claims. 104th Congress. *Immigration in the National Interest Act of 1995.* Hearing 29th June 1995, Washington.

AFL-CIO (1996) *The Labor Movement in '96 - The New Activism,* Speech by John J. Sweeney (President) at the New School for Social Research, New York, 03.06.1996, www.aflcio.org/publ/speech96/ (accessed July 1998).

AFL-CIO (1997a) 'Building a Broad Movement of America's Workers', *Resolutions and Constitutional Amendments Adopted at the Twenty-Second AFL-CIO Convention,* AFL-CIO, Washington.

AFL-CIO (1997b) 'A New Voice for Workers in a Changing Global Economy', *Resolutions and Constitutional Amendments Adopted at the Twenty-Second AFL-CIO Convention,* Washington.

AFL-CIO (1997c) 'Workers and the Global Economy', *AFL-CIO 1997: Resolutions and Constitutional Amendments Adopted at the Twenty-Second AFL-CIO Convention,* Washington.

AFL-CIO (1997d) 'Economic and Social Justice', *Resolutions and Constitutional Amendments Adopted at the Twenty-Second AFL-CIO Convention,* Washington.

AFL-CIO (1997e) 'Civil and Human Rights'. *Resolutions and Constitutional Amendments Adopted at the Twenty-Second AFL-CIO Convention,* Washington.

AFL-CIO (1998a) *Making the Global Economy Work for America,* Speech by John J. Sweeney (President) at the Economic Strategy Institute Conference 05.05.1998, www.aflcio.org/publ/speech98/sp0505.htm (accessed July 1998).

AFL-CIO (1998b) *Speech by John J. Sweeney, (President) at the World Economic Forum in Davos,* Switzerland, 31st January 1998, www.aflcio.org/publ/speech98/sp0131.htm (accessed July 1998).

AFL-CIO (1998c) *Remarks by John J. Sweeney (President) at the Symposium on Corporate Social Responsibility,* Mount St. Mary's College; 04.03.1998, www.aflcio.org/publ/speech98/sp0324.htm (accessed July 1998).

AFL-CIO (2000a) *Immigration.* Executive Council, Adopted Policy Statements. 16.02.2000, New Orleans.

AFL-CIO (2000b) *Campaign for Global Fairness,* Executive Council. Adopted Policy Statements. 16.02.2000, New Orleans.

AFL-CIO (1997) Remarks by Linda Chavez-Thompson, *ORIT Congress Santo Domingo* April 23, 1997, www.aflcio.org/publ/speech97/sp0423.htm (accessed July 1998).

Aggarwal, Vinod K. (1985) *Liberal Protectionism. The International Politics of Organized Textile Trade*, Berkeley: University of California Press.

Alba, Francisco, Jean-Pierre Garson, and El Mouhoub Mouhoud (1998) 'Migration Policies in a Free Trade Area: The Issue of Convergence with the Economic Integration Process', in *Migration, Free Trade and Regional Integration in North America*, Paris: OECD, 261-78.

Allen, John (1992) 'Post-Industrialism and Post-Fordism', in Stuart Hall, David Held, and Tony McGrew, eds. *Modernity and its Futures*, Cambridge and Oxford: Polity Press, 169-220.

Altvater, Elmar (1999) 'Vernetzung ungleicher Partner. NGOs und Gewerkschaften in der Kampagne für "Codes of Conduct"', in A. Klein, H.-J. Legrand, and T. Leif, eds. *Neue Soziale Bewegungen. Impulse. Bilanzen und Perspektiven*, Opladen: Westdeutscher Verlag, 320-40.

Amoore, Louise, Richard Dodgson, Barry Gills, Paul Langley, Don Marshall, and Iain Watson (1997) 'Overturning 'Globalisation': Resisting the Teleological, Reclaiming the 'Political'', *New Political Economy* 2 (1), 93-104.

Andreas, Peter (2000) 'Introduction: The Wall after the Wall', in Peter Andreas and Timothy Snyder, eds. *The Wall Around the West: State Borders and Immigration Controls in North America and Europe*, Lanham, MD: Rowman and Littlefield, 1-15.

Andreas, Peter and Timothy Snyder, eds. (2000) *The Wall Around the West. State Borders and Immigration Controls in North America and Europe*, Lanham, MD: Rowman & Littlefield.

Augelli, Enrico and Craig Murphy (1988) *America's Quest for Supremacy and the Third World*, London: Pinter.

Augelli, Enrico and Craig Murphy (1993) 'Gramsci and International Relations: A General Perspective with Examples From Recent US Policy Toward the Third World', in Stephen Gill, ed. *Gramsci, Historical Materialism and International Relations*, Cambridge: Cambridge University Press, 127-47.

Bach, Robert L. (1992) 'Settlement Policies in the United States', in Gary P. Freeman and James Jupp, eds. *Nations of Immigrants. Australia, the*

United States and International Migration, Melbourne: Oxford University Press, 145-64.

Badie, Bertrand and Marie-Claude Smouts (1995) *Le Retournement du Monde. Sociologie de la Scène Internationale*, Paris: Presses de la Fondation Nationale des Sciences Politiques et Dalloz.

Baer, W. (1972) 'Import Substitution Industrialisation in Latin America: Experiences and Interpretations', *Latin American Research Review* 7 (1), 85-105.

Baker, Gerard (2000) 'Flexibility of Labour Market Key to US Success', *Financial Times 12.07.2000*.

Barry, James (1999) 'Leaner, Meaner OECD Rides the Global Waves', *International Herald Tribune*, 26.05.1997.

BDA – Bundesvereinigung der Deutschen Arbeitgeberverbände

BDA (1992a) *Stellungnahme – September 1992 – zum Vorschlag für eine Richtlinie des Rates über die Entsendung von Arbeitnehmern im Rahmen der Erbringung von Dienstleistungen*, Bonn.

BDA (1992b) *Ausländerbeschäftigung in Deutschland. Grundsätze und Empfehlungen der Arbeitgeber*, Köln.

BDA (1994) *Aktualisierte Stellungnahme – Juli 1994 – zum Vorschlag für eine Richtlinie des Rates über die Entsendung von Arbeitnehmern im Rahmen der Erbringung von Dienstleistungen* (Kommissionsvorschlag vom 30. August 1991; geänderter Kommissionsvorschlag vom 16. Juni 1993 - Kom (93) 225 endg. - Syn. 346), Köln.

BDA (1995a) *Stellungnahme zur Entsenderichtlinie*. Deutscher Bundestag. Ausschuß für Arbeit und Sozialordnung. Öffentliche Anhörung am 28. Juni 1995, Ausschußdrucksache 0160. 13. Wahlperiode, Folge 1, 42-47, Bonn.

BDA (1995b) *Stellungnahme zum Entwurf eines Gesetzes über zwingende Arbeitsbedingungen bei Grenzüberschreitenden Dienstleistungen*. Deutscher Bundestag. Ausschuß für Arbeit und Sozialordnung. Öffentliche Anhörung am 25. Oktober 1995, Ausschußdrucksache 0286, 13. Wahlperiode, 9-28, Bonn.

Beisheim, Marianne, Sabine Dreher, Gregor Walter, Bernhard Zangl, und Michael Zürn (1999) *Im Zeitalter der Globalisierung? Thesen und Daten zur gesellschaftlichen und politischen Denationalisierung*, Baden-Baden: Nomos.

Bernstein, Aaron (2003) 'Waking Up From the American Dream. Dead-end jobs and the High Cost of College Could be Choking off Upward Mobility', *Business Week*, Online edition, December 1, www.businessweek.com (accessed October 2005),

Bernstein, Richard J. (1979) *Restrukturierung der Gesellschaftstheorie*, Frankfurt/M.: Suhrkamp.

Berschens, Ruth (1994) 'Teurer Club', *Wirtschaftswoche*, 20.04.1994.

Betz, Hans-Georg (1994) *Radical Right-Wing Populism in Western Europe*, London: MacMillan.

Bhagwati, Jagdish (1984) 'Incentives and Disincentives: International Migration', *Weltwirtschaftliches Archiv* 120 (4), 678-701.

Bhagwati, Jagdish (1988) *Protectionism*, Cambridge, Mass.: MIT Press.

Bhagwati, Jagdish (1998) 'The Capital Myth. The Difference between the Trade in Widgets and Dollars', *Foreign Affairs* 77 (3), 7-12.

Bieler, Andreas (2000) *Globalisation and Enlargement of the EU: Austrian and Swedish Social Forces in the Struggle over Membership*, London: Routledge.

Bienefeld, Manfred (1991) 'Karl Polanyi and the Contradictions of the 1980s', Marguerite Mendell and Daniel Salée, eds. *The Legacy of Karl Polanyi. Market, State and Society at the End of the Twentieth Century*, London: Macmillan, 3-30.

Biersteker, Thomas J. (1992) 'The 'Triumph' of Neoclassical Economics in the Developing World: Policy Convergence and Bases of Governance in the International Economic Order', in James N. Rosenau and Ernst-Otto Czempiel, eds. *Governance Without Government: Order and Change in World Politics*, Cambridge: Cambridge University Press, 102-31.

Bloom, David and Adi Brender (1993) *Labor and the Emerging World Economy*. NBER Working Paper Series. Working Paper No. 4266, Cambridge, MA: National Bureau of Economic Research.

Böhning, W. R. (1984) *Studies in International Labour Migration*, London: Macmillan.

Borjas, George J. (1999): *Heavens Door: Immigration Policy and the American Economy*, Princeton, N.J.: Princeton University Press.

Bosch, Gerhard and Klaus Zühlke-Robinet (2000) *Der Arbeitsmarkt in der deutschen Bauindustrie: Strukturen und Merkmale sowie*

Herausforderungen der kommenden Jahre. Forschungsbericht für die Hans-Böckler-Stiftung, Gelsenkirchen: Institut für Arbeit und Technik. Wissenschaftszentrum Nordrhein-Westfalen.

Bowley, Graham (1997) 'Drive to Cut Costs Worries New Head of the OECD', *Financial Times*, 21.02.1997.

Broad, Dave. 1995. 'Globalization and the Casual Labour Problem: History and Prospects', *Social Justice* 22 (3):67-92.

Bundesanstalt für Arbeit (1999) *Merkblatt zum Arbeitnehmer-Entsendegesetz. Derzeit nach dem AEntG anzuwendende Tarifverträge*, Nürnberg: Bundesanstalt für Arbeit.

Bündnis 90/Die Grünen (1995) Antrag der Abgeordneten Annelie Buntenbach und der Fraktion Bündnis 90/Die Grünen. *Grundsätze für eine EU- Entsenderichtlinie sowie eine nationale Regelung bis zu deren Realisierung*, Deutscher Bundestag Drucksache 13/786, 15. März 1995, Bonn.

Bündnis 90/Die Grünen (1997a) *"Hoffentlich sozialversichert!?" Zum Regulierungsbedarf bei geringfügiger Beschäftigung, Scheinselbständigkeit und Telearbeit*, Bundestagsfraktion, Bonn.

Bündnis 90/Die Grünen (1997b) *Themenschwerpunkt Arbeit. Illegale Beschäftigung—moderner Menschenhandel*, Bundestagsfraktion, www.gruenebt.de/fachbereiche/ (accessed January 1998), Bonn.

Briggs, Vernon M. (1996) 'International Migration and Labour Mobility: The Receiving Countries', in Julien Van den Broeck, ed. *The Economics of Labour Migration*, Cheltenham, Glos.: Edward Elgar, 115-58.

Bromley, Simon (1995) 'Rethinking International Political Economy', in John Macmillan and Andrew Linklater, eds. *Boundaries in Question: New Directions in International Relations*, London and New York: Pinter Publishers, 228-43.

Brubaker, Rogers (1994) 'Commentary', in Wayne A. Cornelius, Philip L. Martin, and James F. Hollifield, eds. *Controlling Immigration. A Global Perspective*, Stanford: Stanford University Press, 227-32.

Burnham, Peter (1991) 'Neo-Gramscian Hegemony and the International Order', *Capital and Class* 45, 73-94.

Bustamente, Jorge (1994) 'NAFTA and Labour Migration to the United States', in Thomas Balmer, Nikki Crake, and Mónica Serrano, eds. *Mex-*

ico and the North American Free Trade Agreement. Who will Benefit?, Houndmills: Macmillan, 79-94.

Carlson, Tucker (1997) 'The Intellectual Roots of Nativism', *Wall Street Journal*, 02.10.1997.

Cassen, Bernard (2005) 'ATTAC against the Treaty', *New Left Review* 33 (May/June): 27-33.

Castells, Manuel (1989) 'High Technology and the New International Division of Labour', *Labour and Society* 14 (special issue):7-42.

Castles, Stephen, and Alastair Davidson (2000) *Citizenship and Migration. Globalization and the Politics of Belonging*, London: Routledge.

Castles, S. (1986) 'The Guest-Worker in Western Europe: an Obituary', *International Migration Review* 20 (4), 761-768.

Castles, Stephen (1999) 'International Migration and the Global Agenda: Reflections on the 1998 UN Technical Symposium', *International Migration* 37 (1), 5-17.

Castles, Stephen and Godula Kosack (1973) *Immigrant Workers and Class Structure*, Oxford: Oxford University Press.

Castles, Stephen and Mark J. Miller (1998) *The Age of Migration. International Population Movements in the Modern World*, 2nd ed., London: Macmillan.

Castles, Stephen, Heather Booth, and Tina Wallace (1987) *Migration und Rassismus in Westeuropa*, Berlin: Express Edition.

Cavusgil, Tamer S. (1993) 'Globalization of Markets and its Impact on Domestic Institutions', *Indiana Journal of Global Legal Studies* 1 (1), 83-98.

Cerny, Philip G. (1996) 'What Next for the State?', in Eleonore Kofman and Gillian Youngs, eds. *Globalization: Theory and Practice*, London: Pinter, 123-37.

Chaney, Elsa M. (1981) 'Migrant Workers and National Boundaries: The Basis for Rights and Protections', in Peter G. Brown and Henry Shue, eds. *Boundaries: National Autonomy and its Limits*, Lanham, M.D.: Rowman and Littlefield, 37-78.

Chin, Christine B. N. and James H. Mittelman (1997) 'Conceptualising Resistance to Globalisation', *New Political Economy* 2 (1), 25-38.

Clark, Ian (1999) *Globalization and International Relations Theory*, Oxford: Oxford University Press.

Clay, William (1997) United States Congress. Congressional Record. *Introduction of the Stop Sweatshops Act of 1997*, 07.01.1997, p. E 70-71; www.thomas.loc.gov (accessed July 1998).

Clinton, William (1994) *Accepting the Immigration Challenge: The President's Report on Immigration*, Washington: U.S. Government Printing Office.

Clinton, William (1995) 'Deterring Illegal Immigration. Memorandum for the Heads of Executive Departments and Agencies. President of the United States', *Federal Register*, 10th February 1995, 60: 28, 7885-7889.

Cohn, Theodore H. (2000) *Global Political Economy. Theory and Practice*, New York: Longman.

Cooper, Muriel H. (1995a) 'Thai Sweatshop Tip of Iceberg', *AFL-CIO News*, 25.08.1995, www.aflcio.org/newsonline (accessed July 1998).

Cooper, Muriel H. (1995b) 'Retailers Slip Sweatshop Blame', *AFL-CIO News*, 25.09.1995, www.aflcio.org/newsonline/95nov6/sweatny.html, (accessed July 1998).

Cooper, Muriel H. (1995c) 'Unions Rally in Garment District; Reich: Administration will Shut Sweatshops', *AFL-CIO News* 06.11.1995, www.aflcio.org/newsonline/ 95nov6/ sweatny.html (accessed July 1998).

Copeland, Emily (1998), *Welcomed at the Front Door: The Political Economy of Granting Skilled Migrants Access to the U.S. Job Market*, Paper presented at the Annual Conference of the International Studies Association, Minneapolis.

Cornelius, Wayne A., Philip L. Martin, and James F. Hollifield (1994) 'Introduction: The Ambivalent Quest for Immigration Control', in Wayne A. Cornelius, Philip L. Martin, and James F. Hollifield, eds. *Controlling Immigration. A Global Perspective*, Stanford: Stanford University Press, 3-42.

Coughlin, Cletus C., Alec K. Chrystal, and Geoffrey E. Wood (2000) 'Protectionist Trade Policies: A Survey of Theory, Evidence, and Rationale', in Jeffry A. Frieden and David A. Lake, eds. *International Political Economy. Perspectives on Power and Wealth*, 4th ed., Boston and New York: Bedford and St. Martin's, 303-17.

Cox, Robert W. (1986) 'Social Forces, States and World Orders. Beyond International Relations Theory', in Robert O. Keohane, ed. *Neorealism and Its Critics*, New York: Columbia University Press, 204-55.

Cox, Robert W. (1987) *Production, Power and World Order. Social Forces in the Making of History*, New York: Columbia University Press.

Cox, Robert W. (1991) 'The Global Political Economy and Social Choice', in Daniel Drache and Meric S. Gertler, eds. *The New Era of Global Competition. State Policy and Market Power*, Montreal: McGill-Queen's University Press, 335-50.

Cox, Robert W. (1993a) 'Gramsci, Hegemony and International Relations: an Essay in Method', in Stephen Gill, ed. *Gramsci, Historical Materialism and International Relations*, Cambridge, UK: Cambridge University Press, 49-66.

Cox, Robert W. (1993b) 'Structural Issues of Global Governance: Implications for Europe', in Stephen Gill, ed. *Gramsci, Historical Materialism and International Relations*, Cambridge: Cambridge University Press, 259-89.

Cox, Robert W. (1994) 'Global Restructuring: Making Sense of the Changing International Political Economy', in: Stubbs, Richard and Geoffrey R.D. (eds.): *Political Economy and the Changing Global Order*, London: Macmillan, 45-59.

Cox, Robert W. (1996) *Approaches to World Order*, Cambridge, UK: Cambridge University Press.

Cox, Robert W. (1997) 'Economic Globalization and the Limits to Liberal Democracy', in Anthony McGrew, ed. *The Transformation of Democracy? Globalization and Territorial Democracy*, Cambridge: Polity Press, 49-72.

Cox, Robert W. (1999) 'Civil Society at the Turn of the Millennium: Prospects for an Alternative World Order', *Review of International Studies* 25, 3-29.

Cox, Ronald W. and Daniel Skidmore-Hess (1999) *U.S. Politics and the Global Economy*, Boulder, Col.: Lynne Rienner.

Crozier, Michel, Samuel P. Huntington, and Joji Watanuki (1975) *The Crisis of Democracy. Report on the Governability of Democracies to the Trilateral Commission*, New York: New York University Press.

Dahrendorf, Ralf (1994) 'The Changing Quality of Citizenship', in B. v. Steenbergen, ed. *Conditions of Citizenship*, London: Sage, 10-19.

Dawkins, Peter J., William Foster, Lindsay Lowell, and Demetrios G. Papademetriou (1992) 'The Microeconomic Analysis of Immigration in Australia and the United States', in Gary P. Freeman and James Jupp, eds. *Nations of Immigrants. Australia, the United States and International Migration*, Melbourne: Oxford University Press, 111-28.

Deutsche Bundesregierung (1995) *Entwurf eines Gesetzes über zwingende Arbeitsbedingungen bei grenzüberschreitenden Dienstleistungen (Arbeitnehmer - Entsendegesetz)*. Bundestagsdrucksache Nr. 13/2414 vom 25. September 1995, Bonn.

Deutscher Bundestag (1995a) Ausschuß für Arbeit und Sozialordnung. *Wortprotokoll der 18. Sitzung* (Öffentliche Anhörung) am 28. Juni 1995, 13. Wahlperiode, Protokoll Nr. 18, Bonn.

Deutscher Bundestag (1995b) Ausschuß für Arbeit und Sozialordnung. *Wortprotokoll der 28. Sitzung* (Öffentliche Anhörung) am 25. Oktober 1995, 13. Wahlperiode, Protokoll Nr. 28, Bonn.

Deutscher Bundestag (1995c) *Plenarprotokoll* 13/58 vom 28. September, 1995, Bonn.

Deutscher Bundestag (1997) *Plenarprotokoll* 13/151 vom 16. Januar 1997, Bonn.

DGB – Deutscher Gewerkschaftsbund

DGB (1995a) *Stellungnahme zur Entsenderichtlinie. Deutscher Bundestag.* Ausschuß für Arbeit und Sozialordnung. Öffentliche Anhörung am 28. Juni 1995, Ausschußdrucksache 0160, 13. Wahlperiode, (Folge 1), 19-23, Bonn.

DGB (1995b) *Stellungnahme zum Entwurf eines Gesetzes über zwingende Arbeitsbedingungen bei Grenzüberschreitenden Dienstleistungen.* Deutscher Bundestag. Ausschuß für Arbeit und Sozialordnung. Öffentliche Anhörung am 25. Oktober 1995, Ausschußdrucksache 0286, 13. Wahlperiode (Folge 1), 1-7, Bonn.

DGB (1995c) 'Europäische Sozialpolitik – Bilanz der deutschen Ratspräsidentschaft', *Informationen zur Sozial- und Arbeitsmarktpolitik*, No. 21995 vom 9. März 1995, Bonn.

DGB (1999) *.... es kommen Menschen. Herausforderungen an gewerkschaftliche Migrationspolitik*, Düsseldorf.

Dicken, Peter (1998) *Global Shift. Transforming the World Economy*, 3rd ed., London: Paul Chapman Publishing.

Dickerson, Kitty G. (1991) *Textiles and Apparel in the International Economy*, New York: Macmillan.

Dohse, Knuth (1981) *Ausländische Arbeiter und bürgerlicher Staat. Genese und Funktion von staatlicher Ausländerpolitik und Ausländerrecht. Vom Kaiserreich bis zur Bundesrepublik Deutschland*, Berlin: Express Edition.

Dolan, Michael (1993) 'Global Economic Transformation and Less Developed Countries', in Robert Slater et al., eds. *Global Transformation and the Third World*, Boulder: Lynne Rienner, 259-82.

DOL – United States Department of Labor.

DOL (n.d.) *Protecting America's Garment Workers* (www.dol.gov.esa, accessed June 1998).

DOL (1998) *North American Agreement on Labor Cooperation: A Guide*, Washington.

Doomernik, Jeroen and Rinus Penninx (1998) 'Internationale Arbeitsmigration: Weltweiter Arbeitsmarkt?', in Thomas Geisen, ed. *Zukunft ohne Arbeit: Beiträge zur Krise der Arbeitsgesellschaft*, Frankfurt: IKO-Verlag für Interkulturelle Kommunikation, 145-70.

Drainville, André (1994) 'International Political Economy in the Age of Open Marxism', *Review of International Political Economy* 1 (1), 105-133.

Drainville, André (1995) 'Of Social Spaces, Citizenship, and the Nature of Power in the World Economy', *Alternatives* 20 (1):51-79.

Dreher, Sabine (2005) 'Citizenship and Migration in Germany and the United States', in M. Zürn, ed. (with the assistance of G. Walter) *Globalizing Interests. Pressure Groups and Denationalization*, Albany: Suny, 125-186.

Drucker, Peter F. (1986) 'The Changed World Economy', *Foreign Affairs* 64 (4), 768-792.

Ebeling, Richard M. (1995) 'The Case Against the Immigration Laws', in Richard M. Ebeling and Jacob G. Hornberger, eds. *The Case for Free Trade and Open Immigration*, Fairfax: Freedom Foundation, 105-14.

Eichhorst, Werner (1998) *Europäische Sozialpolitik zwischen nationaler und supranationaler Regulierung: Die Entsendung von Arbeitnehmern im Rahmen der Dienstleistungsfreiheit innerhalb der Europäischen Union*, Dissertation, Universität Konstanz.

Eiteljörge, Uwe (1998) 'Das Abkommen über den internationalen Handel mit Dienstleistungen. Ein Schritt vorwärts, einer zurück?', in Martin Klein, Werner Meng, und Reinhard Rode, eds. *Die Neue Welthandelsordnung der WTO*, Amsterdam: Fakultas, 137-73.

Ethier, Wilfried (1995) *Modern International Economics*, 3rd ed., New York: W.W. Norton Press.

European Commission (1993), W*hite Paper on Growth, Competitiveness, and Employment. The Challenges and Ways Forward into the 21st Century*, COM (93) 700 Final (www.europa.eu.int/en/record/white, accessed June 1999).

Evans, Peter (1997) 'The Eclipse of the State? Reflections on Stateness in an Era of Globalization', *World Politics* 50 (1), 62-87.

FAIR – Federation for American Immigration Reform (www.fairus.org)

FAIR (1992) *Immigration 2000. The Century of the New American Sweatshop*, Washington.

FAIR (1997a) *Oaths, Allegiance and the Loss of Common Understandings*, Executive Director Dan Stein at the Brookings Institution: National Issues Forum, 08.12.1997, www.fairus.org (accessed July 1998).

FAIR (1997b) *Making Immigration Great Again*, Speech of Dan Stein to the Commonwealth Club, San Francisco, 28.07.1997, www.fairus.org (accessed July 1998).

FAIR (1997c) *How to Survive Win the Immigration Debate*, Washington.

FAIR (1995) Prepared Statement of Dan Stein, Executive Director, Federation for American Immigration Reform, United States, House of Representatives, Committee on the Judiciary, Subcommittee on Immigration and Claims, *Hearing on H.R. 1915 Immigration in the National Interest Act of 1995*, 29th June 1995, Washington.

Faist, Thomas (1995a) 'Ethnicization and Racialization of Welfare-State Politics in Germany and the USA', *Ethnic and Racial Studies* 18 (2), 219-250.

Faist, Thomas (1995b) 'Migration in transnationalen Arbeitsmärkten: Zur Kollektivierung und Fragmentierung sozialer Rechte in Europa. *Zeitschrift für Sozialreform* 41(1 und 2), 36-47; 108-122.

Faist, Thomas (1997) 'Migration in Contemporary Europe: European Integration, Economic Liberalization and Protection', in Jytte Klausen and Louise A. Tilly, eds. *European Integration in Social and Historical Perspective*, Lanham, MD: Rowman and Littlefield, 223-48.

Faist, Thomas (2000) *The Volume and Dynamics of International Migration and Transnational Social Spaces*, Oxford: Oxford University Press.

Faist, Thomas, Klaus Sieveking, Uwe Reim, and Stefan Sandbrink (1999) *Ausland im Inland. Die Beschäftigung von Werksvertragsarbeitnehmern in der Bundesrepublik Deutschland*, Baden-Baden: Nomos.

Falk, Richard (1994) 'The Making of Global Citizenship', in B. Van Steenbergen, ed. *The Condition of Citizenship*, London: Sage, 127-140.

Falkner, Gerda (1992) '"Sozialdumping" im EG-Binnenmarkt: Betrachtungen aus politikwissenschaftlicher Sicht', *Österreichische Zeitschrift für Politikwissenschaft* 22, 261-276.

Fennema, Meindert, and Kees Van der Pijl (1987) 'International Bank Capital and the New Liberalism', in M. S. Mizruchi and M. Schwartz, eds. *Intercorporate Relations. The Structural Analysis of Business*, Cambridge: Cambridge University Press.

Ferguson, T. and J. Rogers (1986) *Right Turn*, New York: Hill and Wang.

Fernández Kelly, Patricia M. (1989) 'International Development and Industrial Restructuring: The Case of Garment and Electronics Industries in Southern California', in Arthur MacEwan and William K. Tabb, eds. *Instability and Change in the World Economy*, New York: Monthly Review Press, 147-65.

Fix, Michael (1991) *The Paper Curtain: Employer Sanctions' Implementation, Impact, and Reform*, Washington: Urban Institute.

Foreman-Peck, James (1995) *A History of the World Economy. International Economic Relations Since 1850*, 2nd ed., New York: Harvester Wheatsheaf.

Fragomen, Austin T. (1997) 'The Illegal Immigration Reform and Immigrant Responsibility Act of 1996: An Overview', *International Migration Review* 31(2), 438-460.

Fraser, John R. (1994) 'Illegal Immigration in the United States and the Limits of Sanctions Against Employers', in OECD, ed. *Migration and Development. New Partnerships for Co-operation*, Paris: OECD, 75-84.

Freeman, Gary P. (1994) 'Can Liberal States Control Unwanted Migration?', *Annals of the American Academy of Political and Social Science* (534), 17-30.

Freeman, Gary P. (1998) 'The Decline of Sovereignty? Politics and Immigration Restrictions in Liberal States', in Christian Joppke, ed. *Challenge to the Nation-State. Immigration in Western Europe and the United States*, Oxford: Oxford University Press, 86-108.

Friedman, Milton (1962) *Capitalism and Freedom*, Chicago: University of Chicago Press.

Friedman, Milton (1979) *Free to Choose*, New York: Harcourt Brace Jovanovich.

Fröbel, Folker, Jürgen Heinrichs and Otto Kreye (1980) *The New International Division of Labour: Structural Unemployment in Industrialized Countries and Industrialization in Developing Countries*, Cambridge: Cambridge University Press.

Frost, Mervyn (1998): 'Migrants, Civil Society and Sovereign States: Investigating an Ethical Hierarchy', *Political Studies* XLVI, 871-885.

Gamble, Andrew (1994) *The Free Economy and the Strong State. The Politics of Thatcherism*, 2nd ed., London: MacMillan.

GAO (United States General Accounting Office) (1988): *"Sweatshops" in the U.S. Opinions on their Extent and Possible Enforcement Options*, General Accounting Office: Washington.

GAO (United States General Accounting Office) (1994): *Garment Industry. Efforts to Address the Prevalence and Conditions of Sweatshops*. General Accounting Office: Washington.

Garrett, Geoffrey (1998) *Partisan Politics in the Global Economy*, Cambridge: Cambridge University Press.

Garson, Jean-Pierre (1998) 'North America: Migration and Economic Integration', *OECD Observer*, No. 214, October/November, www.oecd.org, html-document (accessed October 1999).

Germain, Randall D. (1997) *The International Organization of Credit: States and Global Finance in the World Economy*, Cambridge: Cambridge University Press.

Germain, Randall D. and Michael Kenny (1998) 'Engaging Gramsci: International Relations and the New Gramscians', *Review of International Studies* 24, 3-21.

Gesamtmetall – Gesamtverband der metallindustriellen Arbeitgeberverbände e.V..

Gesamtmetall (1995) *Stellungnahme zum Entwurf eines Gesetzes über zwingende Arbeitsbedingungen bei grenzüberschreitenden Dienstleistungen.* Deutscher Bundestag. Ausschuß für Arbeit und Sozialordnung. Öffentliche Anhörung am 25. Oktober 1995. Ausschußdrucksache 0286, 13. Wahlperiode (Folge 1), 12-16, Bonn.

Gesamttextil – Gesamtverband der Textilindustrie.

Gesamttextil (1995) *Stellungnahme zum Entwurf eines Gesetzes über zwingende Arbeitsbedingungen bei grenzüberschreitenden Dienstleistungen.* Deutscher Bundestag. Ausschuß für Arbeit und Sozialordnung. Öffentliche Anhörung am 25. Oktober 1995. Ausschußdrucksache 0286, 13. Wahlperiode (Folge 1), 17-18, Bonn.

Gesamttextil (1996) *Ist das Entsendegesetz der Weg in die Zukunft?* Manuskript, 30. Mai 1996, Eschborn.

Gill, Stephen (1986) 'Hegemony, Consensus and Trilateralism', *Review of International Studies* 12, 205-221

Gill, Stephen (1990a) *American Hegemony and the Trilateral Commission.* Cambridge: Cambridge University Press.

Gill, Stephen (1990b) 'The Emerging Hegemony of Transnational Capital: Trilateralism and Global Order', in David P. Rapkin, ed. *World Leadership and Hegemon*, Boulder: Lynne Rienner, 117-46.

Gill, Stephen (1992a) 'The Emerging World Order and European Change', *Socialist Register*, London: Merlin Press, 157-96.

Gill, Stephen (1992b) 'Economic Globalization and the Internationalization of Authority: Limits and Contradiction', *Geoforum* 23, 269-283.

Gill, Stephen (1993a) 'Gramsci and Global Politics: Towards a Post-Hegemonic Research Agenda', in Stephen Gill, ed. *Gramsci, Historical*

Materialism and International Relations, Cambridge: Cambridge University Press, 1-18.

Gill, Stephen (1993b) 'Epistemology, Ontology and the 'Italian School'', in Stephen Gill, ed. *Gramsci, Historical Materialism and International Relations*. Cambridge: Cambridge University Press, 21-48.

Gill, Stephen, ed. (1993c) *Gramsci, Historical Materialism and International Relations*. Cambridge: Cambridge University Press.

Gill, Stephen (1993d) 'Neo-Liberalism and the Shift Towards a US-Centred Transnational Hegemony', in Henk Overbeek, ed. *Restructuring Hegemony in the Global Political Economy*, London: Routledge, 246-82.

Gill, Stephen (1994a) 'Structural Change and Global Political Economy: Globalizing Elites and the Emerging World Order', in Yoshikazu Sakamoto, ed. *Global Transformation: Challenges to the State System*, Tokyo: United Nations University Press, 169-99.

Gill, Stephen (1994b) 'Knowledge, Politics, and Neo-Liberal Political Economy', in Geoffrey R. D. Underhill and Richard Stubbs, eds. *Political Economy and the Changing Global Order*, Basingstoke and London: Macmillan, 75-88.

Gill, Stephen (1995a) 'Globalisation, Market Civilisation, and Disciplinary Neoliberalism', *Millennium. Journal of International Studies* 24, 399-424.

Gill, Stephen (1995b) 'Theorizing the Interregnum: The Double Movement and Global Politics in the 1990s', in Björn Hettne, ed. *International Political Economy: Understanding Global Disorder*, London and New Jersey: Zed Books, 65-99.

Gill, Stephen (1998) 'European Governance and New Constitutionalism: Economic and Monetary Union and Alternatives to Disciplinary Neoliberalism in Europe', *New Political Economy* 3 (1), 5-26.

Gill, Stephen (2003) *Power and Resistance in the New World Order*, Houndmills: Palgrave Macmillan.

Gill, Stephen and David Law (1988) *The Global Political Economy. Perspectives, Problems, and Policies*, Baltimore: Johns Hopkins University Press.

Gill, Stephen and David Law (1993) 'Global Hegemony and the Structural Power of Capital', in Stephen Gill, ed. *Gramsci, Historical Materialism and International Relations*, Cambridge, Cambridge University Press, 93-126.

Gill, Stephen and James H. Mittelman, eds. (1997) *Innovation and Transformation in International Studies*, Cambridge: Cambridge University Press.

Gills, Barry, ed. (1999) *Globalisation and the Politics of Resistance*, London: MacMillan.

Gilpin, Robert (1987) *The Political Economy of International Relations*, Princeton: Princeton University Press.

Gilpin, Robert (2000) *The Challenge of Global Capitalism. The World Economy in the 21st Century*, Princeton: Princeton University Press.

Glahn, Wiltrud (1992) *Der Kompetenzwandel internationaler Flüchtlingsorganisationen: vom Völkerbund bis zu den Vereinten Nationen*, Baden-Baden: Nomos.

Glasmeier, Amy, Jeffery W. Thompson, and Amy J. Kays (1993) 'The Geography of Trade Policy: Trade Regimes and Location Decisions in the Textile and Apparel Complex', *Transactions. Institute of British Geographers* 18, 19-35.

Glassman, J. (1999) 'State Power Beyond the 'Territorial Trap': the Internationalization of the State', *Political Geography* 18, 669-696.

Glyn, Andrew and Bob Sutcliffe (1992) 'Global but Leaderless? The New Capitalist Order', *Socialist Register*, 76-95.

Goff, Patricia (2000) 'Invisible Borders: Economic Liberalization and National Identity', *International Studies Quarterly* 44 (4), 533-562.

Goodin, Robert E. (1992) 'If People Were Money', in Brian Barry and Robert E. Goodin, eds. *Free Movement. Ethical Issues in the Transnational Migration of People and of Money*, New York: Harvester Wheatsheaf, 6-22.

Goodman, John B. and Louis W. Pauly (1994) 'The Obsolescence of Capital Controls? Economic Management in an Age of Global Markets', *World Politics* 46 (1), 50-82.

Gordon, David M. (1988) 'The Global Economy: New Edifice or Crumbling Foundations?', *New Left Review* 168, 24-64.

Gosh, Bimal (1997) 'Magnitude, Trends and Dynamics of Immigration into North America. The Need for a Global Perspective: The Contextual

Framework', in Emek M. Uçarer and Donald J. Puchala, eds. *Immigration into Western Societies: Problems and Policies*, London: Pinter, 145-74.

Gourevitch, Peter (1986) *Politics in Hard Times. Comparative Responses to International Economic Crises*, Ithaca: Cornell University Press.

Gowan, Peter (1999) *The Global Gamble. Washington's Faustian Bid for World Dominance*, London: Verso.

Gowan, Peter (2003) 'The American Campaign for Global Sovereignty', *Socialist Register*, London: Merlin Press, 1-27.

Gowan, Peter (2004) 'Triumphing Toward International Disaster. The Impasse in American Grand Strategy', *Critical Asian Studies* 36 (1): 3-36.

Grahl, John and Paul Teague (1989) 'The Cost of Neoliberal Europe', *New Left Review* (174), 33-50.

Gray, John (1999) *False Dawn. The Delusion of Global Capitalism*, 2nd ed., London: Granta Books.

Greenhill, Romilly, and Ann Pettifor (2002) *The United States as a HIPC - How the Poor are Financing the Rich*, London: Jubilee Research at the New Economics Foundation.

Greenhouse, Steven (1998), 'Anti-Sweatshop Coalition Finds Itself at Odds on Garment Factory Code', *New York Times*, 03.07.1998.

Guild, Elspeth (1996) 'The Legal Framework of Citizenship of the European Union', in David Cesarani and Mary Fulbrook, eds. *Citizenship, Nationality, and Migration in Europe*, London: Routledge, 30-56.

HDB – Hauptverband der Deutschen Bauindustrie.

HDB (1995a) *Stellungnahme zur Entsenderichtlinie*, Deutscher Bundestag, Ausschuß für Arbeit und Sozialordnung, Öffentliche Anhörung am 28. Juni 1995, Ausschußdrucksache 0160, 13. Wahlperiode (Folge 2), 13-18, Bonn.

HDB (1995b) *Stellungnahme zum Entwurf eines Gesetzes über zwingende Arbeitsbedingungen bei grenzüberschreitenden Dienstleistungen*. Deutscher Bundestag, Ausschuß für Arbeit und Sozialordnung, Öffentliche Anhörung am 25. Oktober 1995, Ausschußdrucksache 0286, 13. Wahlperiode (Folge 2), 36-40, Bonn.

Haggard, Stephan and Sylvia Maxfield (1996) 'The Political Economy of Financial Internationalization in the Developing World', in Robert O.

Keohane and Helen V. Milner, eds. *Internationalization and Domestic Politics*, Cambridge: Cambridge University Press, 209-39.

Hammar, Tomas (1990) *Democracy and the Nation State, Aliens, Denizens and Citizens in a World of International Migration*, Aldershot: Gower.

Hammar, Tomas, ed. (1985) *European Immigration Policy. A Comparative Study*, Cambridge: Cambridge University Press.

Hammar, Tomas, Grete Brochmann, Kristof Tamas, and Thomas Faist, eds. (1997) *International Migration, Immobility and Development. Multidisciplinary Perspectives*, Oxford: Berg.

Hansen, Randall and Desmond King (2000) 'Illiberalism and the New Politics of Asylum: Liberalism's Dark Side', *Political Quarterly 71 (4)*, 396-402.

Harrison, Bennett and Barry Bluestone (1988) *The Great U-Turn. Corporate Restructuring and the Polarizing of America*, New York: Basic Books.

Harvey, David (1982) *The Limits to Capital*, Oxford: Blackwell.

Harvey, David (1985) 'The Geopolitics of Capitalism', in D. Gregory and J. Urry, eds. *Social Relations and Spatial Structures*, London: Blackwell, 128-62.

Harvey, David (1990) *The Condition of Postmodernity. An Enquiry into the Origins of Cultural Change*, Cambridge, MA and Oxford, UK: Blackwell.

Harvey, David (2005) *A Brief History of Neoliberalism*, Oxford: Oxford University Press.

Harwood, Richard (1992) 'Signs of a New Politics', *Social Policy* Fall-Winter, 5-16.

Hasenau, Michael (1991) 'ILO Standards on Migrant Workers: The Fundamentals of the UN Convention and Their Genesis', *International Migration Review* 25, 687-697.

Haus, Leah (1995) 'Openings in the Wall: Transnational Migrants, Labor Unions, and U.S. Immigration Policy', *International Organization* 49 (2), 285-313.

Hauser, Heinz and Kai-Uwe Schanz (1995) *Das neue GATT. Die Welthandelsordnung nach Abschluß der Uruguay-Runde*, München: RR. Oldenbourg Verlag.

Hawthorn, Geoffrey (1999) 'Liberalism since the Cold War: an Enemy to itself?', *Review of International Studies* 25 (5), 145-160.

Hayek, Friedrich A. (1944) *The Road to Serfdom*, Chicago: The University of Chicago Press.

Hayek, Friedrich A. (1960) *The Constitution of Liberty*, London: Routledge.

Hecker, Steven (1993) 'US Unions, Trade and International Solidarity: Emerging Issues and Tactics', *Economic and Industrial Democracy*, 14, 355-367.

Held, David (2002) 'Cosmopolitanism: Ideas, Realities and Deficits', in D. Held and A. McGrew, eds. *Governing Globalization. Power, Authority and Global Governance*, Oxford: Polity Press, 303-324.

Held, David, Anthony McGrew, David Goldblatt, and Jonathan Perraton (1999) *Global Transformations. Politics, Economics and Culture*, Cambridge: Polity Press.

Helleiner, Eric (1994) 'From Bretton Woods to Global Finance: A World Turned Upside Down', in Richard Stubbs and Geoffrey R. D. Underhill, eds. *Political Economy and the Changing Global Order*, London: Macmillan, 163-75.

Hellman, Rainer (1997) 'OECD auf dem Prüfstand', *EU Magazin*, Nr. 7/8.

Herod, Andrew (1997) 'From a Geography of Labor to a Labor Geography: Labor's Spatial Fix and the Geography of Capitalism', *Antipode* 29 (1), 1-31.

Hettne, Björn, ed. (1995) *International Political Economy: Understanding Global Disorder*, London and New Jersey: Zed Books.

Hinojosa Ojeda, Raul (1994) 'The North American Free Trade Agreement and Migration', in OECD, ed. *Migration and Development. New Partnerships for Co-operation*, Paris: OECD, 229-39.

Hirst, Paul and Grahame Thompson (1999) *Globalization in Question: The International Economy and the Possibilities of Governance*, 2nd ed., Cambridge: Polity Press.

Hobsbawm, E. J. (1979) 'The Development of the World Economy', *Cambridge Journal of Economy* (3), 305-318.

Hollifield, James F. (1992) *Immigrants, Markets and States*, Cambridge, Mass.: Harvard University Press.

Holman, Otto (1996) *Integrating Southern Europe: EC Expansion and the Transnationalization of Spain*, London: Routledge.

Hoogvelt, Ankie (1987) 'The New International Division of Labour', in R. Bush, G. Johnston, and D. Coutes, eds. *The World Order*, London: Polity, 65-86.

Hoogvelt, Ankie (1997) *Globalisation and the Postcolonial World: The New Political Economy of Development*, Basingstoke: Macmillan.

Hopkins, Terence K. and Immanuel Wallerstein (1986) 'Commodity Chains in the World Economy', *Review* 10 (1), 157-170.

Horsmann, M. and A. Marshall (1994) *After the Nation State*, London: Harper Collins.

Howard, Alan (1997) 'Labor, History, and Sweatshops in the New Global Economy', in Andrew Ross, ed. *No Sweat. Fashion, Free Trade, and the Rights of Garment Workers*, London: Verso, 151-72.

Hunger, Uwe (2000) *Der 'rheinische Kapitalismus' in der Defensive. Eine komparative Policy-Analyse zum Paradigmenwechsel in den Arbeitsmarktbeziehungen am Beispiel der Bauwirtschaft*, Baden-Baden: Nomos.

Hymer, S. (1975) 'The Multinational Corporation and the Law of Uneven Development', in H. Radice, ed. *International Firms and Modern Imperialism*, Harmondsworth: Penguin.

IG BAU – Industriegewerkschaft Bauen Agrar Umwelt.

IG BAU (1994-1996) *Geschäftsbericht*, Frankfurt: Industriegewerkschaft Bauen-Agrar-Umwelt.

IG BAU (1995a) *Stellungnahme zur Entsenderichtlinie*. Deutscher Bundestag. Ausschuß für Arbeit und Sozialordnung. Öffentliche Anhörung am 28. Juni 1995, Ausschußdrucksache 0160, 13. Wahlperiode (Folge 2), 6-12, Bonn.

IG BAU (1995b) *Stellungnahme zum Entwurf eines Gesetzes über zwingende Arbeitsbedingungen bei grenzüberschreitenden Dienstleistungen*. Deutscher Bundestag. Ausschuß für Arbeit und Sozialordnung. Öffentliche Anhörung am 25. Oktober 1995, Ausschußdrucksache 0286, 13. Wahlperiode (Folge 2), 1-8, Bonn.

IG Metall – Industriegewerkschaft Metall.

IG Metall (1995b) *Stellungnahme zum Entwurf eines Gesetzes über zwingende Arbeitsbedingungen bei grenzüberschreitenden Dienstleistungen.* Deutscher Bundestag. Ausschuß für Arbeit und Sozialordnung. Öffentliche Anhörung am 25. Oktober 1995, Ausschußdrucksache 0286, 13. Wahlperiode (Folge 1), 19-29, Bonn.

IG Metall (1995a) *Stellungnahme zur Entsenderichtlinie.* Deutscher Bundestag. Ausschuß für Arbeit und Sozialordnung. Öffentliche Anhörung am 28. Juni 1995, Ausschußdrucksache 0160, 13. Wahlperiode (Folge 2), 19-22, Bonn.

Ikenberry, G. J. (1999) 'Liberal Hegemony and the Future of American Postwar Order' in T.V. Paul and J. A. Hall, ed. *International Order and the Future of World Politics,* Cambridge: Cambridge University Press: 123-146.

ILO (International Labour Organisation) (1999) *Migrant Workers,* Geneva: International Labour Office.

IMF (International Monetary Fund) (1997) *World Economic Outlook. May 1997,* Washington: International Monetary Fund.

INS (Immigration and Naturalization Service) (1997) *Immigration and Nationality Act of 1952. Reflecting Amendments through December 2nd, 1997,* Washington: Immigration and Naturalization Service.

Ireland, Patrick R. (1995) 'Migration, Free Movement, and Immigrant Integration in the EU: A Bifurcated Policy Response', in Stephan Leibfried and Paul Pierson, eds. *European Social Policy: Between Fragmentation and Integration,* Washington: Brookings Institution, 231-66.

Jacobson, David (1996) *Rights Across Borders. Immigration and the Decline of Citizenship,* Baltimore: John Hopkins University Press.

Jenkins, Rhys (1984) 'Divisions over the New International Division of Labour', *Capital and Class* 22, 28-57.

Jones, Barry (1995) *Globalisation and Interdependence in the International Political Economy. Rethoric and Reality,* London: Pinter Publishers.

Jones, Maldwyn Allen (1992) *American Immigration,* 2nd ed., Chicago: The University of Chicago Press.

Kapstein, Ethan Barnaby (1994) *Governing the Global Economy: International Finance and the State,* Cambridge, Mass.: Harvard University Press.

Keohane, Robert O. (1995) 'Hobbes's Dilemma and Institutional Change in World Politics: Sovereignty in International Society', in Hans-Henrik Holm and Georg Sørensen, eds. *Whose World Order*, Boulder: Westview Press, 165-86.

Keohane, Robert O. and Joseph S. Nye (2000) 'Globalization: What's New? What's Not? (And So What?)', *Foreign Policy* (Spring), 104-119.

Keohane, Robert O. and Joseph S. Nye (2001) *Power and Interdependence*, 3rd ed., New York: Longman.

Kindleberger, Charles (1967) *Europe's Postwar Growth: The Role of Labor Supply*, Cambridge, Mass.: Harvard University Press.

King, Desmond and Stewart Wood (1999) 'The Political Economy of Neoliberalism: Britain and the United States in the 1980s', in Herbert Kitschelt, Peter Lange, Gary Marks, and John D. Stephens, eds. *Continuity and Change in Contemporary Capitalism*, Cambridge: Cambridge University Press, 371-97.

Kistler, Ernst and Thomas Schönwälder (1998) 'Eliten und Heloten, herrschen und dienen. Die rechtskonservativen Ideen der bayerisch-sächsischen Zukunftskommission', *Soziale Sicherheit* 47 (4), 121-133.

Klein-Beekman, Chris (1996) 'International Migration and Spatiality in the World Economy: Remapping Economic Space in an Era of Expanding Transnational Flows', *Alternatives* 21, 439-472.

Köbele, Bruno and Karl-Heinz Sahl, eds. (1993) *Die Zukunft der Sozialkassensysteme der Bauwirtschaft im Europäischen Binnenmarkt*, Köln: Bund.

Koch, Jürgen (1991) 'The Completion of the Internal Market and its Impact on the Building Sector in Europe', in Helen Rainbird and Gerd Syben, eds. *Restructuring a Traditional Industry: Construction Employment and Skills in Europe*, Oxford: Berg, 263-83.

Kohler-Koch, Beate (1990) 'Interdependenz', in Volker Rittberger, ed. *Theorien der Internationalen Beziehungen. Bestandsaufnahme und Forschungsperspektiven, Politische Vierteljahresschrift, Sonderheft 21*, Opladen: Westdeutscher Verlag, 110-29.

Kommission für Zukunftsfragen der Freistaaten Bayern und Sachsen (1996) *Erwerbstätigkeit und Arbeitslosigkeit in Deutschland. Entwicklung, Ursachen und Maßnahmen. Teil I: Entwicklung von Erwerbstätigkeit und Arbeitslosigkeit in Deutschland und anderen frühindustrialisierten Ländern*, Bonn.

Kommission für Zukunftsfragen der Freistaaten Bayern und Sachsen (1997a) *Erwerbstätigkeit und Arbeitslosigkeit in Deutschland. Entwicklung, Ursachen und Maßnahmen. Teil II: Ursachen steigender Arbeitslosigkeit in Deutschland und anderen frühindustrialisierten Ländern*, Bonn.

Kommission für Zukunftsfragen der Freistaaten Bayern und Sachsen (1997b) *Erwerbstätigkeit und Arbeitslosigkeit in Deutschland. Entwicklung, Ursachen und Maßnahmen. Teil III: Maßnahmen zur Verbesserung der Beschäftigungslage*, Bonn.

Körner, Heiko (1990) *Internationale Mobilität der Arbeit. Eine empirische und theoretische Analyse der internationalen Wirtschaftsmigration im 19. und 20. Jahrhundert*, Darmstadt: Wissenschaftliche Buchgesellschaft.

Koslowski, Rey (1998) 'European Union Migration Regimes, Established and Emerged', in Christian Joppke, ed. *Challenge to the Nation-State. Immigration in Western Europe and the United States*, Oxford: Oxford University Press, 153-90.

Kostakopoulou, Theodora (2000) 'The 'Protective Union': Change and Continuity in Migration Law and Policy in Post-Amsterdam Europe', *Journal of Common Market Studies* 38 (3), 497-518.

Krasner, Stephen D. (1985) *Structural Conflict: The Third World Against Global Liberalism*, Berkeley: University of California Press.

Krugman, Paul R. and Maurice Obstfeld (1997) *International Economics. Theory and Policy*, 4th ed., Reading, Mass.: Addison-Wesley.

Krupat, Kitty (1997) 'From War Zone to Free Trade Zone. A History of the National Labor Committee', in Andrew Ross, ed. *No Sweat. Fashion, Free Trade, and the Rights of Garment Workers*, London: Verso, 51-78.

Lacher, Hannes (1999) 'Embedded Liberalism, Disembedded Markets: Re-Conceptualising the Pax Americana', *New Political Economy* 4 (3), 343-360.

Lacher, Hannes (2005) 'International Transformation and the Persistence of Territoriality: Toward a New Political Geography of Capitalism', *Review of International Political Economy* 12 (1): 26-52.

Lacher, Hannes (2006) *The International Relations of Modernity: Capitalism, Territoriality and Globalization*, London: Routledge.

Lake, David A. (1999) 'Global Governance: A Relational Contracting Approach', in A. Prakash and J. A. Hart, eds. *Globalization and Governance*, London: Routledge.

Lavenex, Sandra (1997), *Transgressing Borders: The Emergent European Refugee Regime and 'Safe Third Countries'*, Paper presented at the Annual Conference of the International Studies Association, Toronto.

Leblang, David A. (1997) 'Domestic and Systemic Determinants of Capital Controls in the Developed and Developing World', *International Studies Quarterly* 41 (3), 435-454.

Lee, Denise Kelly (1995) *Global Telecommunications Regulation*, London: Pinter Publishers.

Leitner, Helga (1995) 'International Migration and the Politics of Admission and Exclusion in Postwar Europe', *Political Geography* 14 (3), 259-278.

Levy, Carl (1999) 'European Asylum and Refugee Policy after the Treaty of Amsterdam: the Birth of a New Regime?', in Alice Bloch and Carl Levy, eds. *Refugees, Citizenship, and Social Policy in Europe*, Houndmills: MacMillan, 12-50.

Ley, Robert (1996) 'Multilateral Rules to Promote the Liberalisation of Investment Regimes', in OECD, ed. *Towards Multilateral Investment Rules*, Paris: OECD, 69-74.

Lönnroth, Juhani (1993) 'Labour Market Policies for the 1990s', in OECD, ed. *The Changing Course of International Migration*, Paris: OECD, 67-78.

MacEwan, Arthur (1999) *Neo-Liberalism or Democracy. Economic Strategy, Markets, and Alternatives for the 21st Century*, London and New York: Zed Books.

Madeuf, Bernadette and Albert Michalet (1978) 'Global Forces. A New Approach to International Economics', *International Social Science Journal* 30 (2), 253-283.

Maier, Charles S. (1977) 'The Politics of Productivity: Foundations of American Economic Policy After World War II', *International Organization* 31 (4), 607-633.

MALDEF – Mexican-American Legal Defense and Educational Fund.

MALDEF (1993) Statement of Vibiana Andrade, Immigrants' Rights Director, Mexican American Legal Defense and Educational Fund, *Hearing before the Subcommittee on International Law, Immigration and Refugees of the Committee of the Judiciary, House of Representatives*, 103rd Congress, First Session, June 16, 1993, Serial No. 12, 359-383, Washington.

MALDEF and ACLU (1989) *The Human Costs of Employer Sanctions*, Washington and New York.

Mann, Michael (1997) 'Has Globalization Ended the Rise and Rise of the Nation-State?', *Review of International Political Economy* 4 (3), 472-496.

Marks, Jon (1997) 'A Platform for Policy', *Financial Times*, 07.07.1994.

Marshall, T. H. (1992) *Bürgerrechte und Soziale Klassen. Zur Soziologie des Wohlfahrtsstaates*, Frankfurt: Campus.

Martin, Philip (1994) The United States: Benign Neglect towards Immigration, in Wayne Cornelius, Philip Martin and James Hollifield, eds. *Controlling Immigration. A Global Perspective*, Stanford: Stanford University Press, 83-100.

Martin, Philip (1996) 'Trade and Migration: The Case of NAFTA', in David O'Connor, ed. *Development Strategy, Employment and Migration. Country Experiences*, Paris: OECD, 231-59.

Massey, D.S., J. Arango, G. Hugo, A. Kouaouci, A. Pellegrino, J.E. Taylor (1993): 'Theories of International Migration: A Review and Appraisal', *Population and Development Review* 19 (3), 431-466.

Mazur, Jay (1997) 'Labor's New Languages', *The Dissident*, 8-9, 30.

Mazur, Jay (2000) 'Labor's New Internationalism', *Foreign Affairs* 79 (1), 79-93.

McCracken, Paul et al. (1977) *Towards Full Employment and Price Stability*, Paris: OECD.

McMichael, Philip (2000) 'Globalisation. Trend or Project?', in Ronen Palan, ed. *Global Political Economy: Contemporary Perspectives*, London: Routledge, 100-13.

Meissner, Doris (1992) 'Managing Migrations', *Foreign Policy* 86, 66-83.

Meissner, Doris M., Robert D. Hormats, Antonio Garrigues Walker, and Shijuro Ogata (1993) *International Migration Challenges in a New Era. Policy Perspectives and Priorities for Europe, Japan, North America and the International Community. A Report to the Trilateral Commission*, New York: The Trilateral Commission.

Merk, Jeroen (2005) The Private Regulation of Labour Standards: The Case of the Apparel and Footwear Industries, Paper presented at the *Workshop on Private Governance*, ECPR Joint Sessions at Granada.

Messina, Anthony M. (1996) 'The Not So Silent Revolution: Postwar Migration to Western Europe', *World Politics* 49 (1), 130-54.

Miller, Mark J. (1992) 'Evolution of Policy Modes for Regulating International Labour Migration', in Mary M. Kritz, Lin Lean Lim, and Hania Zlotnik, eds. *International Migration Systems. A Global Approach*, Oxford: Clarendon Press, 300-14.

Mills, Kurt (1998) *Human Rights in the Emerging Global Order: A New Sovereignty?*, New York: St. Martin's Press.

Mines, Richard and Jeffrey Avina (1992) 'Immigrants and Labour Standards: The Case of California Janitors', in Jorge A. Bustamante, ed. *U.S. Mexico Relations: Labor Market Interdependence*, Stanford: Stanford University Press, 429-48.

Mines, Richard and Philip Martin (1984) 'Immigrant Workers and the Californian Citrus Industry', *Industrial Relations* 23 (1), 139-149.

Mittelman, James H. (1998) 'Coxian Historicism as an Alternative Perspective in International Studies', *Alternatives* 23 (1), 63-92.

Mittelman, James H. (2000) *The Globalization Syndrome. Transformation and Resistance*, Princeton, N.J.: Princeton University Press.

Mittelman, James H., ed. (1996) *Globalization: Critical Reflections*, Boulder and London: Lynne Rienner.

Moch, Leslie Page (1997) 'Foreign Workers in Western Europe: The "Cheaper Hands" in Historical Perspective', in Jytte Klausen and Louise A. Tilly, eds. *European Integration in Social and Historical Perspective. 1850 to the Present*, Lanham: Rowman & Littlefield Publishers, 103-26.

Moore, Stephen (1999) 'Give Us Your Best, Your Brightest', in Georg McKenna and Stanley Feingold, eds. *Taking Sides. Clashing Views on Controversial Political Issues*, Guilford, Conn.: Dushkin and McGraw-Hill, 329-334.

Mosley, Paul (1992) 'Structural Adjustment: A General Overview, 1980-1990', in Jean-Marc Fontaine, ed. *Foreign Trade Reforms and Development Strategies*, London: Routledge, 27-45.

Mückenberger, Ulrich (1989) 'Non-Standard Forms of Work and the Role of Changes in Labour and Social Security Regulation', *International Journal of the Sociology of Law* 17, 381-402.

Mundell, Robert A. (1957) 'International Trade and Factor Mobility', *American Economic Review* 47 (3), 321-335.

Murphy, Craig N. (1994) *International Organization and Industrial Change: Global Governance Since 1850*, Oxford: Polity Press.

NAM – National Association of Manufacturers (www.nam.org).

NAM (1995) *Resolution on Immigration Reform*, 23rd September 1995, Washington.

NAM (n.d.) *History of the Organisation*, www.nam.org/programs/history.html (accessed July 1998), Washington.

NAM (1997) *Fast Track Myths Refuted. The Truth About International Trade*. Washington, www.nam.org/ (accessed July 1998).

NAM (1998a) NAM Hails Senate Judiciary Committee's Advancement of Immigration Bill to Ease Skilled Worker Shortage. Manufacturers Urge Swift Senate Floor Action on Bill to Allow More Skilled Foreign Professionals into the U.S., Press Release No. 98-102, Washington.

NAM (1998b) Statement. *Temporary Visa Program for High-Tech Workers*. Submitted for the Printed Record of the Hearing before the Committee on the Judiciary, 25th February 1998, United States Senate, Washington.

NAM (1999) *American Manufacturers Support the World Trade Organizations*, Issue Brief, World Trade Organizations, Washington, www.nam.org, (accessed July 1999).

National Consumers League (1997) *Apparel Industry Code of Conduct: A Consumer Perspective on Social Responsitility*. A paper presented by Linda Golodner, President of the NCL to Notre Dame Center for Ethics and Religious Values in Business, 6th October 1997.

Nayyar, Deepak (2002) 'Cross-Border Movements of People', in D. Nayyar, ed. *Governing Globalization. Issues and Institutions*, Oxford: Oxford University Press. UN/WIDER Studies in Development Economics.

NIF – National Immigration Forum (www.immigrationforum.org)

NIF (1996) *Finding Common Ground. A Primer for Environment and Population Advocates Concerned About Immigration,* Washington.

NIF (1997) *Annual Report 1996,* Washington.

NIF (1998a) *National Academy of Science Study Confirms Benefits of Immigration,* Washington, www.immigrationforum.org/national.htm (accessed in July 1998).

NIF (1998a) *Mission Statement,* Washington, www.immigrationforum.org/mission.htm (accessed in July 1998).

NIF (1998b) *Cycles of Nativism in U.S. History,* www.immigrationforum.org/cycles.htm (accessed in July 1998).

NIF (1998c) *Public Opinion on Immigration,* www.immigrationforum.org/USATodayPol.html (accessed July 1998).

NIF (1998d) *Summary of Illegal Immigration Reform and Immigrant Responsibility Act of 1996,* www.immigrationforum.org/goodnews.htm (accessed July 1998).

NIF (1999) *Fix 96,* Various Articles, www.immigrationforum.or/fix96/ (accessed May 2000).

NLC (National Labour Committee) (1992) *Paying to Lose Our Jobs,* Washington.

NRF – National Retail Federation (www.nrf.com).

NRF (National Retail Federation) (n.d.) The NRF Foundation. *Stopping Sweatshops: The View From Main Street.* Washington, www.nrf.com. (accessed July 2000). The following sources are subsections from the main webpage.

    NRF (a) *Stopping Sweatshops: What American Retailers Are Doing..*

    NRF (b) *Retailers and Labor Standards.*

    NRF (c) *Retailers and Labor Standards: What the NRF is doing.*

    NRF (d) *Myths and Truths: US Retailers and Sweatshops.*

    NRF (e) *US Retailers and Sweatshops: A Letter to University Presidents.*

    NRF (f) *How Retailers Soucre. The Supply Chain.*

    NRF (g) *Industry-Wide Initiatives.*

    NRF (h) *The Importance of Vigorous Enforcement of the LaborLaws.*

    NRF (i) *Labor Standards and the World Trade Organization.*

    NRF (j) *U.S. Labor Laws and the U.S. Department of Labor.*

NRF (k) *What is a Sweatshop?*
NRF (l) *Sweatshops in America: From "The Jungle" to El Monte.*
NRF (m) *Why Open Trade is Good for the U.S. Economy.*
NRF (n) *The International Labor Organization.*
NRF (o) *Suppliers and Labor Standards.*
Nevins, Joseph (2000) 'The Remaking of the California-Mexico Boundary in the Age of NAFTA', in Peter Andreas and Timothy Snyder, eds. *The Wall Around the West: State Borders and Immigration Controls in North America and Europe*, Lanham, Maryland: Rowman and Littlefield, 99-114.
Norman, Peter (1994) 'An Economic Think Tank', *Financial Times*, 30.09.1994.
Nuscheler, Franz (1994) *Internationale Migration*, Duisburg: Institut für Entwicklung und Frieden.
O'Brian, Richard (1992) *Global Financial Integration. The End of Geography*, London: Pinter.
O'Connor, David, ed. (1996) *Development Strategy, Employment and Migration. Country Experience. OECD Development Centre Seminars*, Paris: OECD.
OECD (1978a) *Migration, Growth and Development.* Report of a Group of Experts (The Kindleberger Report), Paris: OECD.
OECD (1991a) *Migration: The Demographic Aspects*, Paris: OECD.
OECD (1991b) *Employment Outlook*, Paris: OECD.
OECD (1993): *The Changing Course of International Migration*, Paris: OECD.
OECD (1994a) *The OECD Jobs Study: Facts, Analysis, Strategies*, Paris: OECD (accessed at www.oecd.org, July 2000, html-document).
OECD (1994b) *The OECD Jobs Study - Part I- Labour Market Trends and Underlying Forces of Change*, Paris: OECD.
OECD (1994c) *The OECD Jobs Study. Evidence and Explanations. Part II - The Adjustment Potential of the Labour Market*, Paris: OECD.
OECD (1994d) *Migration and Development. New Partnerships for Cooperation*, Paris: OECD.
OECD (1996a) *Towards Multilateral Investment Rules*, Paris: OECD.

OECD (1996b): *Migration and the Labour Market in Asia. Prospects to the Year 2000*, Paris: OECD.

OECD (1996c) *OECD Jobs Strategy: Enhancing the Effectiveness of Active Labour Market Policies*, Paris: OECD.

OECD (1996d) *OECD Jobs Strategy: Pushing Ahead with the Strategy*, Paris: OECD.

OECD (1996e) *The Provision of Services and The Movement of Labour in the Countries of the European Community*. OECD Working Papers Vol IV. International Migration and Labour Policies, Occasional Paper No. 2.

OECD (1997a) The OECD Report on Regulatory Reform, Volume I: Synthesis Report. Paris: OECD.

OECD (1997b) *The OECD Report on Regulatory Reform: Volume II Thematic Studies*, Paris: OECD.

OECD (1998a) *Open Markets Matter. The Benefits of Trade and Investment Liberalisation*. Paris: OECD.

OECD (1998b) *Migration, Free Trade and Regional Integration in North America*. Paris: OECD.

OECD (1998c) *The OECD Jobs Strategy: Progress Report on Implementation of Country-Specific Recommendations*. Economics Department Working Papers Nr. 196, Paris: OECD.

OECD (1999) *The OECD Jobs Strategy: Assessing Performance and Policy*. Paris: OECD.

Offe, Claus (1987) 'Challenging the Boundaries of Institutional Politics: Social Movements since the 1960s', in Charles S. Maier, ed. *Changing Boundaries of the Political. Essays on the Evolving Balance Between the State and Society, Public and Private in Europe*, Cambridge: Cambridge University Press, 63-106.

Offe, Claus and Susanne Fuchs (1997) 'Wie schöpferisch ist die Zerstörung', *Blätter für deutsche und internationale Politik* (1), 295-300.

Ohmae, Kenichi (1994) *The Borderless World: Power and Strategy in the Global Marketplace*, London: Harper Collins.

O'Rourke, Kevin H. and Jeffrey G. Williamson (1999) *Globalization and History*, Cambridge, Mass.: MIT Press.

Overbeek, Henk (1990) *Global Capitalism and National Decline*, London: Unwin Hyman.

Overbeek, Henk (1995a) 'Globalization and the Restructuring of the European Labour Market', in Mihály Simai, ed. *Global Employment*, London: Zed Books, 204-18.

Overbeek, Henk (1995b) 'Towards a New International Migration Regime: Globalization, Migration and the Internationalization of the State', in Dietrich Thrähnhardt and Robert Miles, eds. *Migration and European Integration. The Dynamics of Inclusion and Exclusion*, London: Pinter, 15-37.

Overbeek, Henk (1998) 'Global Restructuring and Neoliberal Labor Market Regulation in Europe: The Case of Migration Policy', *International Journal of Political Economy*, 28 (1), 54-99

Overbeek, Henk (2000) 'Transnational Historical Materialism', in Ronen Palan, ed. *Theories of Transnational Class Formation and World Order*, London: Routledge, 168-83.

Overbeek, Henk and Kees van der Pijl (1993) 'Restructuring Capital and Restructuring Hegemony: Neo-Liberalism and the Unmaking of the Post-War Order', in Henk Overbeek, ed. *Restructuring Hegemony in the Global Political Economy*, London: Routledge, 1-27.

Önder, Nilgün (1998) 'Integrating with the Global Market: The State and the Crisis of Political Representation. Turkey in the 1980s and 1990s', *International Journal of Political Economy* 28 (2):44-84.

Parkes, Christopher and Henry Tricks (2000) 'Illicit Angels of America's Economic Miracle', *Financial Times*, 23.02.2000.

Passel, Jeffrey S. (1994) 'Illegal Migration to the United States – The Demographic Context', in Wayne A. Cornelius, Philip L. Martin, and James Hollifield, eds. *Controlling Immigration. A Global Perspective*, Stanford: Stanford University Press, 113-18.

Passel, Jeffrey S. (1998) 'Undocumented Immigration', in Peter Duignan and L. H. Gann, eds. *The Debate in the United States over Immigration*, Stanford, Cal.: Stanford University Press, 191-206.

Pauly, Louis W. (1995) 'Capital Mobility, State Autonomy and Political Legitimacy', *Journal of International Affairs* 48 (2), 369-388.

Paye, Jean-Claude (1994) 'Statement. Closing Session of the Conference on Migration and International Co-Operation', in OECD, ed. *Migration and Development. New Partnerships for Co-operation*, Paris: OECD, 303-05.

Peck, Jamie (2002) 'Labor, Zapped/Growth, Restored? Three Moments of Neoliberal Restructuring in the American Labor Market', *Journal of Economic Geography* 2:179-220.

Pellerin, Hélène (1993) 'Global Restructuring in the World Economy and Migration: The Globalization of Migration Dynamics', *International Journal* 48, 240-254.

Pellerin, Hélène (1996) 'Global Restructuring and International Migration: Consequences for the Globalization of Politics', in Eleonore Kofman and Gillian Youngs, eds. *Globalization: Theory and Practice*, London: Pinter, 81-98.

Pellerin, Hélène (1999) 'The Cart before the Horse? The Coordination of Migration Policies in the Americas and the Neoliberal Economic Project of Integration', *Review of International Political Economy* 6 (4), 468-493.

Perot, Ross and Pat Choate (1993) *Save Your Job, Save Our Country. Why NAFTA Must be Stopped -Now*, New York: Hyperion.

Philip, Butt Alan (1994) 'European Union Immigration Policy: Phantom, Fantasy or Fact?', in Martin Baldwin-Edwards and Martin A. Schain, eds. *The Politics of Immigration in Western Europe*, Newbury Park: Frank Cass, 168-92.

Piore, Michael J. (1979) *Birds of Passage*, Cambridge: Cambridge University Press.

Piore, Michael J. (1986) 'The Shifting Grounds for Immigration', *Annals of the American Academy of Political and Social Science* 485, 23-33.

Piore, Michael J. (1997) 'The Economics of the Sweatshop', in Andrew Ross, ed. *No Sweat. Fashion, Free Trade, and the Rights of Garment Workers*, London: Verso, 135-42.

Polanyi, Karl (1957) *The Great Transformation*, Boston: Beacon Press.

Polnischer Sozialrat e.V. (1995) *Stellungnahme zur Entsenderichtlinie*. Deutscher Bundestag. Ausschuß für Arbeit und Sozialordnung. Öffentliche Anhörung am 28. Juni 1995. Ausschußdrucksache 0160, 13. Wahlperiode (Folge 1), 9-17, Bonn.

Portes, A and John Walton (1981): *Labor, Class, and the International System*. Academic Press, New York.

Power, Jonathan (1979) 'The Great Debate on Illegal Immigration - Europe and the United States Compared', *Journal of International Affairs* 33 (2), 239-249.

Proper, Carl (1997) 'New York: Defending the Union Contract', in Andrew Ross, ed. *No Sweat. Fashion, Free Trade, and the Rights of Garment Workers*, London: Verso, 173-93.

Radice, Hugo (1999) 'Taking Globalisation Seriously', *Socialist Register*, London: Merlin Press, 1-28.

Rapley, John (2004) *Globalization and Inequality. Neoliberalism's Downward Spiral*, Boulder and London: Lynne Rienner.

Reder, Melvin W. (1982) 'Chicago Economics: Permanence and Change', *Journal of Economic Literature* 20, 1-38.

Reform Party – (www.reformparty.org).

Reform Party (1997) *Platform of the Reform Party of the United States of America*, Adopted in Kansas City, Missouri National Founding Convention, www.reformparty.org/headquarters/platform.htm (accessed in July 1998).

Reich, Robert B. (1991) *The Work of Nations. Preparing Ourselves for the 21st Century Capitalism*, New York: Alfred Knopf.

Reimers, David M. (1992) *Still the Golden Door. The Third World Comes to America*, New York: Columbia University Press.

Reinicke, Wolfgang (1998) *Global Public Policy. Governing without Government?*, New York: Brookings Institution Press.

Robertson, Daid (1996) 'The OECD Investment Mandate of 1995: Catching up with the Market', in OECD, ed. *Towards Multilateral Investment Rules*, Paris: OECD, 75-84.

Robinson, William I. (1996) *Promoting Polyarchy: Globalization, US Intervention, and Hegemony*, Cambridge: Cambridge University Press.

Robinson, William I. (2001) 'Social Theory and Globalization: The Rise of a Transnational State', *Theory and Society* 30 (2):157-200.

Robinson, William I. (2004) *A Theory of Global Capitalism. Production, Class and State in a Transnational World*, Baltimore: John Hopkins University Press.

Rogers, Rosemarie (1992) 'The Future of Refugee Flows and Policies', *International Migration Review* 26 (4), 1112-1143.

Rogers, Paul (2000) *Losing Control. Global Security in the Twenty-first Century*. Pluto Press, London.

Rosen, Ellen Israel (2002) *Making Sweatshops. The Globalization of the U.S. Apparel Industry*, Berkeley: University of California Press.

Rosenberg, Justin (2005) 'Globalization Theory: A Post Mortem', *International Politics* 42:2-74.

Rosewarne, Stuart (2001) 'Globalization, Migration, and Labour Market Formation - Labour's Challenge', *Capital Nature and Socialism* 12 (3):71-84.

Ruggie, John Gerard (1982) 'International Regimes, Transactions and Change: Embedded Liberalism in the Postwar Economic Order', *International Organization* 36 (2), 379-415.

Ruggie, John Gerard (1995) 'At Home Abroad, Abroad at Home: International Liberalisation and Domestic Stability in the New World Economy', *Millennium. Journal of International Studies* 24 (3), 507-526.

Ruggie, John Gerard (1996) *Winning the Peace. America and World Order in the New Era*, New York: Columbia University Press.

Rupert, Mark (1995) *Producing Hegemony. The Politics of Mass Production and American Global Power*, Cambridge, UK: Cambridge University Press.

Rupert, Mark (2000) *Ideologies of Globalization. Contending Visions of a New World Order*, London: Routledge.

Ryner, Magnus (1997), *Gramscian International Political Economy as Critical Research on European Regionalism: Contributions and Limitations*, Paper presented at the Annual Meeting of the British International Studies Association, University of Leeds.

Sachs, Jeffrey (1998) 'International Economics: Unlocking the Mysteries of Globalization', *Foreign Policy* 110, 97-111.

Salt, John (1976) 'International Labour Migration: The Geographical Pattern of Demand', in John Salt and Hugh Clout, eds. *Migration in Post-War Europe. Geographical Essays*, Oxford: Oxford University Press, 80-125.

Salt, John (1992) 'The Future of International Labor Migration', *International Migration Review* 26 (4), 1077-1111.

Santel, Bernhard and Uwe Hunger (1997) 'Gespaltener Sozialstaat, gespaltener Arbeitsmarkt', *Soziale Welt* 4, 379-396.

Sassen, Saskia (1988) *The Mobility of Labor and Capital: A Study in International Investment and Labor Flow*, Cambridge: Cambridge University Press.

Sassen, Saskia (1994) *Cities in a World Economy*, Thousand Oaks, Calif.: Pine Forge Press.

Sassen, Saskia (1996) *Losing Control? Sovereignty in an Age of Globalization*, New York: Columbia University Press.

Sassen, Saskia (1998) *Globalization and Its Discontents. Essays on the New Mobility of People and Money*, New York: The New Press.

Sassen, Saskia (1999) 'Transnational Economics and National Migration Policies', in Max J. Castro, ed. *Free Markets, Open Societies, Closed Borders. Trends in International Migration and Immigration in the Americas*, Miami: North-South Center Press, 7-32.

Scharpf, Fritz W. (1997) 'Economic Integration, Democracy and the Welfare State', *Journal of European Public Policy* 4 (1), 18-36.

Scharpf, Fritz W. (1997) 'Konsequenzen der Globalisierung für die nationale Politik', *Internationale Politik und Gesellschaft* 2, 184-193.

Scherrer, Christoph (1999) *Globalisierung wider Willen? Die Durchsetzung liberaler Außenwirtschaftspolitik in den USA*, Berlin: edition sigma.

Schmidt, Ingo (1995) 'Von der Standortkonkurrenz zur internationalen Regulation?', *Prokla. Zeitschrift für kritische Sozialwissenschaft* 25 (99), 271-290.

Scholte, Jan Aart (1997) 'Global Capitalism and the State', *International Affairs* 73 (3), 427-452.

Schuck, Peter H. (1998) 'The Re-Evaluation of American Citizenship', in Christian Joppke, ed. *Challenge to the Nation-state. Immigration in Western Europe and the United States*, Oxford: Oxford University Press, 191-230.

Schultz, Theodore W. (1978) 'Migration: An Economist's View', in William H. McNeill and Ruth S. Adams, eds. *Human Migration. Patterns and Policies*, Boston: Indiana University Press, 377-86.

Self, Peter (1993) *Government by the Market? The Politics of Public Choice*, Boulder, Co.: Westview Press.

Senatsverwaltung für Arbeit, berufliche Bildung und Frauen (1998) *Die Sackgassen der Zukunftskommission. Streitschrift wider die Kommission für Zukunftsfragen der Freistaaten Bayern und Sachsen*, Berlin: BBJ Verlag.

Senghaas, Dieter (1996) 'Standort D: Die Dialektik des Erfolgs', *Blätter für deutsche und internationale Politik* 11, 1295-1299.

Shepherd, Matthew (1994) 'U.S. Domestic Interests and the Latin American Debt Crisis', in Geoffrey R. D. Underhill and Richard Stubbs, eds. *Political Economy and the Changing Global Order*, Basingstoke: Macmillan, 302-12.

Simmons, Beth A. (1999) 'The Internationalization of Capital', in Herbert Kitschelt, Peter Lange, Gary Marks, and John D. Stephens, eds. *Continuity and Change in Contemporary Capitalism*, Cambridge: Cambridge University Press, 36-69.

Simon, Julian L. (1989) *The Economic Consequences of Immigration*, Oxford: Basil Blackwell.

Simons, Henry C. (1948) *Economic Policy for a Free Society*, Chicago: University of Chicago Press.

Sinclair, Timothy J. (1994) 'Passing Judgement: Credit Rating Processes as Regulatory Mechanisms of Governance in the Emerging World Order', *Review of International Political Economy* 1 (1), 133-160.

Smith, Alister (1996) 'The Development of a Multilateral Agreement on Investment at the OECD: A Preview', in OECD, ed. *Towards Multilateral Investment Rules*, Paris: OECD, 31-40.

Smythe, Elisabeth (1997), *Your Place or Mine? States, International Organizations and the Negotiation of Investment Rules: The OECD versus the WTO*, Paper presented at the Annual Conference of the International Studies Association, Toronto.

Soltwedel, Rüdiger (1993) 'Structural Adjustment, Economic Growth, and Employment', in OECD, ed. *The Changing Course of International Migration*, Paris: OECD, 55-66.

SOPEMI (1992) *Trends in International Migration. Continuous Reporting System on Migration*, OECD, Paris.

SOPEMI (1998) *Trends in International Migration. Continuous Reporting System on Migration*, OECD, Paris.

Soros, George (1997) 'The Capitalist Threat', *Atlantic Monthly* (February), 45-58.

Soysal, Yasemin Nuhoglu (1994) *Limits of Citizenship: Migrants and Postnational Membership in Europe*, Chicago: University of Chicago Press.

SPD (1995) (Sozialdemokratische Partei Deutschlands), Gesetzentwurf der Fraktion der SPD. *Entwurf eines Gesetzes zur Angleichung der Arbeitsbedingungen bei der Entsendung von Arbeitnehmern.* Deutscher Bundestag, Drucksache 13/2418 vom 22. September 1995, Bonn.

Spener, David (2000) 'The Logic and Contradictions of Intensified Border Enforcement', in Peter Andreas and Timothy Snyder, eds. *The Wall Around the West. State Borders and Immigration Controls in North America and Europe*, Lanham: Rowman & Littlefield, 115-38.

Stahl, Karl-Heinz and Brigitte Stang (1996) 'Das Arbeitnehmer-Entsendegesetz und die Europäische Entsenderichtlinie', *Arbeitsrecht im Betrieb* 11, 652-661.

Stalker, Peter (2000) *Workers without Frontiers. The Impact of Globalization on International Migration*, Boulder, Col.: Lynne Rienner.

Stewart, Frances (1995) *Adjustment and Poverty: Options and Choices*, London: Routledge.

Stienstra, Deborah (1994) *Women's Movements and International Organizations*, Basingstoke: MacMillan.

Stokes, Bruce (1999-2000) 'The Protectionist Myth', *Foreign Policy* 117, 88-102.

Strange, Susan (1995) 'The Limits of Government', *Government and Opposition* 20 (3), 291-311.

Streeck, Wolfgang (1999) *Korporatismus in Deutschland. Zwischen Nationalstaat und Europäischer Union*, Frankfurt: Campus.

Sutcliffe, Bob (1993) 'Immigration and the World Economy', in Gerald Epstein, Julie Graham, and Jessica Newhard, eds. *Creating a New World Economy. Forces of Change and Plans for Action*, Philadelphia:Temple University Press, 84-107.

Sutcliffe, Bob (1998) 'Freedom to Move in the Age of Globalization', in Dean Baker, Gerald Epstein, and Robert Pollin, eds. *Globalization and Progressive Economic Policy*, Cambridge, UK: Cambridge University Press, 325-36.

Sutcliffe, Bob (2004) 'Crossing Borders in the New Imperialism', *Socialist Registe*, London: Merlin Press.

Sutcliffe, Bob and Andrew Glyn (1999) 'Still Underwhelmed: Indicators of Globalization and Their Misinterpretation', *Review of Radical Political Economics* 31 (1), 111-132.

Syben, Gerd (1999) *Die Baustelle der Bauwirtschaft. Unternehmensentwicklung und Arbeitskräftepolitik auf dem Weg ins 21. Jahrtausend*, Berlin: edition sigma.

Talani, Leila Simona (2004) *European Political Economy*, Aldershot: Ashgate.

Tapinos, Georges (1993) 'Can International Co-operation be an Alternative to the Emigration of Workers?', in OECD, ed. *The Changing Course of International Migration*, Paris: OECD, 175-82.

Taplin, Ian M. (1994) 'Strategic Reorientations of U.S. Apparel Firms', in Gary Gereffi and Miguel Korzeniewicz, eds. *Commodity Chains and Global Capitalism*, Westport: Praeger, 205-22.

Teeple, Gary (1995) *Globalization and the Decline of Social Reform*, New Jersey and Toronto: Humanities Press and Garamond Press.

Thränhardt, Dietrich (1997) 'The Political Uses of Xenophobia in England, France, and Germany', in Emek M. Uçarer and Donald J. Puchala, eds. *Immigration into Western Societies: Problems and Policies*, London: Pinter, 175-94.

Thygesen, Niels, Yutaka Kosai, and Robert Z. Lawrence (1996) *Globalization and Trilateral Labor Markets: Evidence and Implications. A Report to the Trilateral Commission. The Triangle Papers 49*, New York, Paris and Tokyo: The Trilateral Commission.

Tilly, Charles (1978) 'Migration in Modern European History', in William H. McNeill and Ruth S. Adams, eds. *Human Migration. Patterns and Policies*, Boston: Indiana University Press, 48-74.

Todaro, Michael P. (1989) *Economic Development in the Third World*, 4th ed., New York: Longman.

Torpey, John (2000a) *The Invention of the Passport. Surveillance, Citizenship and the State*, Cambridge: Cambridge University Press.

Torpey, John (2000b) 'States and the Regulation of Migration in the Twentieth-Century North Atlantic World', in Peter Andreas and Timothy Snyder, eds. *The Wall Around the West: State Borders and Immigration Controls in North America and Europe*, Lanham: Rowman and Littlefield, 31-54.

U.S. Commission on Immigration Reform (1994) *U.S. Immigration Policy: Restoring Credibility: 1994 Report to Congress*, Washington.

Ugur, Mehmet (1995) 'Freedom of Movement vs. Exclusion: A Reinterpretation of the 'Insider'-'Outsider' Divide in the European Union', *International Migration Review* 29 (4), 964-999.

UNCTAD (1994) *World Investment Report*, New York: United Nations.

UNITE – Union of Needletrades and Industrial and Textile Employees (www.uniteunion.org)

UNITE, *Overnite*, several issues.

UNITE (various) *This Week's Sweatshop News*.

UNITE (n.d.a) *The Face of Change*, New York.

UNITE (n.d.b) *The Sweatshop Campaign*, New York.

UNITE (1998) Statement on the White House Apparel Industry Partnership, in *Sweatshop Watch*, 5th November 1998, Sweatshopwatch.org/swatch/headlines/ 1998/aip_nov.98.html (accessed November 1999).

UNITE (1999) Statement on *the "New Interior Enforcement Strategy" of the Immigration and Naturalization Service*, United States House of Representatives, Committee on the Judiciary, Subcommittee on Immigration and Claims (www.house.gov/judiciary/ chis0701.htm, accessed July 2000).

UNITE/AFL-CIO/RWDSU (1998) Joint Statement on the Apparel Industry Partnership by Lenore Miller (Retail, Wholesale and Department Store Union); Jay Mazur (UNITE), and John Sweeney (AFL-CIO), in: *Sweatshop Watch*, 5th November 1998, www. Sweatshopwatch.org/swatch/headlines/1998/aip_nov.98. html (accessed November 1999).

United Nations High Commissioner For Human Rights (1997) *The Rights of Migrant Workers. Fact Sheet No 24*, Geneva: Office of the United Nations High Commissioner for Human Rights.

Utichelle, Louis (2000) 'I.N.S. Looks the Other Way on Illegal Immigrant Labor', *The New York Times*, 09.03.2000.

Van Apeldoorn, Bastiaan (1998) 'Transnationalization and the Restructuring of Europe's Socioeconomic Order. Social Forces in the Construction of "Embedded Neoliberalism"', *International Journal of Political Economy* 28 (1), 12-53.

Van der Pijl, Kees (1984) *The Making of an Atlantic Ruling Class*, London: Verso.

Van der Pijl, Kees (1989) 'Restructuring the Atlantic Ruling Class in the 1970s and 1980s', in Stephen Gill, ed. *Atlantic Relations. Beyond the Reagan Era*, New York: St. Martin's Press, 62-87.

Van der Pijl, Kees (1995) 'The Second Glorious Revolution: Globalizing Elites and Historical Change', in B. Hettne, ed. *International Political Economy. Understanding Global Disorder*, London: Zed Books, 100-128.

Van der Pijl, Kees (1998) *Transnational Classes and International Relations*, London: Routledge.

Van Dijk, Meine Pieter (1995) 'The Internationalization of the Labour Market', in Mihály Simai, ed. *Global Employment*, London: Zed Books, 219-29.

Vogel, Dita (2000) 'Migration Control in Germany and the United States', *International Migration Review* 34 (2), 390-422.

Voswinkel, Stephan, Stefan Lücking, and Ingo Bode (1996) *Im Schatten des Fordismus. Industrielle Beziehungen in der Bauwirtschaft und im Gastgewerbe Deutschlands und Frankreichs*, München. Rainer Hampp Verlag.

Wade, Robert (1996) 'Globalization and it's Limits: Reports of the Death of the National Economy Are Greatly Exaggerated', in Suzanne Berger and Ronald Dore, eds. *National Diversity and Global Capitalism*, New York: Cornell University Press, 60-89.

Wade, Robert and Frank Veneroso (1998a) 'The Gathering World Slump and the Battle over Capital Controls', *New Left Review* (231), 13-42.

Wade, Robert and Frank Veneroso (1998b) 'The Asian Crisis: The High Debt Model Versus the Wall Street-Treasury Complex', *New Left Review* (228), 3-23.

Walzer, Michael (1983) *Spheres of Justice. A Defense of Pluralism and Equality*, New York: Basic Books.

Waever, Ole, Barry Buzan, Morten Kelstrum, and Pierre Lemaitre eds. (1993): Identity, Migration, and the New Security Agenda in Europe, New York: St. Martin's Press.

Weiner, Myron (1995) *The Global Migration Crisis*, New York: Harper Collins.

Weiss, Linda (1998) *The Myth of the Powerless State*, Cambridge: Polity Press.

Weiss, Linda (1999) 'Globalization and National Governance: Antinomy or Interdependence?', *Review of International Studies* 25, 59-88.

White House (1995): *Remarks on Illegal Immigration* by Attorney General Reno; INS Commissioner Meissner, Secretary of Labor Reich, El Paso Chief Border Partrol Agent Reyes, and INS Western Region Director Urs de la Vina. February 7th 1995, www. pubwhitehou...ov.us/1995/2/7/6.txt.1 (accessed July 1998).

Whitworth, Sandra (1994) *Feminism and International Relations: Towards a Political Economy of Gender in Interstate and Non-Governmental Institutions*, London: MacMillan.

Widgren, Jonas (1990) 'International Migration and Regional Stability', *International Affairs* 66 (4), 749-766.

Witherell, William (1996) 'Towards an International Set of Rules for Investment', in OECD, ed. *Towards Multilateral Investment Rules*, Paris: OECD, 17-29.

Wolfrum, Rüdiger, ed. (1991) *Handbuch Vereinte Nationen*, München: Beck.

Wood, Bernard (1994) 'Development Strategies and Migration: Linkages and Possible Lessons', in OECD, ed. *Migration and Development. New Partnerships for Co-operation*, Paris: OECD, 139-52.

Wood, Ellen (2003) *The Empire of Capital*, London: Verso.

World Bank (1995) *World Development Report. Workers in an Integrating World*, Washington: International Bank for Reconstruction and Development.

Zangl, Bernhard (1999), *Internationale Normdurchsetzung. Enforcement, Management oder Adjudication?'* InIIS Arbeitspapier Nr. 15/99. Institut für Interkulturelle und Internationale Studien, Universität Bremen.

Zänker, Alfred (1996) 'OECD für einschneidenden Veränderungen', *Die Welt*, 24.05.1996.

ZDB – Zentralverband des deutschen Baugewerbes.

ZDB (1995a) *Stellungnahme zur Entsenderichtlinie.* Deutscher Bundestag. Ausschuß für Arbeit und Sozialordnung. Öffentliche Anhörung am 28. Juni 1995. Ausschußdrucksache 0160, 13. Wahlperiode (Folge 2), 1-5, Bonn.

ZDB (1995b) *Stellungnahme zum Entwurf eines Gesetzes über zwingende Arbeitsbedingungen bei grenzüberschreitenden Dienstleistungen.* Deutscher Bundestag. Ausschuß für Arbeit und Sozialordnung. Öffentliche Anhörung am 25. Oktober 1995. Ausschußdrucksache 0286, 13. Wahlperiode (Folge 2), 29-35, Bonn.

ZDH – Zentralverband des Deutschen Handwerks.

ZDH (1995a) *Stellungnahme zur Entsenderichtlinie.* Deutscher Bundestag. Ausschuß für Arbeit und Sozialordnung. Öffentliche Anhörung am 28. Juni 1995. Ausschußdrucksache 0160, 13. Wahlperiode (Folge 1), 28-31, Bonn.

ZDH (1995b) *Stellungnahme zum Entwurf eines Gesetzes über zwingende Arbeitsbedingungen bei grenzüberschreitenden Dienstleistungen.* Deutscher Bundestag. Ausschuß für Arbeit und Sozialordnung. Öffentliche Anhörung am 25. Oktober 1995, Ausschußdrucksache 0286, 13. Wahlperiode (Folge 1), 8-11, Bonn.

Zolberg, Aristide R. (1989) 'The Next Waves: Migration Theory for a Changing World', *International Migration Review* 23 (3), 403-430.

Zolberg, Aristide R. (1991) 'Bounded States in a Global Market: The Uses of International Labour Migrations', in Pierre Bourdieu and James S. Coleman, eds. *Social Theory for a Changing Society*, Boulder, Col.: Westview Press, 301-25.

Zolberg, Aristide R. (1994) 'Changing Sovereignty Games and International Migration', *Global Legal Studies Journal* 2 (1), 153-177.

Zürn, Michael (1998) *Regieren jenseits des Nationalstaates. Denationalisierung und Globalisierung als Chance,* Frankfurt am Main: Suhrkamp.

Zürn, Michael ed. (with the assistance of G. Walter) (2005) *Globalizing Interests. Pressure Groups and Denationalization.*

Zysman, John (1996) 'The Myth of a 'Global' Economy: Enduring National Foundations and Emerging Regional Realities', *New Political Economy* 1(2), 257-277.

Politik, Gemeinschaft und Gesellschaft in einer globalisierten Welt

hrsg. von Rainer Dombois (Universität Bremen) und Thomas Faist (Hochschule Bremen)

Kathrin Prümm
Einbürgerung als Option
Die Bedeutung des Wechsels der Staatsangehörigkeit für Menschen türkischer Herkunft in Deutschland
Diese Reihe widmet sich theoretischen Beiträgen und empirischen systematischen Studien zur grenzüberschreitenden Vergesellschaftung und Vergemeinschaftung auf substaatlicher, staatlicher, trans- und internationaler Ebene. Die Studien fokussieren Prozesse der Vergesellschaftung in den Hauptbereichen staatlichen Handelns: Sicherheit, Menschen- und Bürgerrechte, Legitimität von politischen Systemen, soziale Wohlfahrt und Entwicklung im Süd-Nord Kontext. Der erste Band beschäftigt sich mit der Bedeutung von Staatsbürgerschaft. Diese wird theoretisch erörtert und durch eine qualitative Befragung ergänzt.
Bd. 1, 2004, 344 S., 29,90 €, br., ISBN 3-8258-7022-7

Rainer Dombois; Erhard Hornberger; Jens Winter
Internationale Arbeitsregulierung in der Souveränitätsfalle
Das Lehrstück des North American Agreement on Labor Cooperation zwischen den USA, Mexiko und Kanada
Die Globalisierung hat auch die Debatte über die Möglichkeiten und Perspektiven internationaler Arbeitsregulierung, insbesondere die Durchsetzung internationaler Sozialstandards neu entfacht. Im vorliegenden Buch werden die vielfältigen Aushandlungsprozesse und die Wirkungsweise des 1993 zwischen den USA, Mexiko und Kanada als NAFTA-Nebenabkommen ausgehandelten North American Agreement on Labor Cooperation untersucht. Das internationale Arbeitsregime wird als Lehrstück für die Probleme und Dilemmata internationaler Arbeitsregulierung im Spannungsfeld zwischen internationalen Beziehungen und nationalen Arbeitsbeziehungen und Souveränitätsansprüchen analysiert.
Bd. 2, 2004, 328 S., 29,90 €, br., ISBN 3-8258-7694-2

Wissenschaftliche Paperbacks
Politikwissenschaft

Klaus Schubert
Innovation und Ordnung
In einer evolutionär voranschreitenden Welt sind statische Politikmodelle und -theorien problematisch. Deshalb lohnt es sich, die wichtigste Quelle für die Entstehung der policy-analysis, den Pragmatismus, als dynamische, demokratieendogene politisch-philosophische Strömung zu rekonstruieren. Dies geschieht im ersten Teil der Studie. Der zweite Teil trägt zum Verständnis des daraus folgenden politikwissenschaftlichen Ansatzes bei. Darüber hinaus wird durch eine konstruktivspekulative Argumentation versucht, die z. Z. wenig innovative Theorie- und Methodendiskussion in der Politikwissenschaft anzuregen.
Bd. 7, 2003, 224 S., 25,90 €, br., ISBN 3-8258-6091-4

Politik: Forschung und Wissenschaft

Mario Petri; Ulrich Schnier; Jürgen Bellers (Hg.)
Handbuch der transitorischen Systeme, Diktaturen und autoritären Regime der Gegenwart
Gefestigte und intakte sowie gesellschaftlich akzeptierte und vor allem „funktionierende", demokratische Strukturen sind heutzutage keine Selbstverständlichkeit, schon gar nicht in globaler Perspektive. Auf dem steinigen Weg zu demokratischen Strukturen liefert das Handbuch der transitorischen Systeme, Diktaturen und autoritären Regime eine Bestandsaufnahme anhand einer Vielzahl ausgesuchter nationalstaatlicher Beispiele. Die strukturell ähnlich angelegten Beiträge skizzieren neben der Historie das gegenwärtige politische System und liefern einen Ausblick zu Chancen und Perspektiven des weiteren Demokratisierungsprozesses. Ergänzt werden die aktuellen Nationalstaatsbeispiele um Betrachtungen der „klassischen" totalitären, diktatorischen und autoritären Regime des deutschen Nationalsozialismus, des italienischen Faschismus, des spanischen Franquismus sowie des Austro-Faschismus.
Bd. 24, 2006, 584 S., 39,90 €, br., ISBN 3-8258-9070-8

Hartmut Elsenhans
Globalization Between A Convoy Model and An Underconsumptionist Threat
Bd. 25, 2006, 312 S., 29,90 €, br., ISBN 3-8258-9219-0